Wittgenstein and the Philosophy of Language

Throughout his philosophical development, Wittgenstein was more concerned with language than with any other topic. No other philosopher has been as influential on our understanding of the deep problems surrounding language, and yet the true significance of his writing on the subject is difficult to assess, since most of the current debates regarding language tend to overlook his work. In this book, Thomas McNally shows that philosophers of language still have much to learn from Wittgenstein's later writings. The book examines the finer details of his arguments while also clarifying their importance for debates outside the field of Wittgenstein studies. Presenting the issues thematically (as they relate to questions of reference, scepticism about meaning and the social dimension of language, among others), the book explores how the arguments in the *Philosophical Investigations* remain relevant, compelling us to reflect in novel and challenging ways on the nature of language.

THOMAS MCNALLY is a Research Associate in the Department of Philosophy at Trinity College, Dublin.

Wittgenstein and the Philosophy of Language

The Legacy of the *Philosophical Investigations*

Thomas McNally

Trinity College, Dublin

CAMBRIDGE
UNIVERSITY PRESS

CAMBRIDGE
UNIVERSITY PRESS

University Printing House, Cambridge CB2 8BS, United Kingdom

One Liberty Plaza, 20th Floor, New York, NY 10006, USA

477 Williamstown Road, Port Melbourne, VIC 3207, Australia

4843/24, 2nd Floor, Ansari Road, Daryaganj, Delhi – 110002, India

79 Anson Road, #06-04/06, Singapore 079906

Cambridge University Press is part of the University of Cambridge.

It furthers the University's mission by disseminating knowledge in the pursuit of education, learning, and research at the highest international levels of excellence.

www.cambridge.org
Information on this title: www.cambridge.org/9781107197947
DOI: 10.1017/9781108181976

First published 2017

Printed in the United Kingdom by Clays, St Ives plc

A catalogue record for this publication is available from the British Library.

ISBN 978-1-107-19794-7 Hardback

Cambridge University Press has no responsibility for the persistence or accuracy of URLs for external or third-party internet websites referred to in this publication and does not guarantee that any content on such websites is, or will remain, accurate or appropriate.

For Sinéad

Contents

Acknowledgements

I would like to thank the following people who have been very helpful at various points throughout the writing of this book: Jim Levine, Alexander Miller and Peter Simons; my friends and colleagues in the Philosophy Department at Trinity College, Dublin; students in my Wittgenstein seminars at Trinity College, Dublin during the years 2012–14; and the two anonymous readers for Cambridge University Press. I am also grateful for the funding provided by The Irish Research Council during the academic year 2012–13, during which most of Chapter 2 was written. My thanks also to: my mother and father, my siblings Deirdre, Imelda and Frank and all my family; Mary and PJ Phelan; James Kelly; and James Wrest. Most of all, I want to thank my wife Sinéad, to whom this book is dedicated, and our two sons Cathal and Finn.

Parts of Chapters 2 and 6 are based on the following articles, and I hereby gratefully acknowledge the permission of the journal editors to make use of this material:

> "Wittgenstein's Anti-Platonist Argument." *Philosophical Investigations* 39 (3) (2016a).
>
> "More Than a Feeling: Wittgenstein and William James on Love and Other Emotions." *British Journal of the History of Philosophy* 24 (4) (2016b).

Abbreviations

ACL	Wittgenstein's Lectures: Cambridge, 1932–1935 (1979)
BB	The Blue and Brown Books (1969)
BT	The Big Typescript: TS 213 (2005a)
LCL	Wittgenstein's Lectures: Cambridge, 1930–32 (1980a)
OC	On Certainty (1974b)
PG	Philosophical Grammar (1974a)
PI	Philosophical Investigations (2001)
PR	Philosophical Remarks (1975)
RFM	Remarks on the Foundations of Mathematics (1978)
RPP	Remarks on the Philosophy of Psychology (1980b/1980c)
TLP	Tractatus Logico-Philosophicus (2005b)
Z	Zettel (1981)

Introduction

There are a lot of features of Wittgenstein's philosophy that mark it out as unusual or unorthodox in the broader context of twentieth-century philosophy. For example, one could draw attention to the distinctiveness of his writing styles or his methods of philosophical inquiry. But arguably the most unique feature of his thought is his general antipathy towards philosophy itself, or more specifically philosophy as it has been practiced throughout much of the last two thousand years. It is this antipathy – apparent in both *Tractatus Logico-Philosophicus* (*TLP*) and *Philosophical Investigations* (*PI*) – that makes it extremely difficult to promote a constructive dialogue between Wittgenstein and other philosophers (and philosophical debates that extend beyond the exegetical field of Wittgenstein studies). The goal of this book is to open the dialogue by focusing on one broad and far-reaching area, viz. the philosophy of language.

Before outlining how this can be done, it is helpful to be reminded of Wittgenstein's hostility towards traditional conceptions of what philosophy is and of what it can aspire to achieve. In *PI*, he famously writes:

For the clarity that we are aiming at is indeed *complete* clarity. But this simply means that the philosophical problems should *completely* disappear. The real discovery is the one that makes me capable of stopping doing philosophy when I want to. – The one that gives philosophy peace, so that it is no longer tormented by questions which bring *itself* in question. (§133)

According to Wittgenstein, philosophical problems are in a sense pseudo-problems. And since the formulation of the problems and the typical ways of trying to deal with them arise from confusion, the most desirable outcome would not be to perpetuate the same errors but to eradicate or dissolve the philosophical problems themselves (see *PI*, §§119, 254 and 255). On this view, philosophy should not model itself on the sciences by constructing theories to solve the philosophical problems. Instead, it should end in the elimination of the problems, or the recognition that the problems arose in the first place because philosophers were misguided in some distinctive ways (*PI*, §§109, 119, 126 and 128).

1

Reflecting on Wittgenstein's negative attitude may lead us to conclude that there is only one way of viewing the relation between him and other philosophers, i.e. that since his conception of philosophy is so different to most philosophers' there is simply no way for there to be a fruitful dialogue in which, say, philosophers writing today could learn something from Wittgenstein. The seemingly inevitable scenario is one in which Wittgenstein scholars debate among themselves about what he was trying to say in his writings, while more 'constructive' philosophical discussions and debates continue independently in academic journals and books. Although this looks like where things are headed, it is interesting that in the decades that followed the publication of *PI* in 1953 there *was* significant engagement by philosophers with Wittgenstein's texts. For instance, what came to be known as his 'private language argument' was undoubtedly influential, as was his notion of a 'language-game', his discussion of rule-following, his remarks on the relation between meaning and use and his general emphasis on the practical and social aspects of language. However, in most cases this influence came at a high price, which was to distort Wittgenstein by re-constructing what he wrote and moulding him into a more traditional philosopher. In other words, it was as if Wittgenstein was deemed to be an important philosopher only insofar as he was (contrary to what he explicitly stated in his metaphilosophical remarks) engaged in a roughly similar enterprise to other philosophers that involved defending particular views of the mind, language, knowledge etc. Other philosophers engaged with him by implicitly interpreting him as defending proto-theories – if not fully fledged theories – of the same phenomena that they were interested in.

A major concern in this book is with showing that there is a way for philosophers to learn from Wittgenstein, and to engage in a meaningful way with his writings, without overlooking or distorting his highly unusual metaphilosophy. My approach will be to limit myself for the most part to what he writes about language in his later work and to consider how it connects in substantial and hitherto unexplored ways with contemporary debates in the philosophy of language. Before getting into how I propose to do this, it will be instructive to look in more detail at the field of Wittgenstein studies and how it has become much more isolated in recent years.

Wittgenstein Studies, and the Problem of Wittgenstein's Metaphilosophy

Wittgenstein studies appear to be as vibrant now as they have ever been. Every year new edited volumes, monographs and multitudes of journal articles are published that are devoted to the interpretation of his writings. One reason for this is the formation over the last thirty years of different strands that represent strongly opposing ways of reading Wittgenstein. The ensuing debates have been classified using labels such as 'Pyrrhonian vs. non-Pyrrhonian' readings and 'resolute/new vs. traditional' readings. Each side creates identifiable targets for opponents, which has regularly led to ever new statements from philosophers concerning how we should read Wittgenstein. Essentially, the opposition that has developed is between, on the one hand, philosophers including G.E.M. Anscombe, David Pears and Peter Hacker, who have done the most to shape a comprehensive picture of Wittgenstein's philosophy since his death in 1951, and, on the other hand, philosophers including Cora Diamond and James Conant, who more recently have proposed *new* ways of reading Wittgenstein that explicitly reject the dominant interpretive approaches taken or assumed by the former group. Broadly speaking, the opposition is thus between traditional and new methods of interpretation.

The most divisive issues – and which were the principal causes of the development of the new readings – concern Wittgenstein's distinctive metaphilosophy, in both his early and later writings. The major complaint against the traditional readings is that they are not 'resolute' enough in the sense that they purportedly do not take Wittgenstein's metaphilosophical remarks seriously enough. In other words, the new readings maintain that the traditional readings fail to appreciate the full extent of his Pyrrhonianism, or his opposition to defending philosophical theses or theories. Instead, the traditional readings are supposedly more interested in outlining Wittgenstein's arguments and his substantive doctrines or views concerning topics such as the nature of language and the mind. The new readers tend to place Wittgenstein's metaphilosophy at the centre of their interpretations and thus endeavour to show how his methods manage to highlight the errors that traditional philosophy commits, but without Wittgenstein himself falling into the trap of proposing theories of his own (or for some, it may be that he unwittingly fell into this trap in the early work but not in the later).

Although the new (Pyrrhonian/resolute) readings have the merit of being more sensitive to what is unique about Wittgenstein's method or methods of philosophising, they also have the disadvantage that I have been alluding to of isolating him from debates outside of Wittgenstein studies. We thus seem to be confronted with a dilemma: either offer a truly faithful reading of Wittgenstein's writings along the lines of the Pyrrhonian readings and accept that for better or worse Wittgenstein is a radical outsider, which makes dialogue with other philosophers very difficult; or offer a more traditional reading that downplays his metaphilosophical remarks, which makes dialogue possible at the cost of painting a picture of him that is incomplete or distorted in the sense that it makes it seem that he is more like other philosophers.

The Approach Taken in this Book

There are possible ways out of this dilemma, the most obvious being to either argue that the Pyrrhonian readings do not after all make Wittgenstein uninteresting to philosophers who are more optimistic about constructing philosophical theories, or argue that the traditional readings do not distort Wittgenstein's philosophy. The approach I adopt, though, takes its inspiration in part from a rather controversial source, viz. Saul Kripke's reading of Wittgenstein in his 1982 book, *Wittgenstein on Rules and Private Language*. To explain how, it must first be highlighted that Kripke's book occupies a position in the history of Wittgenstein scholarship that is difficult to classify. It is obvious that Kripke does not propose a traditional reading since, as he recognises, his depiction of the later Wittgenstein (which is his focus) is at odds with most other interpreters. Traditional readers recognised this too, which is why his book was so vigorously attacked (see, for instance, Baker and Hacker 1984). Furthermore, his book pre-dates and has very little in common with the Pyrrhonian readings. For example, Kripke offers almost no detailed exegesis of *PI* or any other of Wittgenstein's writings, preferring instead to reconstruct a major line of argument in Wittgenstein's *PI* 'as it struck' Kripke (1982, 5); and he attributes to Wittgenstein what appears to be a substantive philosophical theory or proto-theory concerning the nature of language.

What I find most appealing in Kripke's book is that he depicts Wittgenstein as presenting *arguments* (or at least one argument) and sets about trying to provide the clearest possible formulation of them. The role of arguments in *PI* is difficult to assess – as it is also in *TLP* – but I think Kripke is right to base his reading around a sustained attempt to get clear on what argumentative points Wittgenstein was trying to make. For there can be little doubt that there are arguments or fragments of arguments presented in *PI* (although see Chapter 5 on how this can be challenged). However, a mature and sensitive treatment of the passages where they are found would have to go beyond Kripke and account for what they are doing there. It may, for instance, be that these arguments are presented through Wittgenstein's stylistic device of giving expression to different *voices*, so that the arguments are merely his attempts to mimic the kind of theory-driven and argument-heavy philosophy he opposes. And if so, this would imply that the arguments we find in the book do not have the standard or traditional goal of defending particular philosophical theses. Rather, their goal would be therapeutic – designed to illustrate to his interlocutors some confusion or absurdity inherent in the philosophical assumptions they presuppose. Even if the arguments have this peculiar context within *PI*, they would still be worth investigating; and if they are incomplete or suggestive of more elaborate arguments, we should consider whether they can be completed or given additional support. We can always subsequently hold that

Wittgenstein distanced himself from the arguments or the voices he adopts to express them, but wouldn't it be more interesting if the voices that he distanced himself from were actually presenting pretty compelling arguments?

As I will explain in Chapter 5 in particular, I think that the role of arguments in *PI* is broadly along the lines just sketched. This goes against the view of some prominent Wittgenstein scholars, especially those associated with the new readings. For example, a central claim of Gordon Baker's later writings is that Wittgenstein did not present – and did not need to present – arguments of any kind in *PI*. Instead, according to Baker, he employed a multitude of other methods with the aim of loosening the grip of certain philosophical assumptions or misconceptions about language and the mind. I will attempt to show that while Wittgenstein did employ the kinds of methods Baker identifies, it was imperative that he also employed the method of presenting arguments. This is because these other methods can only go so far in convincing a philosophical opponent; in most cases (for example, highlighting the flaws in the referentialist/'Augustinian' picture of language) arguments are indispensable. This, I hold, is what it means for Wittgenstein to mimic other philosophers. It is as if more traditional-minded philosophers will only be swayed by the kind of method – that of constructing arguments – that they habitually employ themselves.

I will thus defend the reading that there are arguments in *PI*, and moreover often quite intricate arguments; and that in these contexts the interlocutor's voice is typically used to articulate the philosophical conception (for example, referentialism or platonism about meaning) that he is using the arguments to attack. The challenges that my kind of reading face include accommodating his remarks that appear to proclaim that he is not proposing arguments (see *PI*, §§126 and 599) and his metaphilosophical opposition to defending theses of his own. Generally, I endeavour to address these issues by arguing that Wittgenstein developed something like *reductio ad absurdum* arguments. That is, he used his interlocutors' voices to articulate or give vivid expression to the philosophical picture or conception he was attacking; and then, by a chain of reasoning, showed that this conception entailed an absurdity, which motivated the result that we should reject the philosophical conception in question. The only way to defend this strategy for interpreting Wittgenstein is to do so in the context of concrete cases within *PI*. This is what I will do in each of the chapters.

My approach to reading *PI* is, to reiterate, to prioritise the search for, and articulation of, arguments within the book. One of the biggest advantages to this approach is that it provides a fruitful way of connecting Wittgenstein's discussion with the views of other philosophers regarding language. An obvious way in which dialogue can be promoted will be to consider whether particular philosophers writing today are committed to the dominant conceptions of language under attack in *PI*, which would call for a response to Wittgenstein. This has not happened as much as it should because Wittgenstein's arguments have rarely been adequately and clearly presented – perhaps this is partly due to the worry that to present the arguments in a fairly standard way would be to somehow distort Wittgenstein's purpose. A major task of this book is to improve on previous attempts to articulate his arguments, and to explain why the kind of worry that may attach to doing so is misguided.

The book is structured around a set of central topics in the philosophy of language: reference; normativity of meaning; scepticism about meaning; the social dimension of language; and the relation between meaning and use. Most textbooks and handbooks in the philosophy of language contain chapters devoted to most or all of these topics. My strategy will be to follow this approach, but to devote each chapter to what the later Wittgenstein has to say on the topics. This will prove to be illuminating for several reasons. For example, by focussing on the issue of reference in the first chapter and the issue of the normativity of meaning in the second, I will be able to chart the major shift in his middle and later writings away from referentialism and towards the interest in the rules governing the use of words. Furthermore, the discussion of the normativity of meaning will lead naturally into the topic of scepticism about meaning in the third chapter because the main sceptical argument under consideration (as reconstructed by Kripke from Wittgenstein's *PI*) actually contains as a major premise the thesis that meaning is normative; and I will also argue in the fourth chapter that Wittgenstein's so-called private language argument is an extension of his argument against this thesis that meaning is normative. Finally, all of this will prepare the way for the interpretation of Wittgenstein's correlation of meaning and use in the sixth and final chapter.

Overall, my approach will be to devote Chapters 1–4 and 6 to formulating the major arguments in *PI* that bear directly on these five fundamental topics in the philosophy of language. In the process, I will include sections in each chapter on how his arguments impact on debates outside of Wittgenstein studies. Chapter 5 is the exception in this regard; its purpose will be to directly address the major metaphilosophical questions that arise in my reading of Wittgenstein, especially concerning what the arguments I will outline in the rest of the book are doing in *PI*. Most of all, I will attempt to show that there is no internal conflict or inconsistency between Wittgenstein presenting complex arguments throughout much of *PI*, on the one hand, and his metaphilosophical remarks, on the other. The history of scholarship on *PI* is full of claims concerning such a conflict. But I will argue that although Wittgenstein presented numerous arguments throughout the book (and thus brought himself into close alignment with traditional philosophising, despite the stylistic differences), he did so for the sake of the highly unorthodox goal of attacking the presumption in favour of theorising in philosophy. That is, the traditional or non-Wittgensteinian conception of philosophy is one whereby philosophers should strive to develop theories of some sort, such as theories of the nature of language or the mind. Most of Wittgenstein's arguments in *PI* take a set of theoretical claims about language – including those comprising referentialism and platonism – and argue that these claims lead to absurdity. When these arguments are taken together, they demonstrate the repeated failure of the attempt to theorise about the nature of language. According to the reading defended here, this is how Wittgenstein motivates his unorthodox, anti-theoretical standpoint. He proposes an alternative approach to reflecting philosophically on language, one that prioritises the richness of our practices of using language, and that abandons the presumption that philosophising about language must result in a theory that somehow subsumes this complexity or encapsulates it in a general theory.

For Wittgenstein, the complexity and richness of language is never reduced or overlooked. And while he favours an anti-theoretical attitude that acknowledges this, he does not do so dogmatically. On the contrary, a great deal of *PI* is devoted to seriously thinking through the most dominant and tempting general theoretical assumptions about language and particularly with showing how they distort the phenomena they are supposed to be elucidating. This is apparent in the arguments he develops and it is these arguments that I will be most concerned with outlining and evaluating throughout the book.

1   Reference

The analysis of Wittgenstein's reflections on language must begin with the issue of reference, or the referentialist conception of linguistic meaning. Generally, this is the view that the meaning of a word is the object it refers to. This is the necessary starting point because Wittgenstein has traditionally been interpreted as endorsing a version of referentialism in *Tractatus Logico-Philosophicus* (*TLP*) and the opening discussion of *Philosophical Investigations* (*PI*) is devoted to attacking this particular view of linguistic meaning.

Sections 1.1–1.3 of this chapter will address many of the difficult interpretive issues that arise when trying to understand Wittgenstein's attacks on referentialism in the opening sections of *PI*. Sections 1.4–1.8 will also engage with the exegetical problems, but the goal will be to provide a comprehensive picture of the most important stages of Wittgenstein's criticisms of referentialism. I will argue that he provides a powerful case against this view; and despite the fact that his objections are presented simultaneously with his apparent endorsement of a use-based conception, Wittgenstein manages to do so without begging the question and without presupposing a premise that the referentialist does not accept. Finally, in section 1.9, I will consider the relation between his views and the 'descriptivist' theories of reference with which he is often associated.

1.1   Augustine and the Augustinian Picture of Language

Wittgenstein's first remarks in §1 of *PI* are made in response to the following description provided by Augustine of how he was taught to use language:

When they (my elders) named some object, and accordingly moved towards something, I saw this and I grasped that the thing was called by the sound they uttered when they meant to point it out. Their intention was shewn by their bodily movements, as it were the natural language of all peoples: the expression of the face, the play of the eyes, the movement of other parts of the body, and the tone of voice which expresses our state of mind in seeking, having, rejecting, or avoiding something. Thus, as I heard words repeatedly used in their proper places in various sentences, I gradually learnt to understand what objects they signified; and after I had trained my mouth to form these signs, I used them to express my own desires. (Augustine, *Confessions*, I. 8)

8

Wittgenstein comments that this description 'gives us a particular picture of the essence of human language', and he summarises it with two general claims:

(i) 'the individual words in language name objects';
(ii) 'sentences are combinations of such names'.

In addition, he states that this picture contains 'the roots of the following idea', which is expressed in three further claims:

(iii) 'Every word has a meaning.'
(iv) 'This meaning is correlated with the word.'
(v) '[The meaning] is the object for which the word stands.'

These latter three claims (along with a few others that are introduced in subsequent sections) are usually taken to comprise what has since been called 'the Augustinian picture of language'. As indicated especially in (v), the Augustinian picture is representative of any approach to language that characterises linguistic meaning in terms of reference to objects. It is a referentialist picture, or a general conception of 'the essence of human language' as consisting in the reference of words to objects in the world. On one dominant type of reading of *PI*, Wittgenstein is concerned from this point onwards (at least up to §64 or so and possibly for the entire book) with attacking this referentialist approach in a variety of ways.

However, before turning to Wittgenstein's arguments against referentialism, there are some deep interpretive issues that must be addressed. The most important is that of how *Augustinian* the so-called Augustinian picture of language really is. When we look closer at Augustine's description, we will notice that there is a considerable distance between it and the philosophical claims that Wittgenstein states are rooted in it. For example, there is no mention of sentences as being combinations of names, and there is no implication that all words have the same function (viz., to refer to objects in the language-user's environment). Furthermore, Augustine even draws attention to features of language-learning that Wittgenstein himself emphasises later in *PI*, such as shared inclinations and reactions, or what Augustine calls 'the natural language of all peoples' (see Wittgenstein's reference to 'The common behaviour of mankind' at *PI*, §206). Warren Goldfarb provides the clearest expression of doubt concerning the connection between Augustine's description and the philosophical picture extracted from it by maintaining that there is no genuine philosophical claim being made in the Augustine passage:

It is not at all obvious that Augustine *is* expressing a conception of the essence of language. My primary reaction to the citation from the *Confessions*, read by itself, is to think that what it expresses is obvious – it seems trivial, prosaic, well-nigh unobjectionable. It is just a harmless elaboration of the observations that early in life children learn what things are called, and learn to express their wants and needs verbally. It hardly goes beyond the level of the commonplace; surely no capital can be made of it. (Goldfarb 1983, 268)

Goldfarb argues that Wittgenstein's intention is to impose these philosophical claims on Augustine's description in order to 'shock' us into seeing clearly how philosophical notions can be introduced in contexts where there is no call for them (*Ibid.*). The point would then be that it is possible to give a perfectly adequate description of language-learning, as Augustine does, without introducing philosophical notions; and although ordinarily in philosophy these notions are introduced into discussions of language and other topics automatically or without ever drawing attention to them *as* philosophical notions, Wittgenstein is intending to introduce them in a way that is more explicit or obvious so that we can be aware of the move.

This is very much a minority view of what Wittgenstein is doing in the opening of *PI*. What we find in most readings is an unquestioned acceptance that the philosophical claims, (i)–(v), *are* firmly rooted in Augustine's description (see, for example, Baker and Hacker 2005b, 48–50 and Glock 1996, 41). But the decision we take on this issue of whether or not the philosophical referentialist picture is in fact Augustinian will shape how we interpret Wittgenstein's entire opening discussion and his attack on referentialism. I will explain exactly how in the remainder of this section.

The contrast between the two types of readings that result from this issue is best highlighted by considering the relation between the philosophical referentialist picture, on the one hand, and Wittgenstein's example of the builders' language introduced in §2 of *PI*, on the other:

That philosophical concept of meaning has its place in a primitive idea of the way language functions. But one can also say that it is the idea of a language more primitive than ours.

Let us imagine a language for which the description given by Augustine is right. The language is meant to serve for communication between a builder A and an assistant B. A is building with building-stones: there are blocks, pillars, slabs and beams. B has to pass the stones, and that in the order in which A needs them. For this purpose they use a language consisting of the words 'block', 'pillar', 'slab', 'beam'. A calls them out; – B brings the stone which he has learnt to bring at such-and-such a call. – Conceive this as a complete primitive language.

The builders' language consists exclusively of four words: 'block', 'pillar', 'slab' and 'beam'; and it functions as a tool for 'communication' between a 'builder A' and an 'assistant B'. The activity of using the language simply involves A using the words for the building-stones he wants, and B bringing the relevant stones. Crucially, Wittgenstein calls this language one 'for which the description given by Augustine is right'. The divisive issue is that of whether or not Augustine's original description is itself philosophical (i.e. that it implies certain referentialist philosophical claims), and so the two main types of readings follow from their respective views of whether or not the builders' language is supposed to embody a philosophical picture.

The dominant view is that the builders' language does embody a philosophical picture. On this type of reading, Wittgenstein's purpose is to show that the referentialist philosophical picture can be shown to have *limited* applicability by describing a primitive language for which this picture is accurate. This seems plausible because the language only contains words like 'block' and 'pillar', and it is easy to imagine their meaning being fixed by correlating them with objects of a certain size and shape. Wittgenstein's overall point would then be to demonstrate that when we expand this primitive language (as he does in §8) to include, for example, numerals and indexical terms, the applicability of the referentialist philosophical picture becomes questionable. The implication is that when we take account of the complexity of language – not just of the extended builders' language, but of fully fledged natural languages like English – the philosophical claims characteristic of referentialism will be seen to not apply generally; or to put it another way, it will be shown that referentialism does not, after all, capture the essence of human language, but at most a tiny fragment of it. This reading is given strong support by what Wittgenstein states in §3:

Augustine, we might say, does describe a system of communication; only not everything that we call language is this system. And one has to say this in many cases where the question arises 'Is this an appropriate description or not?' The answer is: 'Yes, it is appropriate, but only for this narrowly circumscribed region, not for the whole of what you were claiming to describe.'

It is as if someone were to say: 'A game consists in moving objects about on a surface according to certain rules ...' – and we replied: You seem to be thinking of board games, but there are others. You can make your definition correct by expressly restricting it to those games.

Despite the coherence and wide acceptance of this reading of Wittgenstein's general strategy in the opening of *PI*, there is an alternative reading that has its roots in Goldfarb's 'I Want You to Bring Me a Slab: Remarks on the Opening Sections of the *Philosophical Investigations*' (1983). This other reading emphasises a distinction between Augustine's description and 'the Augustinian picture of language' (represented by claims (i)–(v) above), the main difference being that Augustine's description is non-philosophical, mundane and platitudinous. Therefore, when Wittgenstein calls the builders' language 'a language for which the description given by Augustine is right', this should be read as entailing that it is a description of language use that involves the builders pointing to objects, uttering words, responding to each other's gestures etc. But, importantly, this description is held to be perfectly adequate and intelligible without introducing philosophical notions such as those that are part of the referentialist picture.

If we grant that the non-philosophical description of what the builders are doing with language is intelligible and sufficient (i.e. that it is not in need of philosophical notions like reference to provide a more 'complete' explanation of what they are doing), the point could be generalised to more complex uses of language including our sophisticated use of language in our everyday lives where it is less obvious that we can do without philosophical notions in the description of what we do with words. This approach is suggested in §5 of *PI*:

> If we look at the example in §1, we may perhaps get an inkling how much this general notion of the meaning of a word surrounds the working of language with a haze which makes clear vision impossible. It disperses the fog to study the phenomena of language in primitive kinds of application in which one can command a clear view of the aim and functioning of the words.
>
> A child uses such primitive forms of language when it learns to talk. Here the teaching of language is not explanation, but training.

This quotation depicts the philosophical referentialist picture ('this general notion of the meaning of a word') as 'a haze' that makes it impossible to see clearly how language actually functions. Wittgenstein's proposed method is to look at a limited context, such as the builders' language-game ('the phenomena of language in primitive kinds of application'), where this haze does not exist because the philosophical picture is of no use in the sense that the primitive language use can be described adequately without appealing to philosophical notions. This helps to disperse the fog because if we realise that we can give a sufficient description of primitive language use without invoking philosophical notions, we may come to realise that we can do the same with more complex uses of language. Wittgenstein also mentions 'the example in §1', which is just such an example of an everyday use of language involving an exchange between a person and a shopkeeper who is given a slip of paper with 'five red apples' written on it. Wittgenstein gives a description of the exchange that is as mundane as the (present view of the) description of the builders' language-game and, indeed, of Augustine's description of learning language. The difficulty that arises in this shopkeeper example is that it seems that the description is not sufficient precisely because no philosophical explanation of how the shopkeeper grasps the meaning of the words on the slip of paper is given. On this second, Goldfarbian type of reading, the point of the example of the builders' language is to suggest – not at this early stage to *prove* – that a non-philosophical description of language use may be adequate after all.

In the next section, I will consider how these competing readings of the opening of *PI* generate alternative accounts of Wittgenstein's attack on referentialism.

1.2   Overview of the Steps in Wittgenstein's Attack on Referentialism

Both of the readings just discussed view Wittgenstein's purpose in introducing the builders' language-game to be to target referentialism, but they interpret it in different ways. The first reading holds that Wittgenstein's goal is to show that referentialism has only limited applicability (that it does genuinely apply in the limited context of the builders' language-game), and hence that what is wrong with referentialism is its identification of meaning with reference in *all* contexts. On the second reading, the main point is not that referentialism has limited applicability, but that it is redundant; for on this view, the referentialist picture does not even apply to the builders' language-game because it can be adequately described without introducing the philosophically robust notion of reference.

Although there are these competing readings of the philosophical purpose of the builders' language-game, one thing that we can be reasonably certain about is that the example is supposed to at least make us suspicious of the appropriateness of referentialism as a conception of the essence of linguistic meaning. Furthermore, making us suspicious or wary may be as far as he goes in these opening sections because it could hardly be said that he does enough at this early stage to mount a compelling argument against referentialism. As we will see, some of the steps in his attack seem to involve presenting us with an alternative picture of meaning (a picture that focuses on actual uses of words rather than referential relations) and getting us to appreciate the appropriateness of it, rather than, strictly speaking, proposing an argument that meets the referentialist on her terms and that would worry her. This raises questions about Wittgenstein's method and whether or not he engages in direct or standard argumentation throughout *PI*. My view is that he does at some points, while at others his method is more idiosyncratic and involves encouraging us to adopt a certain critical attitude to a philosophical problem or conception. I will limit my discussion here to trying to articulate his arguments and leave the metaphilosophical questions that arise from them until Chapter 5 (see especially section 5.4).

The following are the main steps in Wittgenstein's attack on referentialism, most of which I will go on to address in this chapter:

(1) The referentialist picture is not an accurate picture of 'the essence of human language' because it has *limited* or *no* applicability (depending on one's reading), i.e. there are many genuine instances of linguistic meaning and language use that do not fit the referentialist picture. (*PI*, §§1–8, §§40–42)

(2) Words – like tools – have a variety of functions; and the referentialist claim that the meaning of a word is the object it refers to presupposes an artificial uniformity of function that overlooks this diversity. (*PI*, §§11–12)

(3) Referentialism has no explanatory power. Rather, its claims concerning the relation between meaning and reference are trivial and uninformative in the sense that they tell us nothing about how a word is to be used. (*PI*, §§13–14)

(4) Ostensive definition – or definition of the meaning of a word by pointing to the thing or kind of thing it refers to – cannot be the foundation of all language learning. The assumption that it is the foundation generates the paradox that the meaning of a word could never be learnt because the success of an ostensive definition depends on some prior linguistic competence (such as understanding of what kind of word is being defined). (*PI*, §§28–32)

(5) *Pure*[1] referentialism about singular terms (for example, names) is false because it relies on a notion of absolute simplicity that is empty or incoherent. (*PI*, §§46–48)

(6) *Pure* referentialism about general terms is false because it relies on the assumption that meanings must be absolutely definite, which is contradicted by a multitude of examples of general terms that have indefinite or vague meanings. (*PI*, §§65–71)

Wittgenstein's reflections on the builders' language-game are an important instance of the first objection, but there are others. His examples in §§40–42 of *PI* of words that have meanings even though they do not have referents or bearers (such as names of people who have died or of things that never existed) serve the similar function of highlighting the inappropriateness of extending the referential picture to all instances of language use.

Of these six types of objections he makes to referentialism, I think it is wise to view the first three as merely preparatory in the sense that they can do no more than plant seeds of doubt in our minds concerning referentialism.[2] Wittgenstein would surely recognise that the referentialist could reply by, for example, discounting the apparent counterexamples to their position (either by denying that the terms in question are really meaningful or arguing that the terms can be analysed away into terms that do fit with the referentialist picture). For example, the second type of objection is based on a comparison between words and tools; and the purpose is to suggest that the different functions that words have in our lives are as varied as the different functions of tools:

---

[1] I am following Robert Hanna in drawing a distinction between pure and moderate versions of referentialism (see Hanna 2010, 16). The pure or strict version – the kind defended in *TLP* – is often viewed as Wittgenstein's main target in *PI*, but I will argue in the following sections that it can be extended to moderate versions.

[2] David Stern makes a similar point, specifically concerning Wittgenstein's method of highlighting the limitations of a philosophical conception by discussing how it applies in very narrow circumstances at best (see Stern 2004, 17).

Think of the tools in a tool-box: there is a hammer, pliers, a saw, a screw-driver, a rule, a glue-pot, glue, nails and screws. – The functions of words are as diverse as the functions of these objects. (*PI*, §11)

In the subsequent section, Wittgenstein makes the same point by drawing an analogy between words and handles in a locomotive cabin, the point being that all of the handles may look alike but their functions are different:

It is like looking into the cabin of a locomotive. We see handles all looking more or less alike. (Naturally, since they are all supposed to be handled.) But one is the handle of a crank which can be moved continuously (it regulates the opening of a valve); another is the handle of a switch, which has only two effective positions, it is either off or on; a third is the handle of a brake-lever, the harder one pulls on it, the harder it brakes; a fourth, the handle of a pump: it has an effect only so long as it is moved to and fro. (*PI*, §12)

These analogies amount to an objection to referentialism because they imply that the referentialist imposes an artificial uniformity of function on words – viz. that of naming or talking about things – that overlooks their diversity of functions in being used to ask questions, make demands, tell jokes, express feelings etc. The objection is persuasive to a point, but someone sympathetic to referentialism could insist that these non-descriptive functions are second-ary to and parasitic on the primary descriptive or naming function, and that the fundamental meaning-determining relation is nevertheless that between a word and the thing it stands for.

   A similar response can be made to the third objection, which is presented in the following passages:

When we say: 'Every word in language signifies something' we have so far said *nothing whatever*; unless we have explained exactly *what* distinction we wish to make. (It might be, of course, that we wanted to distinguish the words of language (8) [i.e. the expanded builders' language] from words 'without meaning' such as occur in Lewis Carroll's poems, or words like 'Lilliburlero' in songs.) (*PI*, §13)
   Imagine someone's saying: 'All tools serve to modify something. Thus the hammer modifies the position of the nail, the saw the shape of the board, and so on.' – And what is modified by the rule, the glue-pot, the nails? – 'Our knowledge of a thing's length, the temperature of the glue, and the solidity of the box' – Would anything be gained by this assimilation of expressions? (*PI*, §14)

Wittgenstein's objection is that the fundamental referentialist assertion that 'Every word signifies something' is trivial and uninformative. The notion of signification or reference does no explanatory work on its own. By this, Wittgenstein means that it does not settle the question of how a word is to be used, any more than the assertion 'All tools serve to modify something' settles the question of how to use pliers or a hammer.

   Once again, it is open to the referentialist to insist that the notion of ref-erence does have explanatory power, that it explains how a word acquires meaning by naming or being about something. Exactly how the referentialist would develop this response would depend on the type of referentialist theory adopted. For example, a 'descriptivist' theory of reference would provide one kind of explanation, while a 'causal-historical' theory would provide another (for more on this see section 1.9). I will return briefly to this objection in the next section when I discuss what it is to be a *theory* of reference, as opposed to a referential *picture*. The main point I want to emphasise is that the first three objections leave room for the referentialist to hold on to their position.

Although the much-discussed fourth objection concerning ostensive definition is significant in that it may genuinely threaten referentialism, I will focus in sections 1.4–1.7 on the more neglected fifth and sixth objections.

1.3   What Is a Theory of Reference? And What Is an Augustinian/Referential Picture of Language?

The practice of philosophising consists almost entirely of the following kinds of activities: formulating problems or questions concerning fundamental notions such as reality, knowledge, goodness etc.; developing and defending theories in response to these problems; identifying weaknesses or errors in the proposed theories; and either refining the existing theories or developing new ones in an attempt to provide better solutions to the core problems we are interested in.

As indicated at the beginning of the book, one of the most distinctive features of Wittgenstein's later philosophy is that he is not engaged in the same kinds of activities as other philosophers (either before or after him). The concern with the above general model of philosophical practice as theory construction and problem solving is nevertheless central to his later writings. But he addresses it in a radically different way in the sense that he is concerned with tracing the first, unnoticed steps that lead to philosophical theorising. He is thus explicitly not concerned with developing his own theories in an attempt to solve philosophical problems; instead he aims to understand how philosophical problems arise in the first place and why the seemingly natural response is to propose a theory to solve the problems.

While this feature of his approach will be explored directly in Chapter 5, at this point it helps to highlight it because it provides some indication as to why he begins *PI* by examining a philosophical 'picture' of language rather than a philosophical theory. Generally speaking, it seems that a philosophical picture pertains to the *source* of philosophising about something, while a philosophical theory is more sophisticated and is the *result* of philosophising. Wittgenstein is interested in the passage from general picture to particular theory because he believes there is something inherently confused or misguided in responding to philosophical problems by constructing theories. The process leading to the construction of a philosophical theory is thus charted as a typical path in which we fall into error when reflecting on notions such as language, reality, the mind etc. Wittgenstein seems to suggest that philosophers are inclined to automatically or unreflectively adopt, for example, the principles constituting the Augustinian picture when they begin theorising about language.

There is a limit to how intelligible we can make this distinction between picture and theory without digressing into the finer details of Wittgenstein's metaphilosophy. For the present purposes of getting clear on his strategy of attacking referentialism, it might be useful to begin with a couple of examples of referential theories of linguistic meaning and to work backwards to the question of what a general referentialist *picture* would be. The two most famous examples of referentialist theories are: 'descriptivism' or the 'description theory', based on the writings of Frege and Russell; and the 'causal-historical theory', defended by Kripke and Putnam. The common feature of these theories is that they attempt to *explain* how it is that a word refers to an object. Hence, they each try to identify some relation that connects the word with the object, and that explains the relation of reference between them. The explanations provided by the description theory and causal-historical theory are along the following lines:

Description Theory of Reference (for proper names):

A name is equivalent in meaning to a certain set of definite descriptions. The relation that ties the name to its referent is that of *satisfaction* (or *application*), i.e. the referent is the individual thing that uniquely satisfies the descriptions (or that the descriptions uniquely apply to) that are equivalent in meaning to the name.

Causal-Historical Theory of Reference (for proper names):

The relation that ties a name to its referent is that of *having a causal-historical link* to the original naming of a thing. That is, the name is connected with a particular individual thing in a naming ceremony; and every subsequent use of that name succeeds in referring to that same thing by virtue of a causal-historical chain of reference borrowings that leads back to the naming ceremony.

Although theories of this sort may be said to be developed within the broad framework of a referentialist or Augustinian picture of language, it is obvious that there is a considerable difference between these theoretical claims, on the one hand, and the rather vague claims such as that '[The meaning] is the object for which the word stands' that are characteristic of the Augustinian picture, on the other.

The most striking difference is that the latter claims are not explanatory. The Augustinian picture merely identifies meaning with reference and – unlike the theories of reference that may be developed in accordance with the picture – simply posits the referential relation between words and objects without attempting to explain it. In this regard, the Augustinian picture resembles what is often called 'the Millian view' of names, based on Mill's assertion that

proper names are not connotative: they denote the individuals who are called by them; but they do not indicate or imply any attributes as belonging to those individuals. (1961, 20)

The Millian view is that names are merely labels for objects and beyond this assertion it provides no explanation concerning the kind of connection that exists between names and objects.

If this comparison with the difference between particular referential theories and the Millian view is appropriate as a guide to clarifying Wittgenstein's distinction between philosophical theories and philosophical pictures, it will have important implications for how we evaluate his strategy for undermining referentialism. Most notably, if we find that his approach is to attack the general referentialist picture and then to assume that his criticisms transfer to any particular theories of reference that are developed in accordance with it, this will be problematic because the particular theories have features that the general picture does not have. For example, if it were to be objected that the Augustinian picture has no genuine explanatory force, this would not transfer to the particular theories of reference that philosophers have proposed.

This will suffice as background to Wittgenstein's attack on the referentialist conception of linguistic meaning. Considerations to do with his unique strategy and the distinction between picture and theory should be kept in mind in what follows. His objections will ultimately have to be judged in light of them.

1.4   Names and Simple Objects

A crucial stage in Wittgenstein's attack on referentialism is provided in §§39–64 of *PI*, where he discusses names and the temptation to hold that 'a name ought really to signify a simple' (§39). In these sections, he offers reasons against thinking that the fundamental relation between language and the world must be the primitive relation of reference holding between absolutely simple names and absolutely simple objects. This view is of course one of the main pillars of logical atomism, and so Wittgenstein is here targeting the position he was attracted to in *TLP* and that was also defended by Russell. Consequently, the argument in these sections may appear to be of little relevance because most of the versions of referentialism defended in the twentieth century are not forms of logical atomism. This assessment, though, would be premature because it may be possible to broaden the scope of Wittgenstein's attack by demonstrating that more moderate versions of referentialism actually presuppose in some sense the legitimacy of the above logical atomist thesis, thus making any attack on the latter applicable to the moderate versions. Therefore, there are two issues to consider: first, Wittgenstein's argument against the logical atomist thesis, and how compelling it is; and second, whether or not this argument can be used against more moderate versions of referentialism. I will devote this section to the first issue and the next section to the second. The emphasis throughout will be on singular terms, and specifically proper names.

In §46 of *PI*, Wittgenstein begins by inquiring into the logical atomist thesis concerning the reference of names to simple objects, and then quotes a passage from Plato's *Theaetetus* that offers a line of reasoning that may be interpreted as leading to the thesis. Wittgenstein's quoting of Plato to introduce a particular philosophical conception is comparable to his quoting of Augustine in §1, but in the present case there seems to be a closer connection between the relevant philosophical claim and the quotation.

What lies behind the idea that names really signify simples?

Socrates says in the *Theaetetus*: 'If I make no mistake, I have heard some people say this: there is no definition of the primary elements – so to speak – out of which we and everything else are composed; for everything that exists in its own right can only be *named*, no other determination is possible, neither that it *is* nor that it *is not* ... But what exists in its own right has to be ... named without any other determination. In consequence it is impossible to give an account of any primary element; for it, nothing is possible but the bare name; its name is all it has. But just as what consists of these primary elements is itself complex, so the names of the elements become descriptive language by being compounded together. For the essence of speech is the composition of names.'

Both Russell's 'individuals' and my 'objects' (*Tractatus Logico-Philosophicus*) were such primary elements. (*PI*, §46)

The fact that Wittgenstein ends the passage by linking the philosophical view with Russell's and his own in *TLP* increases the sense that his interest in these sections is quite narrow.[3]

The subsequent section is one of the most illuminating in the whole of *PI*; it contains some vital clues about his philosophical method, as well as the significance of examples such as the builders' language-game from §2. The section provides the beginning of an attack on the logical atomist thesis, and is continued in §48. §47 provides a good illustration of Wittgenstein's method of taking a philosophical use of language (for example, in asking a philosophical question) and showing that an illicit use of language is actually involved. In this case, the question is 'what are the simple constituent parts of which reality is composed?', but his treatment of it leads him to articulate the kind of error involved in similar philosophical uses of language.

[3] In Wittgenstein's *TLP*, the theory concerning logical simples contains three main claims: (1) that simple objects must exist; (2) that they can only be named; and (3) that the existence of such objects is a condition of genuinely meaningful language. The first two could arguably be attributed to Plato on the basis of the quotation, but the third is quite specific to Wittgenstein's Tractarian doctrine.

Wittgenstein begins by investigating the notions of simplicity and complexity that are presupposed by the logical atomist:

But what are the simple constituent parts of which reality is composed? – What are the simple constituent parts of a chair? – The bits of wood of which it is made? Or the molecules, or the atoms? – 'Simple' means: not composite. And here the point is: in what sense 'composite'? It makes no sense at all to speak absolutely of the 'simple parts of a chair'.

Again: Does my visual image of this tree, of this chair, consist of parts? And what are its simple component parts? Multi-colouredness is one kind of complexity; another is, for example, that of a broken outline composed of straight bits. And a curve can be said to be composed of an ascending and a descending segment. (*PI*, §47)

The point is straightforward. When asking a question using the terms 'simple' or 'complex', the question makes no sense unless it is specified what is meant by the terms. Keeping this in mind, it *is* possible to make sense of questions concerning the complexity of a chair or a visual image of a tree. For example, the complexity could be characterised in terms of 'bits of wood' in the case of the chair or 'multi-colouredness' in the case of a visual image. But Wittgenstein implies that the philosopher who inquires into 'the simple constituent parts of which reality is composed' is attempting to 'speak absolutely' about simplicity and complexity. That is, the philosopher – or the logical atomist – is not concerned with this or that specific sense of 'simple' and 'complex'; he is concerned with a supposedly *deeper* sense of these terms. But Wittgenstein is trying to show that 'It makes no sense at all to speak absolutely' of the simple parts of a thing.

He continues:

If I tell someone without any further explanation: 'What I see before me now is composite', he will have the right to ask: 'What do you mean by "composite"? For there are all sorts of things that that can mean!' – The question 'Is what you see composite?' makes good sense if it is already established what kind of complexity – that is, which particular use of the word – is in question. If it had been laid down that the visual image of a tree was to be called 'composite' if one saw not just a single trunk, but also branches, then the question 'Is the visual image of this tree simple or composite?', and the question 'What are its simple component parts?', would have a clear sense – a clear use. And of course the answer to the second question is not 'The branches' (that would be an answer to the *grammatical* question: 'What are here called "simple component parts"?') but rather a description of the individual branches.

But isn't a chessboard, for instance, obviously, and absolutely, composite? – You are probably thinking of the composition out of thirty-two white and thirty-two black squares. But could we not also say, for instance, that it was composed of the colours black and white and the schema of squares? And if there are quite different ways of looking at it, do you still want to say that the chessboard is absolutely 'composite'? – Asking 'Is this object composite?' *outside* a particular language-game is like what a boy once did, who had to say whether the verbs in certain sentences were in the active or passive voice, and who racked his brains over the question whether the verb 'to sleep' meant something active or passive. (*Ibid.*)

Wittgenstein here reinforces the point that a question involving the term 'composite' makes sense 'if it is already established what kind of complexity – that is, which particular use of the word – is in question', or if it has been given 'a clear sense – a clear use'.

Crucially, he then indicates that what a philosopher does when he asks a question like 'Is this object composite?' without specifying a sense of 'composite' or 'simple' is to ask the question '*outside* a particular language-game'. If this is a characteristic feature of philosophical questions (or of philosophical uses of language generally), it entails that when the words occurring in philosophical questions are given a particular use in a language-game – given a specific sense – they cease to have the kind of deeper significance they were supposed to have in the original philosophical questions. The matter becomes everyday or mundane, and there is therein a rejection of the philosophical question:

To the *philosophical* question: 'Is the visual image of this tree composite, and what are its component parts?' the correct answer is: 'That depends on what you understand by "composite".' (And that is of course not an answer but a rejection of the question.) (*Ibid.*)

This has an important implication for how we view Wittgenstein's method of considering particular philosophical conceptions or pictures in relation to concrete primitive language-games. We encountered an example of this in §2 of *PI* concerning the relation between the Augustinian picture of language and the builders' language-game. As we saw, the question of how to interpret this relation is unclear when these early sections are read in isolation. But what Wittgenstein states in §47 concerning the philosophical use of language as being outside of any particular language-game sheds light on the issue. Taking this remark into account, we would have to conclude that it is impossible for any philosophical claim or picture to be genuinely applicable to such language-games because as soon as they are applied they *cease to be philosophical.* I will elaborate on this point by considering Wittgenstein's example in §48.

Mirroring his introduction of the builders' language-game in §2, Wittgenstein in §48 sets out to construct a language-game for which 'the account in the *Theaetetus*' is 'really valid' (i.e. the conception of names as signifying simples).

The language serves to describe combinations of coloured squares on a surface. The squares form a complex like a chessboard. There are red, green, white and black squares. The words of the language are (correspondingly) 'R', 'G', 'W', 'B', and a sentence is a series of these words. They describe an arrangement of squares in the order:

1	2	3
4	5	6
7	8	9

And so for instance the sentence 'RRBGGGRWW' describes an arrangement of this sort:

r	r	b
g	g	g
r	w	w

Here the sentence is a complex of names, to which corresponds a complex of elements. The primary elements are the coloured squares. (*PI*, §48)[4]

The language in this example thus consists of the terms, 'R', 'G', 'W' and 'B', which are names of red, green, white and black squares, respectively. And sentences of the language describe the coloured arrangements of the squares by means of combinations of names like 'RRBGGGRWW'. Wittgenstein proceeds to ask, 'But are these [coloured squares] simple?', and he replies:

I do not know what else you would have me call 'the simples', what would be more natural in this language-game. But under other circumstances I should call a monochrome square 'composite', consisting perhaps of two rectangles, or of the elements colour and shape. But the concept of complexity might also be so extended that a smaller area was said to be 'composed' of a greater area and another one subtracted from it. Compare the 'composition of forces', the 'division' of a line by a point outside it; these expressions show that we are sometimes even inclined to conceive the smaller as the result of a composition of greater parts, and the greater as the result of a division of the smaller.

But I do not know whether to say that the figure described by our sentence consists of four or of nine elements! Well, does the sentence consist of four letters or of nine? – And which are *its* elements, the types of letter, or the letters? Does it matter which we say, so long as we avoid misunderstandings in any particular case? (*Ibid.*)

In this example, we could say that there is a type of application of the logical atomist thesis (or the *Theaetetus* conception of names as denoting simples) to a particular language-game. But in giving the notion of simples a specific sense, the claim that 'a *name ought really to signify a simple*' has been robbed of its philosophical import. Therefore, it is not that Wittgenstein has established the falsity of the claim; rather, he has shown that insofar as it has sense at all, it

---

[4] In this display, the lower arrangement of boxes is not coloured but marked with 'r', 'b', 'g' and 'w' to indicate what colour they are. We have thus to imagine that the boxes are coloured *red, black, green* and *white*.

could only be quite trivial. This is analogous to his treatment of the claim that 'Every word in language signifies something' in §§13/14, by comparing it to the claim that '*All* tools serve to modify something'. His point is that nothing much is gained by making statements of this sort because the question of how to use words or tools and of what function they have remains unanswered.

The discussion in §§47/48 helps us to understand Wittgenstein's purpose in constructing particular language-games as a way of evaluating certain philosophical claims or pictures. His goal cannot be to construct a language-game for which a particular philosophical conception would be genuinely valid in the sense that it preserves every feature of it. Rather, it must be to show that when you construct a language-game which presents *one* way of specifying a particular use to the words in the philosophical conception (or the questions formulated in accordance with that conception), the result is to give meaning to those words *but* also to strip the philosophical use (the questions etc.) of their intended deep significance. If this is correct, then the Augustinian picture of language is not even genuinely applicable to the builders' language-game. Instead, the builders' language-game is used to show that when the key claims of the Augustinian picture are given a genuine sense, they cease to have the significance they are supposed to have. This supports the second (Goldfarbian) reading I discussed in sections 1.1 and 1.2.

1.5   Referentialism About Singular Terms

Given the fact that Wittgenstein explicitly cites Russell and *TLP* when attacking the view of names as signifying absolutely simple objects, it is not surprising that his target in these sections is interpreted as being quite narrow. But it has also seemed to some that in *PI* as a whole, Wittgenstein is only concerned with undermining a particular type of referentialism, viz. the kind that he and Russell were once drawn to. For example, Robert Hanna argues that

It is Pure Referentialism, and not Referentialism as such, that is the philosophical target of Wittgenstein's deconstructive critique of Referentialism in the *Investigations*. (2010, 21)

And he characterises 'Pure Referentialism' as follows:

All words are names, and the meaning of a word is nothing but the object it names. Furthermore, all names are proper names, and the meaning of every basic proper name in a basic proposition (whether a basic singular term or a basic general term a.k.a. a 'concept word') is nothing but the referent or bearer of the name, i.e. an absolutely simple individual concrete object or a definite abstract concept or universal. (Hanna 2010, 16)[5]

---

[5] See also where Hanna states that the doctrine of Pure Referentialism is exemplified by the view of names in Russell's writings and *TLP*: 'Moreover, the bull's-eye of the philosophical target of

On this reading, the Augustinian picture of language is identified with Pure Referentialism and it applies to both singular and general terms. I will continue to focus on the case of singular terms in this section and turn to general terms in the next section.

I agree with Hanna that Wittgenstein's explicit target is the pure referentialist doctrine, but I think there is a further question that should be considered concerning the possible broader applicability of the argument in §§47/48. The most straightforward strategy would be to demonstrate that more moderate or 'non-pure' versions of referentialism entail or presuppose the legitimacy of pure referentialism, so that any argument against the latter will apply also to the former. A moderate referentialism could, for example, maintain its focus on ordinary proper names like 'Barack Obama' and ordinary general terms like 'red' and state that the meanings of these terms is identical with the objects they refer to. Hence, there would be no presupposition of logically simple names or logical simple objects referred to by the names. This version of referentialism would be formulated in accordance with the general Augustinian picture rather than the more specific logical atomist or *Theaetetus* conception.

However, moderate referentialist accounts of this kind face a number of familiar objections that historically have motivated the defence of the more extreme or 'pure' referentialism. For example, how would such an account deal with non-referring singular terms such as 'Excalibur' and 'the present King of France'? The options are quite stark:

(a) Accept that the terms do not refer to anything. But this requires abandoning or supplementing referentialism because the terms are nevertheless meaningful and hence it must be accepted that there is more to meaning than reference. (The Fregean response.)

(b) Accept that the terms do refer to entities after all, but of a peculiar 'non-actual' kind (non-existent or fictional entities). This preserves referentialism but at the high price of adopting a strange metaphysics. (The Meinongian response.)

(c) Deny that the terms are genuine names or descriptions and argue that when the sentences containing the terms are properly analysed the terms disappear or reveal *genuine* or logically simple names that do refer to objects. This also preserves referentialism but by transforming the initial moderate referentialism into a pure referentialism. (The Russellian and Tractarian response.)

Pure Referentialism is not in fact the semantics of names proposed by Plato's Socrates in the *Theaetetus*, but instead a dual bull's-eye consisting of Russell's semantics of names circa 1912 and early Wittgenstein's semantics of names in the *Tractatus*' (2010, 21).

Other widely discussed problems such as dealing with negative existentials and the substitution of co-referring terms in belief contexts provide additional motivation for adopting one of these options.[6]

The third option is obviously the one that interests Wittgenstein the most because it is the one that he had taken in his earlier work. This is articulated in §39, where he first explains why one may be led from the general Augustinian picture to the more specific atomist thesis:

[O]ne is tempted to make an objection against what is ordinarily called a name. It can be put like this: *a name ought really to signify a simple*. And for this one might perhaps give the following reasons: The word 'Excalibur', say, is a proper name in the ordinary sense. The sword Excalibur consists of parts combined in a particular way. If they are combined differently Excalibur does not exist. But it is clear that the sentence 'Excalibur has a sharp blade' makes *sense* whether Excalibur is still whole or is broken up. But if 'Excalibur' is the name of an object, this object no longer exists when Excalibur is broken in pieces; and as no object would then correspond to the name it would have no meaning. But then the sentence 'Excalibur has a sharp blade' would contain a word that had no meaning, and hence the sentence would be nonsense. But it does make sense; so there must always be something corresponding to the words of which it consists. So the word 'Excalibur' must disappear when the sense is analysed and its place be taken by words which name simples. It will be reasonable to call these words the *real names*.

When Wittgenstein runs through the reasoning behind the claim that names must stand for simple objects, he explicitly employs the Augustinian premise that 'and as no object would then correspond to the name it would have no meaning'. This may make it seem that he is suggesting that if we accept the general Augustinian picture of the meaning of names, we will be led by this line of argument to the conclusion that names must refer to logically simple objects. However, this would be mistaken because Wittgenstein is aware that there are more ways of responding to the problems created by non-referring terms like 'Excalibur' than the one presented in §39 of adopting the view that 'Excalibur' is not a real name, and that real names must refer to existing entities. He is aware, of course, that the Fregean and Meinongian responses are also possible. Therefore, he would acknowledge that the general Augustinian picture does not entail this more specific atomistic or pure referentialist thesis.

From the point of view of our present concern, this means that his attack on pure referentialism cannot *on its own* be used to undermine referentialism

---

[6] I am deliberately using the terms 'Fregean', 'Meinongian', and 'Russellian' because I am more interested at this point in characterising the general strategies that have been adopted in responding to the problems facing referentialism. Although these responses are based in the writings of Frege, Meinong, and Russell, I am not concerned here with any of the exegetical questions that arise regarding attributing these views to them.

in general (including more moderate versions). Rather, in order to undermine referentialism in general, it would have to be shown that the Fregean and Meinongian attempts to preserve or supplement referentialism in the face of problems arising, for example, from apparently non-referring terms are in fact implausible. Without getting into the details of these responses, it is already possible to see that they put pressure on anyone hoping to maintain a moderate version of referentialism (without it collapsing into pure or atomistic referentialism). For the Fregean response involves accepting that there is more to meaning than reference; and depending on how one views this, it will require either abandoning referentialism or supplementing it with a non-referentialist semantic thesis. Strictly speaking, the Meinongian response is perhaps the only way of holding on to moderate referentialism in the face of problems concerning apparently non-referring terms (and other problems), but it is at such a high price that leaves the resulting moderate referentialist vulnerable to charges of metaphysical mysterianism.

The overall lesson is that Wittgenstein's objections to pure referentialism about singular terms are a vital part of his attack on referentialism in general, even though they are not sufficient on their own to undermine all types of referentialism. I will return to the issue of the scope of Wittgenstein's attack on referentialism later in this chapter when I consider the relation of his objections to the description theories of reference (section 1.9).

1.6   Referentialism About General Terms

In this section, I will turn my attention to general terms such as 'blue', 'water', 'game' etc. I will argue that Wittgenstein provides the basis for an argument against the referentialist conception of their meanings that is structurally similar to the attack on referentialism about singular terms. Hence, the argument will begin by targeting a *pure* referentialism about general terms and then be extended in a couple of steps to more moderate versions.

One of the parts of *PI* that directly addresses the issue of the meanings of general terms is the well-known discussion of family resemblance concepts beginning at §65. This discussion is a stepping-stone to Wittgenstein's subsequent reflections on rule-following because it challenges the view that the use of a word is 'everywhere circumscribed by rules' (*PI*, §68). It does this by providing examples of general terms – for example, 'game', 'language' and 'number' – that cannot be given satisfactory analytical or Socratic definitions, i.e. definitions that express the essential characteristics that all instances must possess in order for the terms to be correctly applied to them. I will leave the analysis of this aspect of his discussion to the next two chapters, where the rule-following considerations take centre stage. Here I will be concerned with how these same considerations undermine the view that the meanings of general terms consist in their reference to absolutely definite concepts. Call this view pure referentialism about general terms.

Wittgenstein argues that the pure referentialist requirement cannot be satisfied when it comes to many of the general terms that are of most significance to philosophers, including 'name', 'proposition', 'number', 'believing', 'understanding' and 'language'. His most famous example is of the general term, 'game'. He asks, 'What is common to [all of the activities we call "games"]?' And he responds:

For if you look at them you will not see something that is common to *all*, but similarities, relationships, and a whole series of them at that. To repeat: don't think, but look! – Look for example at board-games, with their multifarious relationships. Now pass to card-games; here you find many correspondences with the first group, but many common features drop out, and others appear. When we pass next to ball-games, much that is common is retained, but much is lost. – Are they all 'amusing'? Compare chess with noughts and crosses. Or is there always winning and losing, or competition between players? Think of patience. In ball games there is winning and losing; but when a child throws his ball at the wall and catches it again, this feature has disappeared. Look at the parts played by skill and luck; and at the difference between skill in chess and skill in tennis. Think now of games like ring-a-ring-a-roses; here is the element of amusement, but how many other characteristic features have disappeared! And we can go through the many, many other groups of games in the same way; can see how similarities crop up and disappear. (*PI*, §66)

Wittgenstein states that 'the result of this examination' is that 'we see a complicated network of similarities overlapping and criss-crossing' rather than a set of characteristic or essential marks that all examples of games possess (*Ibid.*).

He proposes a similar assessment of the meaning of the term 'language' and his view is in strong contrast to his early position that there is a 'general form' shared by all instances of propositions:

Instead of producing something common to all that we call language, I am saying that these phenomena have no one thing in common which makes us use the same word for all, – but that they are *related* to one another in many different ways. And it is because of this relationship, or these relationships, that we call them all 'language'. (*PI*, §65)

Wittgenstein suggests that we call these overlapping similarities between instances 'family resemblances' because

the various resemblances between members of a family: build, features, colour of eyes, gait, temperament, etc. etc. overlap and criss-cross in the same way. – And I shall say: 'games' form a family. (*PI*, §67)

Gordon Baker and Peter Hacker state that although the notions of family resemblance and family likeness had been appealed to by many linguists and philosophers since the late eighteenth century when discussing the similarities between different languages, what is genuinely innovative in Wittgenstein's discussion is his application of the notion of family resemblance 'to *concepts*' and 'to argue that the extension of a concept may be united not by common characteristics but by overlapping similarities between the members' (Baker and Hacker 2005a, 210). Likewise, he applied the notion to the issue of the meanings and applications of general terms by maintaining that the use or application of general terms can proceed smoothly and legitimately when only overlapping similarities or resemblances between the instances exist rather than a unique set of characteristic marks that they all share (see *PI*, §§68–70).

This is his strategy in undermining the pure referentialist requirement that general terms must denote definite concepts, viz. to simply draw our attention to numerous examples of general terms that can be understood and used perfectly well even though the concepts in question are family resemblance concepts. This kind of argumentative strategy may be problematic because it seems to tacitly introduce and rely upon a view of meaning as use, which the pure referentialist would not accept. However, I will postpone the analysis of this significant objection until the next two sections, where the notion of use will be addressed directly.

A different possible objection to Wittgenstein's attack on pure referentialism about general terms is that many of the primary examples of family resemblance concepts that he considers are not concepts of this kind after all because it *is* possible to identify features common to all of the instances in question. For example, Baker and Hacker consider the possibility that Wittgenstein is vulnerable on this point because, for example, someone might object that all games have general features like that of being played:

[T]he matter remains contentious. Games are *played*, and playing a game is a human activity – so games surely have this as *a* common property. Furthermore, it is difficult to deny that games are *rule-governed*. (2005a, 214)

And they cite Bede Rundle's proposed definition of a game:

[G]ames are rule-governed activities, with an arbitrary and non-serious objective lacking significance outside the game, which players set themselves to attain for the sake of the fun or the satisfaction of participating in the activity and/or attaining the objective (Rundle 1990, chapter 3; paraphrased by Baker and Hacker 2005a, 215, footnote 32).

One response is to argue that the definitions are trivial and on a par with statements such as 'Every word in language signifies something' and 'All tools serve to modify something', which do not settle anything about how the defined term is to be applied. However, while this might be the case regarding the general definition mentioned by Baker and Hacker's, it does not seem to apply to Rundle's. A better response is to argue that

if by some feat of ingenuity someone managed to find a non-trivial necessary and sufficient condition for being a game, it would still be clear that *that* was not why we applied the word 'game' in all the cases where we do apply it. (Ahmed 2010, 42–3)

The point is that Wittgenstein could continue to hold that the word 'game' has a legitimate use even in the absence of any such definition that may be formulated.

To conclude this section, I will consider how the Wittgensteinian attack on referentialism about general terms could be generalised to more moderate versions of referentialism. The following is how I propose it could be generalised, which is structurally similar to how the attack on pure referentialism about singular terms was extended in the previous section:

(Step 1) Argue that *pure* referentialism about general terms is false by showing that its requirement that such terms denote absolutely definite concepts cannot be realised in most cases (or in other words, by showing that analytical definitions of these general terms cannot be given).

Wittgenstein attempts to establish this by identifying numerous examples of general terms in which the related concepts are family resemblance concepts and hence that cannot be given analytical definitions.

(Step 2) Argue that moderate versions of referentialism about general terms face a trilemma, which originates from the problem of whether or not general terms such as 'game' and 'language' refer to indefinite, open-ended concepts.

The trilemma is:

(a) Deny that the terms refer to genuine concepts, and thus either reject referentialism or supplement it with a non-referentialist semantic thesis. (The Fregean response.)

(b) Insist that the terms refer, but to indefinite concepts. (The Meinongian response.)

(c) Deny that the general terms in question are genuine concept words, and argue that when the sentences containing the terms are properly analysed the terms disappear or reveal *genuine* general terms that do refer to definite concepts. (The Russellian/Tractarian response, which preserves referentialism but at the cost of transforming the initial moderate referentialism about general terms into a pure referentialism.)

(Step 3) Argue that the first two horns of the trilemma are unacceptable; and thus argue that in order to preserve referentialism, moderate referentialism must be abandoned in favour of pure referentialism. Wittgenstein's original argument in the first step is thus shown to apply to moderate referentialism after all (but supplemented with other arguments to show that the other two horns of the trilemma are unacceptable).

A couple of points of clarification should be made concerning this extension of Wittgenstein's argument. The first is that – like the extension of the argument against pure referentialism about singular terms – the extension is not presented this way by Wittgenstein. Nevertheless, the issues that lead to the trilemma in Step 2 and that lead to the rejection of the first two horns in Step 3 are issues that Wittgenstein does grapple with and address at length. For example, he would have been aware of the possibility of certain opponents clinging to referentialism even in the face of his examples of family resemblance concepts. And the horns of the trilemma merely concern the three most obvious ways of holding on to referentialism, which mirror the ways he would be very familiar with from reading Frege and Russell. Furthermore, it is quite clear from what Wittgenstein says about family resemblance concepts why he would consider the first two horns to be unacceptable. Against the Fregean response, there is no reason to suppose that the family resemblance concepts are not genuine concepts since they can be grasped and are perfectly usable. And regarding what I called the Meinongian response, it is correct that there are such open-ended concepts, but the motivation for positing them in the context of referentialism has arguably been lost.[7] This latter point, though, requires additional discussion of the relative merits of a view of meaning based on use rather than on reference.

1.7   Vague Meanings

The issue of family resemblance is easily confused with that of vagueness, but it is important to distinguish them. Robert Fogelin points out that the distinction may not occur to us in examples like games because the concept is both a family resemblance concept and a vague concept (1987, 134). It counts as a family resemblance concept for the reasons just highlighted concerning overlapping similarities between its instances and the absence of any single set of characteristics present in every instance. But vagueness has to do with 'the existence or at least possibility of borderline cases', which means that there are instances in which it is impossible to determine whether or not the concept applies (see Ahmed 2010, 46). For example, colour concepts like *green* are vague because there are borderline cases in which we cannot say whether an object is green or blue, or whether some other object is green or yellow etc.

Timothy Williamson notes that although family resemblances 'do not themselves constitute vagueness', 'family resemblance concepts are obviously susceptible to borderline cases' (1994, 86). There are, for example, borderline cases of games; Wittgenstein's example of 'when a child throws his ball at the wall and catches it again' (*PI*, §66) is arguably one. The point, though, is that the reasons for its being vague are distinct from the reasons for its being a family resemblance concept. The distinction is brought out in Wittgenstein's example of the concept of number, which is a family resemblance concept but not a vague concept. He states that 'the kinds of number [for example, cardinal numbers, rational numbers, irrational numbers, complex numbers etc.] form a

---

[7] Rather than think of words like 'game' as referring to indefinite or open-ended concepts, Wittgenstein holds that indefiniteness or open-endedness is a matter of the rules for the use of the words. These rules are open-ended in the sense that they are specified by pointing to examples (of games, propositions etc.) and stating 'these and similar things are called 'X'. The rules might also be called indefinite in the sense that they are open to competing interpretations as to how they should be applied. As we will see in the next chapter, this raises a whole host of questions including what a rule is, how it guides/compels and whether we need to posit rules for the use of words at all (definite or indefinite).

family in the same way' (*PI*, §67). However, each type of number is rigorously defined and does not admit of borderline cases (see Ahmed 2010, 46–7).

With the introduction of the separate notion of indefiniteness qua family resemblance, Wittgenstein implicitly broadens the remit of his investigation. Instead of being concerned merely with the meanings of general terms (and the pure referentialist assumption that these meanings are exhausted by reference to absolutely definite concepts), his discussion also addresses the more general issue of the possibility of linguistic expressions of any kind possessing indefinite meanings. Hence, it is helpful to draw attention to two main assumptions that Wittgenstein targets, the first more general than the second:

(i) Linguistic expressions can only have definite meanings because an indefinite meaning is not a meaning at all. (See *PI*, §§71 and 99–101.)

(ii) General terms must denote absolutely definite concepts.

For present purposes, I am using 'indefinite' as a general term to cover both linguistic expressions with vague meanings and those with instances bearing only a family resemblance to one another. What connects them is that their use is 'not everywhere circumscribed by rules' (*PI*, §68) either because there are borderline cases in which their application cannot be determined (indefinite qua vague) or because the concept in question is open-ended in the sense that it may be expanded to include instances that bear similarities to some instance but not to others (indefinite qua family resemblance).

Wittgenstein gives expression to the general assumption, (i), in the following passage:

The sense of a sentence – one would like to say – may, of course, leave this or that open, but the sentence must nevertheless have *a* definite sense. An indefinite sense – that would really not be a sense *at all*. – This is like: An indefinite boundary is not really a boundary at all. Here one thinks perhaps: if I say 'I have locked the man up fast in the room – there is only one door left open' – then I simply haven't locked him in at all; his being locked in is a sham. One would be inclined to say here: 'You haven't done anything at all'. An enclosure with a hole in it is as good as *none*. – But is that true? (*PI*, §99)

This is a view that he held in *TLP* (see, for example, the Preface and 3.251), and he mentions Frege as another example of a philosopher who adopted it (see *PI*, §71).

Wittgenstein's approach to undermining assumption (i) is the same as with assumption (ii). He identifies numerous examples of linguistic expressions that have possible functions or uses in our lives even though their meanings are indefinite in either of the above senses. He gives the example of the command 'Stand roughly there' as being indefinite, but useful in certain situations nevertheless.

Frege compares a concept to an area and says that an area with vague boundaries cannot be called an area at all. This presumably means that we cannot do anything with it. – But is it senseless to say: 'Stand roughly there'? Suppose that I were standing with someone in a city square and said that. As I say it I do not draw any kind of boundary, but perhaps point with my hand – as if I were indicating a particular *spot*. (*PI*, §71)

The implication is supposed to be that if indefinite expressions such as these have a use, they must by meaningful in some sense. Likewise, if I can 'explain to someone what a game is' by giving him examples and declaring that 'This *and similar things* are called "games"' ', and if the person goes on to use the term 'game' correctly, it suggests that it is meaningful even though it can only be given an open-ended definition (see *PI*, §§69 and 71).

An objection to this is that Wittgenstein's counterexamples are not compelling to anyone sympathetic to pure referentialism because they actually rely on a notion of meaning that is roughly equivalent to use, which the pure referentialist need not accept. The counterexamples are deemed to be meaningful (to possess an indefinite meaning) on the grounds that they have uses. But – the objection goes – these only count as genuine counterexamples if the view of meaning as use is presupposed.

At this point in the discussion, I merely want to draw attention to Wittgenstein's approach to accepting indefinite meanings and to indicate a point at which it may be vulnerable to objections. I will return to the significance of Wittgenstein's appeal to use in the next section, and in the subsequent chapters.

1.8   From Reference to Use: Evaluating Wittgenstein's Attack on Referentialism

In my presentation of the different stages in Wittgenstein's objections to referentialism, I have sought to highlight where the objections meet the referentialist on her own terms and where they implicitly or explicitly rely on an alternative, non-referentialist view of meaning. This alternative view characterises meaning in terms of use, and it crops up frequently in the sections of *PI* devoted to undermining the referentialist picture. His view of the relation between meaning and use is stated after the opening round of his objections to referentialism, as if his discussion has been leading to it as an alternative:

For a *large* class of cases – though not for all – in which we employ the word 'meaning' it can be defined thus: the meaning of a word is its use in the language.

And the *meaning* of a name is sometimes explained by pointing to its *bearer*. (*PI*, §43)

Hence, it is understandable that some interpreters hold that Wittgenstein takes this definition of meaning in terms of use 'for granted from the outset of his book and relies on it throughout' (Horwich 2012, 106).

Whichever way we view the relation between the attack on referentialism, on the one hand, and the correlation of meaning with use, on the other, it is clear that they are presented more or less simultaneously in the opening sections of *PI* (up to around §80). My discussion of Wittgenstein's individual objections has revealed that in most cases they *do* rely on the broad characterisation of meaning in terms of use – or on the view that if a word has a use, it is meaningful in some sense. Assuming that this is correct, does it genuinely undermine his attack on referentialism? On first consideration, it looks as though it does because surely a more compelling way of arguing against an opponent is to only rely on assumptions that the opponent accepts. Specifically, if an argument against referentialism presupposes an anti-referentialist premise, it is guilty of begging the question.

The matter is not quite that simple, though. This judgment concerning the objections must be balanced by an appreciation of the manner in which Wittgenstein continually appeals to the use we make of words. If Wittgenstein were presupposing a use theory of meaning and criticising referentialism from the point of view of that theory, then his objections would be severely weakened. But his intention at least is not to defend a theory of any sort, much less a fully fledged theory of meaning. As Wittgenstein states, 'The work of the philosopher consists in assembling reminders for a particular purpose' (*PI*, §127). And the purpose in the present context is to draw our attention to certain facts and circumstances concerning language that are obvious and mundane, but that somehow tend to be overlooked when we are engaged in philosophy (see *PI*, §38). Chief among these mundane facts is that the use of language is an activity ('words are also deeds', *PI*, §546), that learning to use language is learning how to do something (like acquiring a practical skill or ability; see *PI*, §§150 and 199). Wittgenstein's assertion that for 'a *large* class of cases–though not for all', 'the meaning of a word is its use in the language' is supposed to draw attention to these ordinary facts rather than to propose a philosophical thesis. Or if it can be called a thesis at all, it would have the quality that he alludes to when he writes:

If one tried to advance *theses* in philosophy, it would never be possible to debate them, because everyone would agree to them. (*PI*, §128)

The important point is that in drawing attention to the use we make of words, Wittgenstein is not making a claim that his opponent – the referentialist – would not accept. Rather, he is drawing attention to something his opponent has for some reason overlooked or forgotten in the process of philosophising. When his attention is drawn to it, he cannot but accept that words are used in such-and-such ways (or in the case of imagined language-games like that of the builders, that language can be used in such-and-such ways).

This is crucial to the evaluation of the strength of Wittgenstein's objections to referentialism. The challenge when reading Wittgenstein is to appreciate the philosophical significance of his method that involves making these 'reminders' regarding language – not as substantial philosophical theses proposed against other theses, but as something of an altogether different kind proposed against the very inclination to theorise or propose theses. This challenge is even greater now that many decades have passed since the publication of *PI*, i.e. now that these reminders often take the form of slogans that create the general sense that Wittgenstein was defending a theory that was characterised by them. It is as if the tendency of philosophers to theorise has, ironically, led them to interpret these reminders as theoretical principles that Wittgenstein wanted to defend (as if philosophers couldn't help themselves because theorising is what they do).

The uniqueness of Wittgenstein's approach can be clarified by considering cases in which the appeal to use *would* be non-trivial and would contain a commitment to substantial theoretical principles concerning meaning. These non-Wittgensteinian cases involve providing an explanation of the use of words. They explain in virtue of what we are able to use words and what it is that underlies the correct use of words in particular instances. For example, within the context of referentialism it could be held that once the referent of a word is identified, the correct way of using the word is thereby determined. Hence, what constitutes the pattern of correct use of a word would be explained by the relation of reference that has supposedly been established between the word and an object. Wittgenstein casts doubt on such referentialist explanations of correct use:

One thinks that learning language consists in giving names to objects. Viz., to human beings, to shapes, to colours, to pains, to moods, to numbers, etc. To repeat – naming is something like attaching a label to a thing. One can say that this is preparatory to the use of a word. But *what* is it a preparation *for*? (*PI*, §26)

'We name things and then we can talk about them: can refer to them in talk.' – As if what we did next were given with the mere act of naming. As if there were only one thing called 'talking about a thing'. (*PI*, §27)

Wittgenstein's complaint is that correlating a word with an object (naming it or attaching a label) is of no consequence in itself. What matters is the use that is subsequently made of the word. Naming is at best 'preparatory to the use of a word'; and it is mistaken to assume that how we go on to use the word is somehow already settled or 'given with the mere act of naming'.

A similar attempt to explain the basis for the correct use of a word is provided in the context of a platonist conception of meaning and rules, which is central to Wittgenstein's discussion in §§138–242 of *PI* (see the next chapter). On this view, understanding a word or grasping its meaning is a mental state of some sort that in some sense 'predetermine[s]' or 'anticipate[s]' all of the steps in correctly using the word, 'as only the act of meaning can anticipate reality' (*PI*, §188). But for reasons that will be explored in detail in the next chapter, this kind of mentalist-platonist explanation also runs into great difficulty.

My point is that any attempt of this kind to explain what underlies our use of words will contain substantial theoretical commitments. Of course, one of these explanatory accounts might be correct. But it is important to note that Wittgenstein's frequent appeal to the use of words does not involve committing himself to any of these kinds of controversial explanatory accounts. His appeal merely consists of observations concerning how words are *actually* or as a matter of fact used (or again, how words would be used in an imagined language-game). This is all that he requires in framing his objections to referentialism. The objections do not rest on any additional claims – which would be non-trivial – of what underlies the use or what makes certain uses correct and others incorrect. When we recognise Wittgenstein's purely descriptive and non-explanatory approach to use, we can see that his objections to referentialism are not weakened by relying on descriptions of use.

1.9   Wittgenstein and Description Theories of Reference

When considering Wittgenstein's relation to prominent debates and theories in the philosophy of language, an obvious place to begin is with what are known as 'descriptivist' or 'description theories' of reference because he is often interpreted as endorsing a weak or moderate version of the theory. Historically, descriptivism is associated with Frege and Russell. Focussing on the case of proper names, descriptivism holds that the meanings of proper names can be specified or analysed in terms of certain descriptions, i.e. descriptions that are uniquely satisfied by the person or thing named. For example, the meaning of 'Barack Obama' can be specified in terms of descriptions such as 'the 44th president of the United States' and 'the only US president to have been born in Hawaii'. A feature of the theory is thus that the meanings of proper names have a degree of *complexity* that allows them to be analysed or specified in terms of descriptions. In this regard, the theory is directly opposed to the 'Millian' view, which we briefly encountered in section 1.3, and holds that proper names are like labels, with simple and unanalysable meanings.

The issue that links this theory to Wittgenstein is that of the exact nature of the relation between proper names and the relevant descriptions. The classical or Russellian version posits the strong thesis that proper names are literally abbreviations of certain descriptions. This is the theory that emerges from Russell's view that ordinary proper names are not really (i.e. at the deeper level of logical form) proper names at all but disguised definite descriptions. However, this is the most radical version of the theory and it seems to be vulnerable to major objections, including: that it is impossible in most cases to specify in a non-arbitrary way the exact set of descriptions that a proper name is to be analysed in terms of; and that it is implausible to hold that what speakers literally mean by the proper names they use is given by the set of associated descriptions (whatever they are, and even if a speaker is unaware of some of those descriptions actually applying to the bearer of the name).

One type of response to these objections has been to develop a weaker version of the theory. For example, instead of holding that proper names are abbreviated or disguised definite descriptions, it could be maintained that proper names are equivalent in meaning to certain descriptions (see Lycan 2000, 40). On this weaker view, proper names like 'Aristotle' are genuine names; but their meanings are equivalent to certain descriptions that apply to the person or thing named. Therefore, the meanings of the proper names can be specified or articulated in terms of the associated descriptions. This weaker version of descriptivism, though, can be developed in a couple of different directions, depending on whether or not one has a strict or loose view of what meanings are. For instance, if one holds with Frege that meanings must be definite, then the 'equivalence in meaning' claim will be interpreted in such a way that the meaning of a name such as 'Aristotle' must be exactly equivalent to whatever meaning is expressed by the conjunction of descriptions such as 'the student of Plato', 'the author of *De Anima*' etc. However, it looks as though this view would be as vulnerable as the Russellian version to the objections mentioned above. For how are we supposed to arrive at a complete list of the descriptions of, for example, Aristotle that together express the meaning of 'Aristotle'? And there are other problems. It is extremely implausible to hold that anybody who understands the name 'Aristotle' must grasp a meaning that is equivalent to that of the conjunction of the relevant descriptions.

The most influential solution to these problems was to interpret the relation between names and the associated descriptions as weaker still. This is where Wittgenstein comes in because it is an essential feature of this weaker position that meanings may be indefinite. John Searle proposed the view that the meaning of a proper name is *roughly* equivalent in meaning to a loose grouping or cluster of descriptions (Searle 1958, 171). This is generally known as the 'cluster theory', but it is important to note that it is still a version of descriptivism. It is a version that attempts to provide an account of proper names that retains the benefits of descriptivism while avoiding the objections against the more radical or strict versions of it.

Wittgenstein has been interpreted as endorsing something like this weak version of descriptivism primarily on the basis of §79 of *PI*, which opens with this paragraph:

Consider this example. If one says 'Moses did not exist', this may mean various things. It may mean: the Israelites did not have a *single* leader when they withdrew from Egypt – or: their leader was not called Moses – or: there cannot have been anyone who accomplished all that the Bible relates of Moses – or: etc. etc. – We may say, following Russell: the name 'Moses' can be defined by means of various descriptions. For example, as 'the man who led the Israelites through the wilderness', 'the man who lived at that time and place and was then called "Moses"', 'the man who as a child was taken out of the Nile by Pharaoh's daughter' and so on. And according as we assume one definition or another the proposition 'Moses did not exist' acquires a different sense, and so does every other proposition about Moses. – And if we are told 'N did not exist', we do ask: 'What do you mean? Do you want to say ... or ... etc.?'

The first apparent piece of evidence that Wittgenstein held a version of descriptivism is his explicit mention of Russell's theory in this passage. Fogelin, for example, cites this in his reading of Wittgenstein as a descriptivist (1987, 138/9). However, Wittgenstein's wording ('Nach Russell können wir sagen') does not suggest straightforward endorsement, but a mere statement of the position for the purposes of reflecting on it.

It is rather in the subsequent paragraphs of §79 that the more compelling evidence is to be found. There we find him distancing himself from the Russellian descriptivist position, but primarily on the grounds that no single definition or fixed set of descriptions can give the meaning of a name like 'Moses'. As Wittgenstein writes:

But when I make a statement about Moses, – am I always ready to substitute some one of these descriptions for 'Moses'? I shall perhaps say: By 'Moses' I understand the man who did what the Bible relates of Moses, or at any rate a good deal of it. But how much? Have I decided how much must be proved false for me to give up my proposition as false? Has the name 'Moses' got a fixed and unequivocal use for me in all possible cases? – Is it not the case that I have, so to speak, a whole series of props in readiness, and am ready to lean on one if another should be taken from under me and vice versa?

Although Wittgenstein objects to the Russellian version of the descriptivist view of proper names, it is not so clear that he objects to a more moderate version that holds that the meaning of a proper name can be specified by certain descriptions of the person or thing named provided that it allows for the fact that the meaning may be indefinite. Wittgenstein's concern in the above passage and subsequently seems to be with highlighting that the descriptions associated with a name may be more or less incidental, and that 'the bounds of the incidental' are difficult or impossible to identify, which means that it is impossible to identify the descriptions that are non-incidental or genuinely constitutive of the meaning of a name.

The ambiguity in the text concerning whether Wittgenstein is attacking descriptivism per se or merely the strict Russellian version of it has led to competing interpretations concerning his attitude to descriptivism. For example, while (as noted) Fogelin interprets him as endorsing a moderate version of descriptivism, Baker and Hacker state that 'The attribution to [Wittgenstein] of a cluster theory of proper names has no textual warrant' (2005b, 176).

Despite this opposition, Fogelin and Baker and Hacker agree that the deeper issue for Wittgenstein in §79 is not that of the truth or falsity of the descriptivist theory, but the issue of the indefiniteness of meanings (in this case, the meanings of proper names). This is brought to the fore at the end of the section:

And this can be expressed like this: I use the name 'N' without a *fixed* meaning. (But that detracts as little from its usefulness, as it detracts from that of a table that it stands on four legs instead of three and so sometimes wobbles.)
    Should it be said that I am using a word whose meaning I don't know, and so am talking nonsense? – Say what you choose, so long as it does not prevent you from seeing the facts. (And when you see them there is a good deal that you will not say.)

According to Fogelin, Wittgenstein's main claim concerning proper names is that 'we do not always (or even usually) use words under the governance of strict rules' (1987, 140). And although Wittgenstein chooses to articulate this point in the context of a descriptivist account – probably (again according to Fogelin) because he was somewhat sympathetic to it – 'it could have been presented as easily within the context of [an] alternative account of proper names', such as the causal theory of reference (*Ibid.*). Baker and Hacker make a similar claim about Wittgenstein's main concern, but with the qualification that Wittgenstein is critical of descriptivism and thus articulates the general point about the indefiniteness of meaning in the context of an objection to descriptivism (see Baker and Hacker 20005b, 175/6).

Despite their underlying agreement concerning Wittgenstein's deeper concern, their disagreement on the issue of his relation to descriptivism is important to address because it impacts on the question of the plausibility of Wittgenstein's view of the meanings of proper names. In particular, there are some well-known and compelling objections to even the moderate, 'cluster theory' versions of descriptivism. And so we need to consider whether Wittgenstein is vulnerable to these too. An obvious way of determining this is to get a clearer sense of his proximity to moderate descriptivism.

Saul Kripke provides the famous example of the name 'Kurt Gödel', and asks us to imagine that the only thing that you know about Gödel is that he proved the Incompleteness Theorems in mathematical logic (see 1980, 83–5). Hence, on the description theory, you use this description to refer to Gödel; and what you mean by the name 'Gödel' is given by the description 'the man who proved the Incompleteness Theorems'. But imagine that it was not really Gödel who proved them but a man named 'Schmidt', and whose proof was stolen and merely published by Gödel. Kripke's objection is that even if this scenario were true, when you utter the name 'Gödel' you would still succeed in referring to Gödel rather than to Schmidt (who you are totally unaware of). The point is that we can understand the meaning of a proper name without having *any* accurate description of the person corresponding to the name. Therefore, the conclusion is that the meaning of the proper name is independent of, and different to, the associated description.

It should be noted that this objection applies to any version of descriptivism, or any theory that posits an essential link between the meanings of names and the meanings of associated descriptions (even if the latter is conceived as comprising an indefinite or changeable grouping or cluster). For Kripke's example is supposed to show that the link can be severed and yet a speaker can still mean the same thing by it, or at least use it to refer to the same thing. The example looks like an extension of Wittgenstein's point in §79 about 'the bounds of the incidental' being impossible to identify. After discussing the various descriptions we associate with a person, Wittgenstein asks 'But if some point now proves false?' Kripke's example in effect asks the related question: 'What if all of the descriptions we associate with a proper name are false?'

I think Wittgenstein would agree with Kripke that in this kind of case, the speaker *does* nevertheless succeed in talking about the same individual; and that he would do so for reasons that genuinely distance him from even moderate versions of descriptivism. Wittgenstein allows for cases where a speaker gives meaning to a name and succeeds in talking about them without having any descriptions to hand, but instead by virtue of the person being pointed out to the speaker or being shown a picture of the person (see the second paragraph of *PI*, §79; see also Baker and Hacker 2005a, 234).

Therefore, on final reckoning, Baker and Hacker are correct in claiming that Wittgenstein did not endorse even a moderate version of descriptivism because such an endorsement goes against his view that the meaning of a proper name can be given in the absence of descriptions. Baker and Hacker, though, overstate the difference when they claim that the interpretation of Wittgenstein as a cluster theorist 'has no textual warrant'. On the contrary, there is an affinity between the cluster theory and what Wittgenstein states in §79 about the blurred distinction between incidental and non-incidental descriptions. Wittgenstein does acknowledge that in many cases descriptions are useful in specifying what a name refers to. But the difference between his view and that of the cluster theory comes down to the specific point that he holds that it is also possible to specify the reference of a proper name by other means (such as pointing); and that there are cases where descriptions of the thing named are not available, and hence where these other means must be relied on. It is this difference that puts Wittgenstein in a better position than the cluster theorist to avoid Kripke's objection.

1.10   Conclusion

The so-called Millian view may be put forward as the purest example of referentialism in that it holds that words are like labels of objects; and insofar as it proposes a conception of the meaning of words at all, the meaning is exhausted by this labelling function. Meaning is simply reference qua labelling objects. Most other referential theories, though, have more to say about the relation of reference. For example, they may state that a name refers to an object only if that object uniquely satisfies certain descriptions (descriptions that are equivalent in meaning to that name); or that a name refers to an object only if there is the relevant kind of causal connection between them (in which any use of the name is linked back to the original ceremony of naming the object). As we have seen, the difference between the Millian view, on the one hand, and these other theories of reference, on the other, can be expressed in terms of the issue of the complexity of meaning; whereas the Millian view holds that meanings are simple and unanalysable, the other theories view meanings as complex and analysable in terms of some other relation. The latter theories are thus explanatory in a way that the Millian view is not.

When the distinction is drawn in this way, there appears to be a parallel between the Millian view and the Augustinian picture of language. The Augustinian claim that the meaning of a word 'is the object for which the word stands' says no more than the Millian view. This raises questions about the scope of Wittgenstein's arguments against referentialism. The issue can be stated as follows: Since he directs most of his objections to the Augustinian picture of language, does this mean that more complex theories like descriptivism and the causal-historical theories of reference are unaffected by his objections? It is difficult to say. What it does mean is that we cannot simply assume that any argument that may be made against the Augustinian picture applies automatically to the more complex theories of reference. This is important to note because it is often assumed that Wittgenstein's argumentative strategy is to attack the general framework within which particular referential theories like descriptivism are developed, and therefore by attacking the framework (the Augustinian picture) he is thereby attacking the particular theories. It is rather the case that each theory must be treated on its own merits. We see this in how Wittgenstein discusses the Russellian version of the description theory. He puts forward additional considerations against it, rather than recycling the objections he made to the general claims in the Augustinian picture.

The issue of the scope of Wittgenstein's attack on referentialism is perhaps the hardest to be clear on. Often it can look as though the scope is narrow, that he is targeting only specific versions of referentialism such as the strict version that he adopted in *TLP*. But I have tried to show in this chapter that the scope is wider than usually assumed and that it can be easily extended to apply to more moderate versions of referentialism. In conclusion, it cannot be said that Wittgenstein has refuted referentialism. He has, though, significantly weakened it and provided compelling reasons for thinking that it promotes a distorted view of the nature of language.

Summary of Main Points

(1a) A fundamental concern for philosophers of language is that of how words (marks on a page, vocalised sounds etc.) can have meaning at all. One prominent view that philosophers have been attracted to is that words acquire meanings by standing for, or referring to, things in the world.

(1b) Wittgenstein was attracted to this referentialist conception of meaning in *TLP*, but the opening sections of *PI* present a sustained attack on it.

(1c) Wittgenstein's approach when laying out his objections to referentialism is rather idiosyncratic. Instead of outlining the doctrine or discussing particular examples of referentialist theories and developing his objections, he chooses to isolate a passage from Augustine's *Confessions* in which Augustine describes how his elders taught him the meanings of certain words. Wittgenstein then asserts that this description contains 'a particular picture of the essence of human language' (which is clearly a referentialist picture) and he proceeds to raise various objections to it.

(1d) This approach is problematic for several reasons. For example, there seems to be considerable distance between Augustine's description and the philosophical picture of meaning extracted from it.

(1e) From the point of view of the wider significance of Wittgenstein's discussion, the most worrying consequence of his distinctive approach is that it makes it difficult to assess the scope of his objections. More specifically, even if the objections directed against the general Augustinian/referentialist picture are found to be strong, it is not clear how these objections are supposed to affect the much more sophisticated referentialist theories that philosophers have actually defended.

(1f) It cannot be assumed that Wittgenstein's objections merely transfer to particular referentialist theories because these theories contain significant features that the general Augustinian picture lacks. For example, whereas the Augustinian picture simply identifies meaning with reference and thus has no real explanatory force, the different referentialist theories (such as descriptivism and the causal-historical theory) do attempt to provide explanatory accounts of the referential or meaning-constituting relation that words have with objects. It seems that additional considerations would have to be developed against these referentialist theories.

(1g) Nevertheless, Wittgenstein has done a great deal to undermine the general assumption that a word acquires meaning by standing for an object. His comparison of words with tools and his discussion of the enormous variety of ways in which we use words in our everyday lives forces us to reflect on the complexities of linguistic meaning that tend to be overlooked by the referentialist. And when it comes to discussing (however briefly) particular examples of referentialist theories, such as

Russell's radical version of descriptivism, he does provide additional points against them.

(1h) Wittgenstein has also provided compelling objections against pure or strict referentialism, or the kind of logical atomist version of the doctrine that he and Russell were once drawn to. However, Wittgenstein's attack is not limited to this narrow version of referentialism, but can be extended to more moderate versions.

(1i) Despite holding that the meaning of a proper name can often be specified in terms of descriptions that apply to the person or thing named, Wittgenstein is not a descriptivist (or 'cluster theorist' like Searle) because he also holds that the meaning can in many cases be given in other ways when no descriptions are available. Hence, objections to the description theory of reference presented, for instance, by Kripke do not apply to Wittgenstein.

(1j) Throughout his discussion of referentialism, Wittgenstein seems to presuppose an alternative conception of meaning as broadly identifiable with use. He appears to assume that if a word or expression has a use, it must be meaningful in some sense.

(1k) His appeal to how words are used, though, does not undermine his objections to referentialism because he does not assume anything that the referentialist would not accept. If he were presupposing a particular explanatory account of meaning as use, then he would be begging the question. But he is clearly not, and thus his objections to referentialism stand.

2   The Normativity of Meaning

When Wittgenstein returned to Cambridge to resume his work in philosophy in 1929, the emphasis in his study of language shifted. While his *Tractatus Logico-Philosophicus* (*TLP*) is dominated by reflections on the relation of reference between words and objects, his writings after 1929 are more concerned with rules and the conception of language as a rule-governed system. It is this shift that eventually leads to his fruitful analogy between linguistic activities and playing games (as being rule-governed in similar ways) in his later writings. Wittgenstein maintains his interest in referentialism in *Philosophical Investigations* (*PI*) but mainly to highlight its shortcomings, which were discussed in detail in the previous chapter. To achieve an adequate grasp of Wittgenstein's philosophical reflections on language in *PI*, we must also consider his criticisms of the alternative view of language as rule-governed. This latter issue is arguably the most central issue regarding language in *PI*. In this chapter I will introduce his discussion of it, which is located primarily at §§138–242. Most of the points that are raised in this context are so intrinsic to Wittgenstein's later view of language that much of the arguments and analyses of the rest of this book will be developed directly from the present chapter.

Regarding the wider significance of this aspect of Wittgenstein's later work, it should be noted that the issues of rules and rule-guidedness have become central in recent philosophy of language. These tend to be treated in relation to the question of whether or not meaning is *normative* (see section 2.2), i.e. whether or not there are semantic rules or other semantic entities (such as what we call 'meanings') that govern the use of words and thus determine how words ought and ought not to be used. On the reading I will defend in this chapter, Wittgenstein's discussion in §§138–242 of *PI* engages deeply with the same contentious topics in this recent debate and in ways that have not yet been explored.

Sections 2.3–2.8 of this chapter will take on the difficult task of interpreting this fundamental part of *PI*, while sections 2.9 and 2.10 will show how it links up with the contemporary debates concerning the normativity of meaning. With respect to the interpretation of §§138–242, my main claim will be that Wittgenstein provides an extremely complex *reductio ad absurdum* argument against what could be called a platonist or classical realist conception of meaning. In sections 2.9 and 2.10, I will argue that this reductio argument provides compelling reasons for rejecting the thesis that meaning is normative; and that Wittgenstein is a more radical opponent of this thesis than any recent philosopher of language.

First, though, I will consider how Wittgenstein's concern with rules governing words first emerges in his writings.

2.1   From Referentialism to a Rule-Based Conception of Meaning: Wittgenstein's Middle Period

It is customary to distinguish three main phases in Wittgenstein's philosophical development: the early period (culminating in the publication of *TLP* in 1921); the middle period (his writings from 1929 to 1935);[1] and his later period (his writings after 1936, most notably *PI*, *Remarks on the Foundations of Mathematics* (*RFM*) and *On Certainty* (*OC*)). Although these divisions are imperfect for a number of reasons – for example, there is considerable overlap between the middle and later periods, and there is a question over whether or not *OC* is continuous with *PI* – they are helpful in charting Wittgenstein's constant struggle with certain philosophical problems and confusions, as well as the changes in his responses to them. While Wittgenstein was occupied by roughly the same problems concerning meaning and rule-following in both his middle and later periods, he offered a more consistent and satisfactory response to them in his later period.

The philosophical problems that Wittgenstein grapples with from his middle period onwards first arise in the context of his attempt to replace his Augustinian or referential conception of meaning from *TLP* with an alternative conception.[2] I shall refer to his non-Augustinian, middle-period conception as his 'rule-based' conception of meaning because it accounts for the meanings

---

[1] Regarding Wittgenstein's middle period texts, I will focus mainly on his Cambridge lectures from 1930 to 1935, his *Philosophical Remarks (PR)* (written between 1929 and 1930), *The Big Typescript (BT)*(written between 1929 and 1933; note that this time period pertains to the typescript itself – the 2005 'Scholars' Edition' of *BT* also contains Wittgenstein's handwritten notes and corrections from 1933 to 1937), *Philosophical Grammar (PG)* (the first half of which contains revisions made in 1933/1934 of selected parts of *BT*), and *The Blue and Brown Books (BB)* (dictated between 1933 and 1935).

[2] The claim that the early Wittgenstein held a referential conception of meaning-constitution is based on remarks such as: 'The name means [*bedeutet*] the object. The object is its meaning [*Bedeutung*]' (*TLP*, 3.203; see also 3.22 and 3.221). However, this overlooks certain crucial features of his conception in that period. Most notably, he famously held that logical terms do not denote objects (*TLP*, 4.0312). Nevertheless, it is a basic commitment of his view in this period that any meaningful language must contain names, the meanings of which consist in the objects they stand for. The qualification is that this model does not extend to every single sign in the language.

of terms, not on the basis of corresponding entities denoted by those terms, but by appealing to grammatical rules or rules for the use of those terms. He states repeatedly in this transitional period that 'It is grammatical rules that determine meaning (constitute it)' (*PG*, §184) and that 'The meaning of a word is its place in the symbolism' (*LCL*, 28), where the symbolism is essentially a network of grammatical rules. For example, he states:

What justifies us in using any particular word? Suppose I say 'This gown is black'. The word 'black' is arbitrary in one sense; another sound or scratch would serve. And the correlation of the word 'gown' to a particular object is in itself arbitrary and has no consequence. But if a proposition is to have sense we must commit ourselves to the use of the words in it. It is not a matter of association; that would not make language work at all. What is essential is that in using the word I commit myself to a rule of use. A word only has meaning in a grammatical system, and what characterises it is the way in which it is used. (*LCL*, 36)

The general picture of meaning that emerges from these middle-period writings is of the meanings of words determined by rules for the use of those words, and with those rules belonging to a larger symbolism or calculus of rules. A word, then, is meaningless (a mere 'sound or scratch') unless it belongs to such a symbolism with rules governing its use. Moreover, merely correlating the word with some entity in the world is held to be wholly ineffective at giving it meaning unless it succeeds in establishing a rule for its use.

However, even as Wittgenstein proposed this alternative conception of meaning he recognised that it generates its own problems, and it is the different responses to these problems that distinguish his middle and later views. The deepest problems of all have to do with the particular issue of what it is to grasp and follow a rule. As Wittgenstein states, to understand a word and to use it requires me to 'commit myself to a rule of use'. But what are such rules? How do they determine meaning? How do we grasp them? How do we follow just these rules when using words? And how are these rules related to their applications? These are the sorts of questions that Wittgenstein struggled with, but did not ultimately resolve (or at least partially resolve) until his later period. A crucial difference between Wittgenstein's middle and later periods is that in his middle period he proposed various mentalistic responses in an attempt to save his rule-based conception, while in his later period he rejected these responses and this particular conception of meaning. Before offering a defence of my interpretation of this difference between the two periods regarding this issue, I will first look at the central problems concerning meaning and rule-following that occupied him.

Throughout most of his middle period, we find Wittgenstein attempting to provide support for his rule-based conception by underpinning it with one or another account of what it is to follow a rule and to mean something by a word. The natural conviction that holds sway is that there must be something that following a rule consists in, or some fact in virtue of which I follow a rule. Most of the proposals that he makes are that some type of *mental state* is decisive in our capacity to follow rules. For example, in his *PR* he appeals to an 'act of insight' to account for rule-following:

Something of the following sort: Supposing there to be a certain general rule (therefore one containing a variable), I must recognize each time afresh that this rule may be applied *here*. No act of foresight can absolve me from this act of *insight*. Since the form to which the rule is applied is in fact different at every step. (*PR*, §149)

The problem that this passage alludes to is of how we are capable of correctly applying a general rule in particular cases given that these cases (which are potentially infinite) are not written into the rule itself; i.e. given that grasping the general rule does not settle the separate issue of how it is to be applied in particular instances. The response that Wittgenstein considers is that an act of intuition or insight is what enables us to grasp how the general rule is correctly applied in these particular cases. However, this response did not satisfy him for very long and within the same period we find him abandoning it. For example, in *PG* the above passage is re-stated, but with the following line added at the end: 'But it is not a matter of an act of *insight*, but of an act of *decision*' (*PG*, 301). Baker and Hacker claim that there is still a 'residue' of the appeal to insight in *PG* (see, for example, *PG*, 347), but that it is gradually eliminated in favour of the notion of decision (Baker and Hacker 1985, 72). In a lecture from 1935 Wittgenstein states:

If any mental process is involved, it is one of decision, not of intuition. We do as a matter of fact all make the same decision, but we need not suppose we all have the same 'fundamental intuition'. (*ACL*, 134).

Wittgenstein thus entertains the suggestion that following a rule consists in some sort of decision, before rejecting this too (see *BB*, 143.).

The other main candidates that he considers in this period are the mental states of intention and interpretation. To appreciate his motivation for appealing to these types of mental states, we need to look at another specific problem about rule-following that troubled him and which is best expressed by considering the distinction between following a rule and merely conforming to a rule. To take one of Wittgenstein's favourite examples (see *BT*, §§62 and 64; *LCL*, 37; and *PG*, §57), when I follow a rule of copying, the result – say, a drawing – will be compatible with an indefinite number of different rules. The task is to explain that I was guided by one rule in particular, even though the result would have been the same if I had been guided by any of the other rules. He reflects on the particular example of copying a line by drawing another line parallel to it.

I order someone to draw a line parallel to a, starting at A. He tries (intends) to do this, but with the result that the line turns out parallel to b.

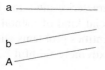

Now was the process of copying the same as if he had intended to draw a line parallel to b and had carried out his intention? I think: obviously not. He let himself be guided by the line a.

... Now the question is: If I have (now) copied a drawing in this way, is it possible to correctly describe the process of copying, as it took place, in accordance with another general rule as well? Or can I reject such a description, saying: 'No, I really only let myself be guided by *this* (general) rule (and not by that other one which, to be sure, would also have had the same result here)'. (*BT*, §62)

The task is to account for this distinction between according with a rule and following (or being guided by) a rule. Since the result of drawing the line A is compatible with having been guided by a rule of copying line a or a rule of copying line b, the drawing itself or the act of drawing it cannot help us to account for this distinction. Wittgenstein's response is that 'intention' is what distinguishes them. This is why he claims that the process of copying line b is different to what is depicted in the passage; the difference is that I was *in fact* guided by the rule of copying line a, or that my intention was to copy line a. Intention, for Wittgenstein, is thus constitutive of following a rule or being guided by a rule. It is precisely what distinguishes it from merely being in accord with the rule. He sums this up by stating:

Then one can say: Even if my pencil doesn't capture the original, my intention always does. Only intention can measure up to the original. (*BT*, §62)

Although Wittgenstein here takes intention to be crucial in accounting for rule-following, he struggles to adequately characterise it. Even in *BT*, he seems to be uncomfortable with characterising it as a mental process accompanying an action or behaviour or manipulation of signs because it suggests the false picture of something happening at a particular time inside me while I use or utter words or follow rules (see *BT*, §65; see also §§62 and 64). He thus struggles with assigning the constitutive role to intention without thinking of intention as a mental process, or at least not as a mysterious mental process of the above kind that can somehow accomplish 'more than written signs on paper' (*BT*, §64). See, for example, where he writes:

So choosing the lines when portraying a model is a different process, to be sure, from simply drawing these lines when I am 'not being guided by the model', but this difference is an external, describable one, like the difference between [a] group of signs ... and it is on a level with this difference. (*BT*, §64)

In this period, though, Wittgenstein does also characterise intention in terms of 'interpretation', which suggests that it is a special kind of mental state or process after all. But while he discusses this, he identifies problems with it too.

He writes that an intention must contain 'an extremely faithful picture of what it intends', and that:

a picture, whatever it may be, can be variously interpreted; hence this picture too in its turn stands isolated. When one has the picture in view by itself it is suddenly dead, and it is as if something had been taken away from it, which had given it life before. (*PG*, §100)

His characterisation of intention in terms of an act of interpretation could be summarised as follows: an intention contains a picture of what it intends; considered in itself, though, the picture does not represent and needs to be interpreted; but the result of each interpretation is itself in need of interpretation. The problem that Wittgenstein articulates regarding the notion of intention here in the middle period prefigures his later discussion of the regress of interpretations in *PI* (see section 2.5 below). Importantly, though, he seems to respond to the regress differently in the middle and later periods and hence we get a good glimpse of the differences in his approach in these two periods. In *PI*, Wittgenstein is explicit that what the regress shows is that 'Interpretations by themselves do not determine meaning' (§198) and that 'there is a way of grasping a rule which is *not* an *interpretation*' (§201). By contrast, there are points in his middle period when he appears to be willing to countenance the idea of a 'final interpretation', or an act of interpretation that puts an end to the regress:

The intention seems to interpret, to give the final interpretation; which is not a further sign or picture, but something else, the thing that cannot be further interpreted. (*PG*, §98)

This strategy preserves the view that meaning something by a term or following a rule consists in an act of intention or interpretation, albeit at the expense of positing a rather mysterious type of mental state (a special act of interpretation). We should, however, acknowledge that this does not represent a settled view of Wittgenstein's in this period. For example, later in the middle period when he discusses this notion of the final interpretation, he puts the reference to it in the interlocutor's voice, thus distancing himself from it (see *BB*, 34).

Finally, I will mention one further variant in the middle period of the suggestion that intention is constitutive of rule-following. One of the claims he frequently makes at this time is that the intention 'contains a general rule', i.e. contains the rule that one actually follows as opposed to the rules that are compatible with what one does (see, for example, *BT*, §62; and *LCL*, 40). While in *BT* Wittgenstein sought to appeal to intention without characterising it as a mysterious mental process, in *BB* he suggests that for the rule to be '*involved* in' what I do is simply for 'the symbol of the rule' to be involved in it (*BB*, 13). Although this succeeds in not positing a strange type of constitutive mental process to account for rule-following, it is not very compelling in its own right and it does not survive the critical remarks he develops in his later period.

The important point to note is that Wittgenstein was far more sympathetic to the notion of a state or process underlying rule-following (and hence meaning) in the middle period than in the later period. This is evident from the fact that in this transitional period he proposes numerous candidates of states to fill this role. In most cases these are mental states, or states that it is difficult to view in any way other than as mental. Even though it is debatable whether he was satisfied for very long with any of these proposals, the mere fact that he continued to propose such candidates is remarkable and is distinctive of this period. The concern of most of the rest of this chapter will be with how Wittgenstein's approach to the philosophical problems regarding rules and meaning changed in his later period. First, though, I will provide a brief sketch of the closely related issue of the normativity of meaning and rules, which is a major topic in the philosophy of language from over the last thirty years. This will give a broader context to Wittgenstein's discussion and further highlight the significance of his reflections on rules and meaning.

2.2   The Normativity of Meaning

A central feature of my reading of Wittgenstein is that much of what he writes about language in the middle and later periods of his career is deeply engaged with what has come to be known as the issue of semantic normativity (or the normativity of meaning). The origins of his interest in this issue may reside in two of the main analogies he makes: in the middle period, between language and a calculus of rules; and in the middle and later periods, between language and games. However, I will begin by looking at the issue itself, before going on to discuss Wittgenstein's relation to it.

The thesis that meaning is normative can be formulated more specifically in different ways depending on which normative distinction one focuses on: correct/incorrect, may/may not, ought/ought not etc. Hence, on one formulation, the thesis states that the meaning of a word entails *correctness conditions* for the application of the word (i.e. that the meaning determines what counts as correctly or incorrectly applying the word). Paul Boghossian puts it succinctly:

Suppose the expression 'green' means *green*. It follows immediately that the expression 'green' applies *correctly* only to these things (the green ones) and not to those (the non-greens).... The normativity of meaning turns out to be, in other words, simply a new name for the familiar fact that ... meaningful expressions possess conditions of *correct use*. (1989, 513)

Similarly (but not equivalently)[3], we could formulate it as holding that the meaning of a word entails *obligations* for how the word is used. For example, given what the word 'green' means, we ought not or should not say that tigers are green, although we may say that grasshoppers are green.

However, problems arise for the normativity thesis as soon as we begin to inquire into the nature of the correctness conditions or obligations that are supposed to be in play in contexts of language use. An essential aspect of the view that meaning is normative is that the obligations involved are distinct from other types of obligations. For instance, when it is stated that we should not say that tigers are green, we are not talking about violating a moral norm or a legal norm or a norm of etiquette. The claim is that we would be violating a *semantic* norm, which is a norm that is supposed to be engendered by nothing but the meaning of the word in question. Hence, the view is that when we attach meaning to a word, a semantic norm is thereby established and our uses of the word are evaluated relative to that norm; the uses are evaluated as correct or incorrect, or as something we should or should not say etc. Problems arise because it is difficult to characterise norms that are intrinsically semantic, as opposed to being reducible to other types of norms. In defending the view that there are semantic norms, it seems that we require an account of meaning that explains not only what meanings are (an enormous task in itself) but also how meanings give rise to norms or rules concerning the correct applications of words. Is there any way to provide such an account or must we simply posit that words have meanings with these special powers?

Although Wittgenstein has a great deal to contribute to this debate concerning semantic normativity, this has rarely been acknowledged and very little has been written on it.[4] Ironically, the recent interest in semantic normativity arose in large part as a result of Kripke's 1982 book on Wittgenstein. Kripke appears to take the thesis that meaning is normative to be obvious or platitudinous and his sceptic uses it as a major premise in his sceptical argument (see the next chapter, especially section 3.3). The irony is that while Kripke may have been motivated to adopt the principle in response to reading Wittgenstein's *PI*, neither he nor most of the philosophers who responded to Kripke actually sought to clearly identify an endorsement or rejection of the thesis in Wittgenstein's writings.[5] Instead,

---

[3] For we can accept that there are correctness conditions without accepting that there are obligations. See below.

[4] A notable exception is Hans-Johann Glock, whose interpretation will be discussed in section 2.9.

[5] This is the case even though I will argue in Chapter 3 that the 'sceptical argument' that Kripke attributes to Wittgenstein can be used as a way of attacking the semantic normativity thesis. It will be seen that it is unclear whether Kripke himself recognised this because he is not sufficiently explicit about the ultimate outcome of the sceptical challenge.

what happened was that the semantic normativity thesis became a significant topic of debate between philosophers of language, but the debate was conducted in almost complete isolation from what Wittgenstein had to say about it.

At first, many philosophers followed Kripke in accepting the thesis and held that any adequate theory of meaning would have to account for the normative dimension of meaning. Boghossian's remark, quoted above, that semantic normativity is 'simply a new name for the familiar fact ... that meaningful expressions possess conditions of *correct use*' is such an example. Other philosophers, including John McDowell and Crispin Wright, adopted a similar stance to the thesis:

We find it natural to think about meaning and understanding in, as it were, contractual terms. Our idea is that to learn the meaning of a word is to acquire an understanding that obliges us subsequently – if we have occasion to deploy the concept in question – to judge and speak in certain determinate ways, on pain of failure to obey the dictates of the meaning we have grasped; that we are 'committed to certain patterns of linguistic usage by the meanings we attach to expressions'. (McDowell 1984, 21)[6]

It is usual to make free use of the idea of an application of a concept *according* with, or failing to accord with, its content. It is in accordance with the meaning of 'red', as we understand it, that it should be applied to red things rather than blue ones. We think of giving the meaning of an expression in contractual terms. Once the meaning has been fixed in a certain way, we are all obliged to make a certain kind of use of the expression; only that kind of use *conforms* with the sense of the expression that was fixed. We are, so to speak, constrained by our understanding. If we are to use the expression in conformity with the way we understand it, or the way the community at large has generally used it in the past, we *have* to use it in certain sorts of ways. (Wright 1980, 19–20)

The appeal of the view that there are semantic norms is that it highlights the obvious fact that we cannot simply use words any way we like and still expect to be making sense. Given the meanings that the words of our language have, it seems undeniable that we are obliged to use the words in such-and-such ways and not others; and that this is what being competent in using the language amounts to. Therefore, the semantic normativity thesis merely draws attention to this fundamental dimension of linguistic meaning. However, despite the initial intuitive appeal of the view, numerous powerful objections have since been raised against it. The opponents accept that there must be a distinction between correctly and incorrectly using words, but they attack the assumption that the normativity involved is intrinsically semantic.

In this chapter, I will attempt to show how the issue of the normativity of meaning is central to Wittgenstein's philosophy in the middle and later periods, despite the fact that he does not of course employ the same terminology as more recent philosophers of language. In short, I will argue that while Wittgenstein implicitly endorsed the semantic normativity thesis in his middle

---

[6] In the last line, McDowell is quoting from Wright (1980, 21).

period, his later reflections on meaning and rule-following are dominated by a radical rejection of the thesis. What I have said in the previous section gives an indication of how he accepted the thesis, for he repeatedly sought to provide an account of what it is to follow a rule (and, given his rule-based conception of meaning, an account also of what it is to mean something by a word). If such an account could have been given – if a distinctive type of mental state could have been identified that is constitutive of rule-following – then it would have also accounted for why a language user is compelled or obligated to follow a rule or use a word one way rather than another in particular instances.

There is an important difference, though, between Wittgenstein's middle-period view and the more recent way of characterising the semantic normativity thesis. In the latter type of formulation, the meaning of a word is taken to be primitive and to engender or entail the semantic norms; whereas in Wittgenstein's middle-period view, the semantic norm or rule is primitive and it determines or constitutes the meaning (this is just what the rule-based conception states). Despite this difference, they can both be viewed as different ways of adopting the semantic normativity thesis. They both hold that there are semantic norms governing the use of words; they merely differ concerning the priority of the semantic norms/rules over meanings.

Sections 2.3–2.8 of what follows will be devoted to how Wittgenstein's attitude to semantic normativity changed dramatically in the later period. The reasons for this change, I will argue, lie in a complex and powerful argument presented mainly in §§138–201 of *PI*. After outlining the various stages in his argument, I will return to a more explicit discussion of the semantic normativity issue in 2.9 and 2.10; and I will evaluate the implications of the argument for the recent debates concerning this issue in the philosophy of language.

2.3   Semantic Normativity and the Platonist Conception in §§138–201 of the *Philosophical Investigations*

Perhaps the primary reason why Wittgenstein's relevance to the semantic normativity debate has rarely been appreciated is that he attacked the semantic normativity thesis in the context of what appears to be a separate issue. Put simply, he attacked the thesis in his arguments against what is often called 'platonism' about meaning and rules.[7] I will argue, though, that the platonist is committed to the semantic normativity thesis; and that not only did Wittgenstein recognise this, he made it the basis of his attacks on platonism (i.e. he identified it as the weak point of the platonist doctrine). My approach will be to first articulate his

---

[7] I will use the term 'platonist' with a small 'p' to distinguish the position from the writings and theories of Plato. The term, as will soon be discussed, refers to a position concerning the nature of meanings and rules as abstract entities with sorting powers regarding the application of words and rules.

anti-platonist argument, and then to show how the argument turns on targeting the normativity thesis. That is the bigger picture in what follows. But for now we need to move away from considering general theses and doctrines, and towards the finer points of Wittgenstein's discussion.

When reflecting on meaning, we find that there are two quite different aspects that must be distinguished and clarified. The first concerns what is involved in understanding or grasping the meaning of a word. Broadly speaking, understanding seems to be something that happens in the mind, and so the first aspect of meaning concerns what must be going on in our minds when we use language to think, speak or write. The second aspect has to do with how we use a word that we understand. How a word is used in particular instances is often how we tell what a word means or how we judge whether a particular language user understands a word. These two aspects of meaning can seem disconnected because the first has to do with what is going on in a person's mind, while the second pertains to the activity of using language in publicly surveyable circumstances.

Wittgenstein begins his discussion of meaning and rules in *PI* by drawing attention to these two aspects. In §§138/139, he makes a distinction between two 'ways of determining meaning'. The first involves determining the meaning of a word 'in an instant' or 'in a flash', which seems to happen whenever we encounter a word we are familiar with or when the meaning of an unfamiliar word is explained to us and we suddenly understand it. The second way is that of determining the meaning of a word by the 'use' we make of it, which – unlike the first way – is extended in time. These ways of determining meaning correspond to the two aspects distinguished above, and they arise at different points of his opening discussion in *PI* (§§1–89).[8] However, the question that he addresses beginning at §138 concerns how they are related and whether they conflict. As we shall see, this question shapes a great deal of Wittgenstein's subsequent discussion of meanings and rules.

But before we consider some of the details, it will be helpful to get a sense of where it eventually leads. What I am calling the platonist conception crops up frequently in the later sections of Wittgenstein's discussion in *PI*. The following are two of the clearest expressions of it:

Here I should first of all like to say: your idea was that that act of meaning the order had in its own way already traversed all those steps: that when you meant it your mind as it were flew ahead and took all the steps before you physically arrived at this or that one.

[8] The second of these two ways is most clearly evident in the opening discussion, especially in §§40–43. §§41 and 42 both contain examples of a sign having a meaning by being given a particular use or function within a language-game; and in §43, we find the definition of meaning in terms of 'its use in the language'. The first way of determining meaning is not quite so obvious in these opening sections. But the Augustinian conception of learning the meaning of a word by identifying the object it stands for is an instance of this way. Wittgenstein does not state that the meaning is grasped in an instant but if the relevant meaning-determining object is present, there is no other way of taking this.

Thus you were inclined to use such expressions as: 'The steps are *really* already taken, even before I take them in writing or orally or in thought.' And it seemed as if they were in some *unique* way predetermined, anticipated – as only the act of meaning can anticipate reality. (§188)

'All the steps are really already taken' means: I no longer have any choice. The rule, once stamped with a particular meaning, traces the lines along which it is to be followed through the whole of space. (§219; see also §§186–187, 192–7, 213, and 218).

Both of these sections articulate the platonist conception in terms of the relation between an 'act of meaning' (for example, an order or rule, 'Add 2') and the pattern of correct application extended over time (for example, '2, 4, 6, 8, …'), which again corresponds to the two aspects of meaning distinguished above. The platonist conception is that once an expression is 'stamped with a particular meaning' in the first, instantaneous sense, the entire pattern of correctly using the expression is thereby 'predetermined' or 'anticipated', 'as only the act of meaning can anticipate reality'. These two aspects of meaning thus fit or accord with one another in this conception; or rather, they are held to be two sides of a single notion of meaning in the sense that in order for the meaning of a word to be genuinely determined in an instant, the correct way of using it over time must be thereby determined. The appropriateness of the platonist label may be disputed (since, of course, it is not Wittgenstein's own), but I will continue to use it here with the qualification that it merely pertains to the way of determining meaning just outlined, which is reflected in the imagery of the application of a word or rule as 'rails invisibly laid to infinity' (*PI*, §218).

Although this is where Wittgenstein's discussion is leading, it is not so clear whether this platonist conception is directly relevant and in question in the earlier sections of *PI*, i.e. §§138–155. I will argue that even at this early stage he is operating with the *assumption* that the platonist conception is legitimate because his goal is to show that doing so ultimately leads to the paradox that there is no such thing as correctly applying a word or following a rule. Exactly how this plays out, though, will require a great deal of further discussion.

2.4   A first look at Wittgenstein's Anti-Platonist Argument: Pears and Child

A good place to start examining the details of Wittgenstein's attack on platonism about meaning and rules is with David Pears' interpretation, which is superficially similar to the interpretation I will defend in the sense that I also hold that Wittgenstein's general target is a platonist conception of meaning and that he adopted a type of reductio argument to undermine it. However, I will argue that Pears' formulation leaves Wittgenstein vulnerable to objections, while mine shows the argument to be more compelling.

Pears poses three questions concerning Wittgenstein's reductio argument: 'What are the premises? What absurdity is deduced from them? And which premise is responsible for it?' (1988, 464). Based on what he states at pp. 467–70 (1988), the main premises seem to be:

(1) It is 'necessary that something in the rule-follower's mind should connect him with the pattern of correct applications of a rule' (1988, 469).
(2) But 'nothing could possibly fill the post, because any single thing in anyone's mind would always be connectible with more than one set of applications' (*Ibid.*).

These premises are intelligible when we take account of the issues and the conception of platonism discussed in the previous section. The first premise states that when a person understands a word or follows a rule, there must be something in his mind that connects with how that word or rule is correctly used or applied in particular instances. The platonist conception is implicit in this premise because the connection is one in which whatever is in the person's mind determines what counts as a correct application of the word or rule. The second premise asserts that nothing can play this role because every candidate of mental state we consider is compatible with different applications of the word or rule (and so does not determine anything).

According to Pears, the absurdity that is deduced from these premises 'is the abolition of the very distinction that the theory was designed to make more secure, the distinction between obeying and disobeying a rule' (1988, 467). The theory in question is platonism and so this also answers the final question of which premise he believes to be responsible for the absurdity. He states that 'Wittgenstein's target is the theory that the guidance given by a rule is complete, covering every possible case in advance' (1988, 465). The reason why platonism can seem attractive is that it is supposed to provide a strong foundation for the distinction between obeying and disobeying a rule, or between applying a word or rule correctly and incorrectly. But on Pears' view, it is just these platonist standards that ultimately undermine the notions of following a rule or applying a word correctly because nothing in a person's mind can meet these standards. Once this absurdity is deduced and the platonist conception is shown to be responsible for it, Wittgenstein's reductio argument is completed by rejecting the platonist conception.

William Child argues that this Wittgensteinian reductio argument is weak and contains little to trouble the platonist about meaning and rules. His main objection is that the absurdity cannot be deduced from the premises identified by Pears without making additional assumptions that the platonist would not accept. Child agrees that Pears' Wittgenstein has shown that there are '*indefinitely many* different ways' of taking a given rule[9], but he argues that this is compatible with platonism (2001, 85). What the platonist cannot accept is the further claim 'that none of these [ways of taking the rule] is any simpler or more natural than the others' (*Ibid.*). That is, the platonist must hang on to the claim that even though there are many ways of taking a given rule, there are nevertheless 'objective, mind-independent standards of simplicity and naturalness' that determine one way as the correct way of applying it in particular instances. According to Child, the Wittgensteinian argument as Pears presents it cannot establish this stronger claim, and therefore it is powerless against the platonist.

Another way of putting this is to say that the paradox cannot be shown to follow from the platonist conception because that would depend on establishing the stronger claim. Child argues that Pears fails to see this because he implicitly presupposes a non-platonist assumption in his attempt to show that the paradox follows from the platonist conception. To see what he means by this, consider the following passage from Pears:

[T]he indefinitely prolonged sequence of correct applications of a word cannot be fixed unequivocally by any example or set of examples. It will always be possible to continue the sequence in more than one way ... The correct continuation of a series can be determined only by what *we, who continue it, find it natural to do*. So if our contribution is ignored, it will not be possible to pick out the right continuation from the others. Anything will pass as correct, and the distinction between obeying the rule and disobeying it will collapse. This distinction must be based on our practice, which cannot be completely anticipated by any self-contained thing. (1988, 208; emphasis added)

In this formulation, Pears seems to be claiming that the platonist conception leads to the rule-following paradox because it ignores 'our contribution', i.e. it ignores what we 'find it natural to do' when using a word or applying a rule. Child's point is that Pears' Wittgenstein is guided by the conviction that in order for there to be one determinate way of applying a rule – among the indefinite amount of alternative ways – we must take account of the way we find it natural to continue applying a rule; and since platonism ignores this and seeks to determine the correct way of applying the rule by means of some strange abstract entity, it leads to the paradox that there is no genuine distinction between correctly and incorrectly applying a rule. Hence, on Child's view, Pears' Wittgenstein merely assumes the strong claim that there is no objectively simple way of correctly applying a rule, and then goes on to conclude that platonism must be defective because it does not have the resources to salvage a distinction between correctly and incorrectly applying a rule. The Wittgensteinian argument would thus beg the question by assuming an anti-platonist premise in its attack on platonism (see Child 2001, 88).

---

[9] Child focuses on rules given by means of ostensive definitions. The points he makes about Pears' interpretation of Wittgenstein's anti-platonist argument, though, are clearly supposed to pertain to any type of rule regardless of how it is specified.

In the next two sections, I will present a much more detailed analysis of Wittgenstein's reductio argument against platonism about meaning and rules. And I will argue that this formulation is not vulnerable to this kind of objection.

2.5 Wittgenstein's Regress-of-Interpretations Argument

According to the reading I will defend, there are two stages to Wittgenstein's reductio argument leading up to the derivation of the paradox. Each of these stages contains a separate argument within the overall reductio and both are necessary to derive the paradox. The first stage is a regress argument and this will be my focus in this section. I will address the second stage in the next section.

After presenting the form of the regress argument, I will attempt to show how it assumes the legitimacy of the platonist conception and how this ends up generating the regress. However, I will also prepare the way for the defence of my claim in the next section that the regress argument does not lead to the paradox stated at §201 and that Wittgenstein's attack on platonism is thus incomplete without a further argument.

The Regress

One of Wittgenstein's clearest statements of the considerations leading to the regress argument are stated at §§85–87 of *PI*, prior to his more sustained discussion of rule-following and meaning beginning at §138. In §86 he asks us to imagine a variant of the builders' language-game, which had been introduced in §2. Recall that the language-game is played by a builder A and his assistant B and consists of A calling out one of four different words – 'block', 'pillar', 'slab' and 'beam' – and B bringing the type of object that he has learnt to bring when hearing the relevant call. The additional feature introduced in §86 is that the language-game is now played 'with the help of a table':

The signs given to B by A are now written ones. B has a table; in the first column are the signs used in the game, in the second pictures of building stones. A shews B such a written sign; B looks it up in the table, looks at the picture opposite, and so on. So the table is a rule which he follows in executing orders. (*PI*, §86)

The table, then, is a rule for the use of the words in the language. B employs it as a guide to correctly responding to A's linguistic utterances. The problem, though, is that this rule can itself be applied in different ways, which may make it seem as if we need a further rule for interpreting this rule. For example, one quite natural way of interpreting the table would be as follows:

One learns to look the picture up in the table by receiving a training, and part of this training consists perhaps in the pupil's learning to pass with his finger horizontally from left to right; and so, as it were, to draw a series of horizontal lines on the table. (*Ibid.*)

Wittgenstein gives this visual representation of the rule:

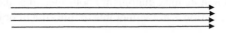

But we can just as easily imagine an alternative rule for applying the table, represented as below:

Wittgenstein continues:

Can we not now imagine further rules to explain *this* one? And, on the other hand, was that first table incomplete without the schema of arrows? And are other tables incomplete without their schemata? (*Ibid.*)

We generate an infinite regress of rules because for each rule we introduce for applying a rule, there is an open question as to how to correctly apply that rule and so it does not get us any further.

These regress considerations also arise in Wittgenstein's discussion of the different candidates of determining the meaning of a word 'in an instant' at §§138–155. For example, if we suppose that a *mental image* determines the meaning of a word, there will be different ways of 'projecting' that image on to objects – different rules for applying the word in accordance with the image – and so we seem to need a further rule for applying it; but this does not get us any further because there are different possible ways of applying this further rule etc.

The common feature in these separate instances is that the object that is supposed to determine the meaning is itself non-semantic or 'normatively inert', as John McDowell puts it (2009a, 100; 2009b, 81). The table in §86 or the mental image of a cube in §139 merely 'stands there like a sign-post' (*PI*, §85); it is something that on its own cannot instruct us on how it is to be correctly applied. The regress arises in each case because each thing we introduce to determine how it should be correctly applied is merely another object of this kind (for example, arrows connecting columns in the table, or imagined lines of projection from a mental image to an object), which is also in need of interpretation. Although this is how the regress is generated, the overall regress argument draws an ultimate conclusion on the basis of this regress. If we take each new rule that we introduce to be an interpretation of some other rule, the conclusion is that 'Interpretations by themselves do not determine meaning' (*PI*, §198). That is, the regress shows that our mistake was to assume that a word or rule was incomplete unless supplemented by a further rule that removed all doubt as to how it should be applied (see *PI*, §87).

This is the form that the regress argument takes and it is quite familiar from the amount of discussion that has been devoted to it in the secondary literature. I will now address the more contentious issue of how this argument relates to the platonist conception and the broader context of Wittgenstein's discussion of rule-following and meaning.

The Regress Argument, Platonism and the Paradox of Rule-Following

The discussion that begins at §§138/139 of *PI* on the relation between the two ways of determining meaning reaches a conclusion with the statement of a 'paradox' concerning the notions of meaning and rule-following at §§198 and 201:

> But how can a rule show me what I have to do at *this* point? Whatever I do is, on some interpretation, in accord with the rule. (*PI*, §198)
> This was our paradox: no course of action could be determined by a rule, because every course of action can be made out to accord with the rule. The answer was: if everything can be made out to accord with the rule, then it can also be made out to conflict with it. And so there would be neither accord nor conflict here. (*PI*, §201)

Both statements of the paradox seem to be articulating the same point, viz. that a rule cannot determine what actions count as the correct applications of the rule, and hence that there is no such thing as a correct or incorrect application of a rule. Both formulations also state similar causes of the paradox: the correct applications cannot be determined by the rule because 'every course of action' ('Whatever I do') can be construed as the correct way of applying the rule. The same issue can be expressed in terms of the notion of meaning: the meaning we attach to a word cannot determine the correct ways of applying it because any way of applying it can be construed as correct.

How does Wittgenstein's discussion arrive at this conclusion? If we consider the wording of §§198 and 201, the most compelling conclusion to draw is that it is the regress argument that leads to the paradox. The connection is made explicit in both passages:

> [A]ny interpretation still hangs in the air along with what it interprets, and cannot give it any support. Interpretations by themselves do not determine meaning. (*PI*, §198)
> It can be seen that there is a misunderstanding here from the mere fact that in the course of our argument we give one interpretation after another; as if each one contented us at least for a moment, until we thought of yet another standing behind it. (*PI*, §201)

The paradox arises, it would seem, because there is nothing to bridge the gap between the rule or the meaning that has been attached to the word and the actions of correctly applying the rule or word. Anything we appeal to – such as a mental picture or formula – is itself separated by a gulf from the actions and in need of something further to bridge the gap between it and the actions. Therefore, no course of action can be determined by a rule.

The role of the platonist conception in the regress argument becomes clearer when we consider each of the candidates that are discussed as potentially determining meaning, viz. a mental 'picture', a picture combined with its 'method of projection' or application, and a 'formula' (see *PI*, §§139–141, 146, and 151–152). None of these candidates can prevent the regress from arising because *none of them satisfy the platonist standards* for determining meaning, i.e. they do not determine the correct way of applying the word or rule and thus fail to bridge the gap between the word or rule and the actions of correctly applying it. Hence, it can be seen that Wittgenstein is operating with the assumption that the platonist conception is legitimate at this stage of the discussion because each of the candidates for determining meaning that are considered in §§138–155 are judged by the standards of this platonist conception. Furthermore, they are all found to fall short of these standards; none of them can determine meaning in the relevant platonist sense. And *this* is what generates the regress in each case.

I will elaborate on this point in section 2.7. However, I will argue in the next section that, despite Wittgenstein's formulations at §§198 and 201, the regress argument is not after all sufficient to derive the paradox. Therefore, on its own it is not capable of constituting a convincing attack on the platonist conception. A further argument is required, and it is to this that I now turn.

2.6   Wittgenstein's Gerrymandering Argument

Many interpreters of *PI* have made a distinction between the regress argument and a second argument running through §§138–242. This second argument has been given different names, including the 'sceptical argument' (Kripke 1982, 7–54), 'gerrymandering argument' (Brandom 1994, 26–30), and the 'Paradox' or 'Paradox-of-Interpretation' argument (Williams 2007, 64). I will use Robert Brandom's label because it is the most neutral. For example, it leaves open the question of the relation between the argument and the paradox of rule-following. However, I adopt Brandom's label without sharing his particular characterisation of the argument.

The gerrymandering argument is not as explicit as the regress argument in Wittgenstein's discussion. I will begin by providing a reading of the relevant sections in which I hold the regress argument to end and the gerrymandering argument to begin; and then I will present an outline of the argument and the role of the platonist conception in it. The basic claim that I want to defend is that it too presupposes the platonist conception, but that it does so in such a way as to make the regress considerations no longer relevant. This prepares the way for the defence of my view that this argument presents the crucial stage in Wittgenstein's attack on platonism that shows that it leads to the paradox at §201 of *PI*.

The Emergence of the Gerrymandering Argument

What are the considerations leading to the gerrymandering argument and in what sense are they distinct from those leading to the regress of interpretations? To answer this, we need to consider where Wittgenstein's discussion stands at §155 of *PI*. In §143, he asks us to imagine a person who has been instructed to 'write down series of signs according to a certain formation rule'. Taking the example of the series of natural numbers in decimal notation, Wittgenstein asks: 'But how far need he continue the series for us to have the right to say' that he has mastered the system or that he understands it? 'Clearly you cannot state a limit here' (§145). He pursues this question with the following:

Suppose I now ask: 'Has he understood the system when he continues the series to the hundredth place?' ... Has he got the system, if he continues the series correctly so far? – Perhaps you will say here: to have got the system (or, again, to understand it) can't consist in continuing the series up to *this* or *that* number: *that* is only applying one's understanding. The understanding itself is a state which is the *source* of the correct use. (*PI*, §146)

It is important to note that this state of understanding which is supposed to be 'the *source* of the correct use' is *distinct* from the various mental states or candidates that Wittgenstein has considered in the preceding sections.[10]

He makes this point in §151 when he gives the example of a person A writing down the numerals, '1', '5', '11', '19', '29', and a person B watching this and suddenly exclaiming 'Now I understand!' Wittgenstein writes:

So this capacity, this understanding, is something that makes its appearance in a moment. So let us try and see what it is that makes its appearance here. (*PI*, §151)

He considers various mental states including thinking of a 'formula', watching 'with a certain feeling of tension', and having 'the sensation "that's easy!"' But he then asks: 'are the processes which I have described here *understanding*?' (§152) He answers this in the negative by stating that, for example, B's understanding the series does not mean simply that the formula occurs to him because 'it is perfectly imaginable that the formula should occur to him and that he should nevertheless not understand' (*Ibid.*). Wittgenstein generalises this

---

[10] In §149, Wittgenstein refers to the state of understanding that is manifested in applying the relevant rule or word as a 'disposition'. In what follows, I will refer to it simply as a 'state' and focus on the feature that it is supposed to possess of being the 'source' of the correct use of a rule or word.

assessment by claiming that understanding 'must have more in it than ... any of those more or less characteristic *accompaniments* or manifestations of understanding' (*Ibid.*).

The importance of this is that it is, I hold, precisely at this point of the discussion that Wittgenstein is moving away from the considerations leading to the regress argument and towards the considerations leading to the gerry-mandering argument. This becomes clearer when we appreciate the distinction between the state of understanding, on the one hand, and the mental states such as having mental images, thinking of formulae, sensations etc., that are '*accompaniments* or manifestations of understanding', on the other. When Wittgenstein writes that understanding 'must have more in it' than these other mental states, he is articulating the viewpoint of his interlocutor who is concerned with identifying a state that is the source of the correct use of a word. By engaging with this interlocutor, Wittgenstein is taking seriously this task and thinking through what such a state of understanding would have to be, and concluding that it would have to be more than any of the accompanying mental states. The only reason he gives at this point for claiming that understanding is distinct from these accompaniments is that they are neither necessary nor sufficient for understanding (see *PI*, §152).

However, there is a crucial sense in which it is distinct from these accompaniments, viz. the state of understanding is by definition 'the *source* of the correct use' of the understood word. This is what, in the philosophical interlocutor's voice, we say the state 'must' be; but it is also exactly what all the other mental states are not. It is the failure of all of these other mental states to fill this role that leads to the regress, or to the gap between the word and actions of correctly using it remaining un-bridged. Conversely, if there is such a state of understanding that is distinct from them, it would put a stop to the regress and bridge this gap.

At this point in the discussion, though, Wittgenstein breaks off this dialogue with the interlocutor who posits such a state of understanding, or rather he postpones any further treatment of the issue. Instead, what we get is an anticipation of what we could call Wittgenstein's favoured response to the difficulties that arise concerning meaning and rule-following; we get the appeal to the 'circumstances' in which we use terms and the rejection of the notion that understanding is a mental state or process at all:

If there has to be anything 'behind the utterance of the formula' it is *particular circumstances*, which justify me in saying I can go on – when the formula occurs to me.

Try not to think of understanding as a 'mental process' at all. – For *that* is the expression which confuses you. But ask yourself: in what sort of case, in what kind of circumstances, do we say, 'Now I know how to go on,' when, that is, the formula *has* occurred to me? (*PI*, §154; see also §155)

The interpretive claim I want to defend is that Wittgenstein returns to this issue of there being a state of understanding at §185 of *PI*, and that the discussion from §186 up to the statements of the paradox at §§198 and 201 is dominated by the attempt to take this notion seriously and to highlight the difficulties inherent in it. Furthermore, for reasons to be outlined in a moment, this is the point of *PI* at which I take Wittgenstein's concern to move from the regress argument to the gerrymandering argument. Hence, I will also argue that it is at this stage that his attack on the platonist conception reaches its conclusion.

The Gerrymandering Argument

§185 of *PI* takes up the discussion of continuing a series (and therewith a state of understanding), which had been introduced at §143. Wittgenstein considers the example of a child being taught how to continue a numerical series in accordance with the order 'Add 2'. The child extends the series as we do up to '1000', but then diverges from us by writing '1004', '1008' etc. Furthermore, the child takes himself to be following the rule he was taught, to be continuing on in the same way. The teacher objects that writing '1004' after '1000' does not accord with the rule of 'Add 2' as it *should* be taken.[11] But this just raises the question of what determines that the rule should be taken one way rather than another. For example, if we hold that the teacher understood the rule in such a way that writing '1002' is the correct next step after '1000' (and '13382' after '13380', '88716' after '88714' etc.), and that he *meant* it to be taken in this way (see §186), this raises the question as to how such a state of understanding or meaning could determine the correct step in each instance.

This opening discussion of the example does not shed any light on the mental state that supposedly underlies the teacher's or child's performances of applying a word or rule. Most of the sections beginning with §186 and leading up to the statements of the paradox are, though, concerned with this state. For example, Wittgenstein writes:

To carry it out correctly! How is it decided what is the right step to take at any particular stage? – 'The right step is the one that accords with the order – as it was *meant*.' – So when you gave the order + 2 you meant that he was to write 1002 after 1000 – and did you also mean that he should write 1868 after 1866, and 100036 after 100034, and so on – an infinite number of such propositions? – 'No: what I meant was, that he should write the next but one number after *every* number that he wrote; and from this all those propositions follow in turn.' – But that is just what is in question: what, at any stage, does follow from that sentence. Or, again, what, at any stage we are to call 'being in accord' with that sentence (and with the *mean*-ing you then put into the sentence – whatever that may have consisted in). (*PI*, §186)

---

[11] I follow Goldfarb in translating 'so *soll* ich's machen' as 'how I *should* do it', rather than Anscombe's 'how I was *meant* to do it' because the notion of an act of meaning is not introduced until §186, and thus should be viewed as strictly speaking separate to the presentation of the example in §185 (but as nevertheless a significant next step in Wittgenstein's characterisation of what is involved in applying a rule as we should). See Goldfarb (2012, 74, footnote).

He is clearly concerned with the same issue discussed in §146, viz. that of how a mental state could provide the standard of correctness for the use of a word or rule in particular instances. These sections are unified by Wittgenstein's critical engagement with an interlocutor who is 'inclined' to hold that the pattern of correct application of a word or rule is 'in some *unique* way predetermined, anticipated – as only the act of meaning can anticipate reality' (*PI*, §188).

The question then is that of the role of this state of meaning or understanding in the overall context of the gerrymandering argument. I hold that the most significant move in this argument is presupposing that there is such a state. Wittgenstein's discussion of the state in these sections (through the voice of his interlocutor and his critical engagement with it) provides some support for this, but I will attempt to provide a more compelling case by showing that the only way in which the paradox at §§198 and 201 can be derived is by positing such a state and assuming for the sake of the argument that it is legitimate. The argument proceeds in a reductio fashion by demonstrating that this assumption leads to the paradox and the ultimate conclusion is that this assumption is flawed. I will explain in the next section how this goes against some prominent ways of reading the argument, but I will first present my analysis of it.

The steps from making the assumption of the state of understanding to the paradox are best discussed by considering in more detail the example in §185 of the child following the rule of 'Add 2'. In line with how I propose to interpret the argument, let us assume that if the child understands 'Add 2' as it 'should' be understood, this is in virtue of a primitive mental state that is 'the *source* of the correct use', and hence which determines that '1002' is the correct next step after '1000', '1004' after '1002' etc. But a problem now arises when we recognise that there are an indefinite number of other such states of understanding that would be consistent with the steps leading up to '1000', but would diverge after this. For example, we can conceive of a state that determines that the child adds 2 up to 1000, 4 up to 2000, 6 up to 3000 etc. The problem then is that of how to demonstrate that the child's state of understanding determines that he should write '1002' rather than '1004' after '1000'. This, of course, generalises to other language users and their understanding of words and their correct use in particular instances.

This may at first appear to be a rather straightforward problem to deal with. But when we consider the features of the state of understanding, the difficulties become more apparent. From the earlier discussion at §§143–155 of *PI*, we can already make a couple of points regarding this state. Firstly, whatever it is, it must be *distinct* from other mental states such as imagining or picturing an object, thinking of a formula or having a sensation because they have all been shown to not possess the relevant sorting power to predetermine the correct applications of a word or rule. Secondly, the mental state is in some sense *hidden*; it is the 'source' of correct application, and what is open to view are either 'manifestations' (for example, particular applications) or 'accompaniments' (for example, other mental states such as sensations) of this mental state. As Wittgenstein states, again articulating the task of his interlocutor: 'We are trying to get hold of the mental process of understanding which seems to be hidden behind those coarser and therefore more readily visible accompaniments' (*PI* §153).

This implies that in any person's attempt to defend the claim that his state of understanding determines that he should use a word one way rather than another, it would be pointless to appeal to any of the mental states that may accompany that understanding; since they are neither necessary nor sufficient for understanding the word in one way rather than the others, they are not a reliable guide to what state of understanding they accompany. The hiddenness of this state adds to the difficulties of demonstrating which way a person understands a word. Wittgenstein suggests these difficulties earlier, in §153:

And how can the process of understanding have been hidden, when I said 'Now I understand' *because* I understood?! And if I say it is hidden – then how do I know what I have to look for? I am in a muddle.

We could ask the same questions about this hidden state of understanding that he later asks about the notion of 'intuition' as removing doubt regarding how I should apply a word:

If intuition is an inner voice – how do I know *how* I am to obey it? And how do I know that it doesn't mislead me? For if it can guide me right, it can also guide me wrong.

    ((Intuition an unnecessary shuffle.))   (*PI*, §213)

There is more to say about Wittgenstein's discussion of the difficulties that arise if we view the use of words or the following of rules as underpinned by mental states of understanding. At this point, I merely want to highlight that these considerations lead directly to the paradox that 'no course of action could be determined by a rule, because every course of action can be made out to accord with the rule'. This result follows if we are unable to provide grounds for claiming that I understand a word or rule one way rather than any of the other ways that are consistent with my behaviour up to this point. Anything I write – for instance, '1004' rather than '1002' after '1000' – can be construed as correct, i.e. as precisely that which I *should* write in accordance with my state of understanding which is the source of the correct use. Whatever I do can be justified by positing some hidden mental state that *compels* me to do this.[12]

These are the considerations that generate the paradox, but the overall gerrymandering argument that includes these steps concludes by rejecting the

---

[12] See section 2.9 on the important distinction that Wittgenstein makes between two senses of being 'compelled'.

assumption that using a word or following a rule rests on a distinctive mental state of understanding. The paradox can only be derived by making this assumption.

2.7   The Plausibility of Wittgenstein's Overall Anti-Platonist Argument

In this section I will explain how the two Wittgensteinian arguments I have identified link up in mounting a powerful challenge to platonism about rules and meaning. In my defence of this anti-platonist challenge, I will argue against Meredith Williams' formulation of Wittgenstein's arguments and also return to Pears' formulation.

Platonism and the Regress and Gerrymandering Arguments

My analysis of the relation between the platonist conception, the two Wittgensteinian arguments and the paradox can be represented as follows:

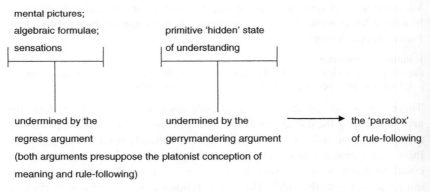

mental pictures;

algebraic formulae;   primitive 'hidden' state

sensations   of understanding

undermined by the   undermined by the   ⟶   the 'paradox'

regress argument   gerrymandering argument   of rule-following

(both arguments presuppose the platonist conception of

meaning and rule-following)

Mental pictures, formulae, sensations and the primitive state of understanding are all candidates of what is involved in determining the meaning of a word in an instant (which seems to occur when one understands the word). According to my reading, the arguments are directed against different candidates, but they both presuppose the legitimacy of the platonist conception in the sense that any such candidate is judged by the standards of this conception. This plays out in different ways corresponding to the differences between the candidates considered in each argument. As outlined in the previous sections, candidates such as mental pictures or algebraic formulae fail to genuinely determine meaning because they do not determine the correct way of applying the relevant word or rule in particular instances (i.e. they do not determine meaning when judged by the platonist standards). Moreover, the failure of these candidates is demonstrated by the fact that they lead to an infinite regress (of mental pictures, formulae etc.).

The role of the platonist conception in the gerrymandering argument is different because it operates with the assumption that there is a primitive mental state of understanding that corresponds to this conception; it is assumed that this state determines (is the 'source' of) the correct use of the word or rule. This assumption leads us away from the regress argument because it effectively takes the gap between words/rules and actions to be bridged at the outset, thus blocking the opening that the regress needs to get started. What we encounter instead are difficulties of an altogether different kind that follow from assuming that the correct use could have its source in such a mental state of understanding.

Finally, there is the relation between the two arguments and the paradox stated at §§198 and 201. The main point to note is that the paradox does not in fact follow from the regress argument alone. Wittgenstein perhaps gives this impression by making reference to the regress in both statements of the paradox. But the regress argument only gets us as far as the claim made at §152 that understanding must be 'more than any of those more or less characteristic *accompaniments* or manifestations of understanding' (for example, having a mental picture of an object). A further inquiry into what it is, if anything, that these mental states accompany or manifest is required. In other words, at this earlier point it is more appropriate to say that *nothing* rather than *anything* I do can be construed as according with the rule or the understood word. For at this point, there is no link between the rule/word and the actions. The paradox that anything I do can be made out to accord with the rule/word follows only when we assume that there is a mental state that bridges the gap and determines the correct way of applying the rule/word in each instance. The regress argument is useful in showing that, for example, having a mental picture or a certain sensation cannot play the role of this meaning-constituting mental state. But the derivation of the paradox depends on additional considerations that are separate to the regress argument.

These stages of Wittgenstein's discussion add up to the overall reductio argument that presupposes the legitimacy of the platonist conception at each stage in the way outlined, derives the paradox and concludes by rejecting this conception. To conclude, I will contrast this reading with Meredith Williams' because it provides a representative example of how Wittgenstein's anti-platonist argument can look weak even when the intention is to defend it.

Response to Williams and Pears on Wittgenstein's Anti-Platonist Argument

Concerning the paradox of rule-following, Williams writes:

Given the fact of multiple interpretations, for any action, that action can be characterised both in a way that accords with a given rule and conflicts with it – even if the interpretation of the rule were transparent. This is the source of the paradox: even if the application of a rule is correct, the action could be made out to conflict with it. Nothing in the application of objectified meaning guarantees what the particular actual action really is. This renders the notion of accord or conflict, hence of rule-governedness itself, meaningless. (2007, 64).

The paradox that Wittgenstein derives in this argument, according to Williams, is that – even if the meaning of the word or the rule for its use is given (or 'transparent') – any action can be characterised as either according with that rule or conflicting with it. But how is this the case? It seems to be that the conception of meaning involved here is that of an abstract standard for the application of a term, but in which it is left undetermined exactly which actions count as correctly applying it. That is, there is a gulf between this abstract standard and the particular actions of applying that standard. See, for example, where she writes:

Even a transparent rule carries no constraint on *what* action is performed, as any action can be characterised to accord with the rule or not. So the idea that the rule imposes constraints on what we do is empty. The rule doesn't 'hook up' with action in any substantive way. (*Ibid.*)

The 'transparent rule', or what she also calls an 'objectified meaning', does not impose constraints on what action is to be performed when applying the relevant word because any action can be 'characterised' or 'made out to' accord or conflict with that rule (*Ibid.*). This is how the paradox is derived in her formulation of the gerrymandering argument.

My main objection to this formulation is that it makes the argument weak, particularly when faced with the platonist position. To explain why, we need to note that on Williams' analysis, the paradox arises because there is a separation or gulf between an interpreted word or rule and the actions that count as correctly applying it. But this implies that the overall gerrymandering argument – in which the derivation of the paradox is an essential part – can only establish its conclusion by assuming *at the outset* that there is no primitive state of understanding corresponding to the platonist conception that would bridge the gap between words/rules and the actions of applying them. In other words, Williams' reading entails that the gerrymandering argument begs the question against the platonist. Her version of the argument cannot be used against the platonist because it must assume at the outset that there is no state of understanding corresponding to the platonist conception. On my reading, this is avoided because the gerrymandering argument is characterised as a reductio that assumes the legitimacy of the platonist state of understanding and proceeds to show that even if we assume that the gap between rules and actions is bridged by such a state, we still end up with the paradox.

This feature of my formulation of the argument is also what separates it from Pears'. Child's main objection to Pears' Wittgenstein's reductio argument was that it is incapable of deriving the rule-following paradox without presupposing a crucial non-platonist premise. The version of the reductio argument presented here does not have this shortcoming because it interprets Wittgenstein as genuinely taking the platonist conception seriously and seeing where it leads. Pears' version of the argument mirrors Williams' because it implicitly assumes something that the platonist does not accept. On my formulation, the chain of inferences beginning with the assumption of the platonist conception and leading to the paradox is complicated, but it does not contain any premise that the platonist would not accept. For instance, the derivation does not depend on assuming that there is no objectively simplest way of continuing to apply a rule; on the contrary, it grants the platonist the notion of a primitive mental state that determines such a way (out of the indefinite number of alternatives). On my reading, Wittgenstein accepts for the sake of argument that a person may have mental states of the kind the platonist requires. But he highlights the problem of demonstrating that a person has a particular mental state, MS_1, rather than other mental states, MS_2, MS_3, MS_4 etc., of the same kind but that would determine alternative patterns of correct applications beyond a certain point. For if such 'sources' of correct application are hidden and distinct from accompanying mental states like sensations and from manifestations of that state (i.e. previous applications), how are we to tell from these accompaniments and manifestations alone exactly which platonist mental state a person possesses? Any application at any point would be justifiable relative to some such hidden state.

2.8   Problems with McDowell's Reading

John McDowell's reading is also worth considering in this context because it too (unwittingly) entails that Wittgenstein's argumentation in this part of *PI* is weak, but in a different way to Williams' reading. McDowell views the regress argument as fundamental – calling it Wittgenstein's 'master argument' (2009a, 108) – and he characterises its outcome as follows:

the thrust of Wittgenstein's reflections is to cast doubt on the master thesis: the thesis that whatever a person has in her mind, it is only by virtue of being interpreted in one of various possible ways that it can impose a sorting of extra-mental items into those that accord with it and those that do not. (1998, 270)

This suggests that the ultimate source of the regress is not strictly speaking the assumption that meaning requires an act of interpretation, but the assumption that the contents of our minds are like dead signs and thus do not themselves succeed in 'sorting' actions into those that accord with them and those that do not. McDowell clarifies this in a later paper by stating that:

We learn [from the regress] that it is disastrous to suppose there is always a conceptual gap between an expression of a rule and performances that are up for assessment according to whether or not they conform to the rule. (2009a, 100)

It is this deeper assumption of the 'conceptual gap' between mental contents or signs and actions that is purportedly at the root of Wittgenstein's regress argument because this assumption is what makes it seem that something like an act of interpretation is needed to bridge the conceptual gap, and thus to determine what a thought is about or how to correctly apply a word or rule. On this reading, then, Wittgenstein's conclusion is to reject the conceptual gap assumption, or what McDowell also calls the 'master thesis'.

I agree that the regress argument functions by exploiting such a gap, but I do not share McDowell's view that the difficulties are eliminated by abandoning the conceptual gap assumption because (as I have argued) if we do so we then face the gerrymandering considerations that ultimately lead to the paradox. Therefore, the ultimate lesson cannot be that we must reject the conceptual gap assumption. It could be responded that when it comes to the gerrymandering argument, the difficulties arise by adopting the wrong conception of how this gap is bridged, viz. in terms of a primitive mental state of understanding corresponding to the platonist conception. But then the onus is on the opponent to show how this gap can be bridged in some other way that does not fall prey to the gerrymandering considerations.

The error in McDowell's reading is to suppose that Wittgenstein's ultimate negative conclusion is to reject the conceptual gap assumption, rather than to reject the platonist assumption. On my reading, it is the platonist assumption that lies at the root of the regress argument because it is the standards that it enforces that make it impossible for the conceptual gap to be bridged, and thus allow for the regress to arise in the first place. But also, this argument does not have the resources to undermine this assumption and so should be viewed in the context of a broader discussion (that includes the gerrymandering argument) that ultimately leads to the negation of the platonist conception. My analysis has shown that if we take the conceptual gap assumption to be fundamental, we succumb to the gerrymandering considerations when we assume that the gap is bridged. McDowell's reading thus fails to realise the importance of the gerrymandering argument and the sense in which it leads to a conclusion that is separate to the conceptual gap assumption.[13] This reinforces my claim that if we take proper account of the arguments at both stages of Wittgenstein's discussion, we must view his ultimate target to be the platonist conception, and that when taken together they offer a compelling case against it.

---

[13] See McDowell (2009a, 107), where he states that the gerrymandering argument is secondary to the regress argument.

2.9   Wittgenstein's Opposition to the Normativity of Meaning and Rules

As indicated in section 2.3, Wittgenstein's attack on the platonist conception of meaning is implicitly an attack on the thesis that meaning is normative. The relation between them becomes clear when we state them side-by-side:

The semantic normativity thesis:

The meaning of a linguistic expression determines what counts as correctly or incorrectly applying the expression in particular instances.[14]

The platonist thesis:

When a linguistic expression is 'stamped with a particular meaning', the entire pattern of correctly using the expression is thereby 'predetermined' or 'anticipated', 'as only the act of meaning can anticipate reality'.

Both statements essentially make a claim about the relation between the 'meaning' of a linguistic expression and the correct/incorrect uses of the expression, viz. that the latter are somehow determined by the meaning. That this notion of determination is mysterious or obscure is, of course, part of Wittgenstein's point. Depending on the precise formulations of the theses, they are very close and possibly equivalent. At the very least, we can observe that the platonist conception stands and falls with the semantic normativity thesis. This is crucial because what I have called Wittgenstein's overall anti-platonist argument seeks to highlight the defects in the conception by demonstrating the falsity of the semantic normativity thesis. It attempts to show that the distinction between correct and incorrect applications of a word cannot be determined by any semantic entity or rule that is correlated with the word. If successful, this amounts to arguing that there are no such normative distinctions that follow from meaning alone.

Where does this leave us? If the source of the correct and incorrect uses of words is not in the meanings of the words, where is it? Furthermore, we cannot eliminate the fact that as speakers of a language there is *some* sense in which certain ways of using words are correct and others incorrect, and some sense in which we are obligated to use words in certain ways rather than others. So how do we account for this while taking account of the lessons from Wittgenstein's discussion of meaning and rules?

Wittgenstein anticipates an answer to these questions at the beginning of that discussion when he makes a distinction between 'psychological' and 'logical' compulsion; the distinction also appears in *RFM*. First I will introduce the

---

[14] There are different versions of this thesis that will be discussed later in this section. This will suffice for the moment as a general formulation that is representative of them all.

distinction, and I will proceed to explain how it is useful in answering the above questions. Wittgenstein writes:

For we might also be inclined to express ourselves like this: [when we use a word] we are at most under a psychological, not a logical, compulsion. And now it looks quite as if we knew of two kinds of case. (*PI*, §140)

It looked at first as if these considerations were meant to show that 'what seems to be a logical compulsion is in reality only a psychological one' – only here the question arose: am I acquainted with both kinds of compulsion, then?! (*RFM*, 82)

The distinction is elucidated in *PI* in the context of his example of the use of the word 'cube' and specifically of whether a mental picture of a cube can determine the correct use of the word. Logical compulsion seems to pertain to the platonist notion of the correct applications being determined in advance by something like a mental picture (or some other mental item). To be *logically* compelled is to be compelled to use a word in accordance with these predetermined correct applications. Psychological compulsion, by contrast, seems to be weaker in the sense that it is not bound up with this imagery of a rigid pattern that we must align our use of words with. Rather, it has to do with our natural tendencies that come into play when following rules or using words, which can be considered independently of the 'rules as rails' imagery. In terms of the cube example, to be psychologically compelled would simply be to take a certain application to be natural (for example, applying the word to this square shaped object rather than to a triangular prism).

It is significant that in both quotations above, Wittgenstein ends by raising a doubt or question about whether we are really acquainted with both types of compulsion. I read this as him raising a doubt about the stronger, platonist notion of logical compulsion. Psychological compulsion is relatively unproblematic because – as our tendency to agree in how words like 'cube' are applied demonstrates – there are as a matter of fact ways that we find natural to apply words. The question that Wittgenstein's entire discussion appears to be addressing is whether we require a stronger notion of compulsion. And his answer, as we have seen, is an emphatic 'no'. What we are left with, then, is some weaker notion like psychological compulsion.

The issue of where Wittgenstein's negative arguments leave us will be central to the discussion in the subsequent chapters. For the moment, the important thing to keep in mind is that Wittgenstein does accept that there is a sense in which we are compelled to apply words and follow rules. Or to put it another way, there is a sense in which there are *correct* and *incorrect* ways of applying words and following rules, and correspondingly of being *obligated*. What he objects to is to locating these correctness conditions and obligations in a mysterious entity or mental state that is attached or related to a word; he objects to locating them in the 'meaning', which would have to be some strange entity with extraordinary sorting powers. The source rather lies in the community of language users, but exactly what this means is difficult to clarify and it will form the subject of Chapters 4 and 6.

Before moving on, though, more needs to be said about my interpretive claim that the later Wittgenstein is opposed to the view that meaning is normative. This is in direct opposition to Hans-Johann Glock's reading, who is among the few scholars to address Wittgenstein's relevance to this issue in the philosophy of language. Glock makes a distinction between different versions of the semantic normativity view and he uses this distinction to explain the exact senses in which he believes Wittgenstein *defended* it (see Glock 2008, 162–8). For the present purposes, the two versions that are most important to consider are the following (2008, 162):[15]

Bare normativity of meaning

If a word is meaningful, there are conditions for the correct use of the word.

Rule-based normativity of meaning

If a word is meaningful, there are rules for the use of the word.

The first is the most general characterisation we can give of the normativity claim and is supposed to capture 'the idea that a certain phenomenon which is semantic in a highly general sense entails the existence of certain normative phenomena' (Glock, *Ibid.*). The second version, though, states specifically that the conditions for the correct use of the word 'are laid down by such rules'. One may hold the first without holding the second (Glock cites Davidson and Boghossian as examples of philosophers who take a position like this).

Glock sets himself the task of arguing that Wittgenstein defended the above rule-based semantic normativity claim. Interestingly, he notes that even those who deny that Wittgenstein held a rule-based version accept that he held the more general, 'bare' or 'rule-free' version of the normativity view (2008, 163). My reading, then, differs from these also in denying even that Wittgenstein accepted the bare version. To clarify, my rationale for maintaining this is that I believe there is no basis for calling the normativity in question *semantic*. It is accepted by everyone that there is a distinction to be made between the correct and incorrect uses of words. But why call it semantic if the normative distinction is not based in anything semantic – i.e. not based in 'meanings' or 'rules' or anything else that are constitutive of meanings? I have suggested rather vaguely that the normativity in question is based in the community or communal practices of using the words. Although this has yet to be explained, it can be confidently asserted at this point that the justification for calling the

---

[15] Another version he distinguishes is 'prescriptive normativity of meaning', which concerns the distinction between correctness conditions and prescriptions or obligations. The other two versions he highlights relate to the normativity of content rather than meaning (see 2008, 163).

normative distinction 'semantic' has been eliminated by Wittgenstein's anti-platonist argument. Any semantic phenomenon we identify is going to be vulnerable to the same considerations raised in that argument.[16]

2.10   Conclusion: The Relevance of Wittgenstein's Arguments to Current Debates on Semantic Normativity

Wittgenstein's anti-platonist argument is interesting in its own right, but the scope of the argument and its broader significance can be seen by how much of what he argues has a direct bearing on the issues discussed in the contemporary debates concerning semantic normativity. The latter notion was taken by many philosophers in the 1980s (when it first became a central topic of discussion) to be legitimate and as possibly pertaining to the trivial fact that there are correct and incorrect ways to use the words of a language. While critics of the view that meaning is normative have emerged since then, Wittgenstein's arguments not only predate them but surpass them in many cases.

Early in this chapter, I noted how we can talk about the semantic normativity issue either in terms of the *correct/incorrect* use of words or in terms of how we *ought/ought not* (or *should/should not*) use words. The difference between these normative distinctions is not prominent in Wittgenstein's writings, but it is central to the more recent literature on this topic. Following Daniel Whiting, 'where "*w*" is a word, "*F*" gives its meaning, and "*f*" is that feature in virtue of which *w* applies', a statement of the correctness conditions for the application of a particular meaningful word can be given along the following lines (2007, 134):

(C) *w* means $F \to (x)(w$ applies correctly to $x \leftrightarrow x$ is $f)$

Most philosophers (including, crucially, opponents of semantic normativity) *accept* that it follows trivially from the fact that a word has meaning that it possesses conditions of correct application, as expressed in the above way (see Hattiangadi 2006, 222 and 2009, 55 and 60; Glüer and Wikforss 2009, 35). Statements of correctness conditions, though, are to be distinguished from the statements of the following form, which are more controversial (see Whiting 2007, 136):

(P) *w* means $F \to (x)(w$ ought to be applied to $x \leftrightarrow x$ is $f)$

---

[16] Prior to the discussion of the social dimension of language in Chapter 4, we can also disregard one possible view of the claim that the normative distinction between correct and incorrect use is based in the community of language-users. Namely: this claim cannot mean that the community or communal practices are constitutive of the *meanings* of words, which would in turn somehow entail the relevant normative standards of use. This would be yet another version of the semantic normativity view that is as vulnerable to the Wittgensteinian argument as the non-communal or mentalistic versions. Therefore, the appeal to the community of language-users must be separated from any attempted explanatory or constitutive account that can be undermined by Wittgenstein's argument.

Such statements are directive or prescriptive; they concern what *ought* to be done with a word, or how it ought to be applied given its meaning. The defender of semantic normativity – as it is now understood – holds that the meaning of a term entails not only conditions of correct use (as expressed in (C)), but also obligations for how we ought to use the term.

From this contemporary standpoint, it looks as though Wittgenstein is among the most radical opponents of semantic normativity because he would apparently reject statements of the form (C). However, I think he would accept that statements of this form are trivial but hold that they are empty; i.e. that they still leave open the question of how to correctly apply words in particular instances. Or rather, if they are held to be non-trivial and as thus positing some robust notion of meaning that establishes a standard of correctness for applying the word, he would reject them for the reasons given in his anti-platonist argument. He would attack the notion of semantic obligations on the same grounds.

It is easier to clarify the precise sense in which Wittgenstein is opposed to semantic normativity by considering another major issue that is prominent in the current debate regarding the prescriptivity of semantic rules. I will call it the 'practical guidance issue' because it is concerned with 'in what sense a rule can be a reason of acting at all' (see Glüer and Pagin 1999, 208). This issue is relevant to the semantic normativity thesis because if there are serious problems with the view that semantic rules can provide practical guidance in the actions they apparently prescribe (as many philosophers maintain there are), the notion that there are obligations following directly from the rules that are in force will be threatened (see Glüer and Pagin 1999, 221; Hattiangadi 2007, 201–6; and Glüer and Wikforss 2009, 57–9).

The connection between this issue and Wittgenstein's discussion of rules and meaning (as presented here) should be obvious. Wittgenstein's regress and gerrymandering arguments expose the different ways in which the notion of a rule guiding our actions or use of words can be easily misconstrued. His arguments can thus be used against any conception that inflates the notion of rule-guidance, or views it in terms of the platonist 'rule as rails' imagery or of being 'logically compelled' by a rule. But does this mean that we are not guided by rules at all when using words?[17] As stated in the previous section, Wittgenstein is willing to make the platitudinous claim that we tend to agree, broadly speaking, in how we use words. Whether this amounts to our language being rule-guided is unclear. But what is clear is that we cannot hold that we are rule-guided in the way that his arguments oppose (for example, guided in the way the platonist maintains we must be).

[17] A positive answer is defended by Glüer and Wikforss (2010), while a negative answer is defended in Wright (2007).

This 'practical guidance issue' is at the centre of Wittgenstein's discussion of rule-following and meaning. It is the issue that creates the strongest link between *PI* and the recent debates, and his critical reflections on it establish him as a major opponent of semantic normativity.

Summary of Main Points

(2a) Throughout Wittgenstein's middle- and later-period writings, there is a concern with a conception of meaning that is distinct from referentialism. According to this alternative conception, the meaning of a word is determined by a *rule* for the use of the word. Wittgenstein thus became preoccupied with the notion of language as rule-governed.

(2b) In §§138–201 (and certain other sections) of *PI*, Wittgenstein identifies what he views as fundamental misconceptions of the nature of meaning and of rules governing the use of words. This entire discussion contains an intricate *reductio ad absurdum* argument of a 'platonist' conception of meaning and rules.

(2c) The platonist conception states that when the meaning of a word (or the rule governing its use) is given, the correct way of applying that word in particular instances is thereby predetermined or anticipated.

(2d) Wittgenstein's approach to undermining the platonist conception is to assume that this conception is legitimate, show that it leads to threatening the entire notion of understanding a word or following a rule and on this basis to conclude by rejecting the conception.

(2e) This reductio strategy is what saves Wittgenstein from the objection that he begs the question against the platonist. Rather than assuming that the platonist is wrong at the outset as many other interpreters imply, he actually assumes for the sake of argument that the platonist has the right conception of meaning and rule-following. But because this leads to a paradoxical conclusion, there are grounds for rejecting the conception.

(2f) The intricacy of Wittgenstein's reductio is best illuminated by distinguishing between his 'regress argument' and his 'gerrymandering argument'. These should be viewed as two distinct stages within his overall reductio of the platonist conception.

(2g) Both the regress and gerrymandering arguments operate with the assumption that the platonist conception is legitimate in order to show that it entails the rule-following paradox (that there is no such thing as correctly or incorrectly applying any rule or using any word). This paradox, though, can only be shown to follow from the platonist conception by employing both arguments. Neither is sufficient on its own.

(2h) Although Wittgenstein does not use the terminology of the 'normativity of meaning' or 'semantic normativity', his concern with rules for the use of words leads him to engage with this issue.

(2i) The thesis that meaning is normative states that the meaning of a word determines what counts as correctly or incorrectly applying the word in particular instances (or similarly, that it determines how we ought or ought not to apply it). Defending this thesis involves holding that the normativity in question is intrinsically semantic, i.e. not reducible to other types of normativity (for example, ethical).

(2j) The platonist must hold that meaning is normative in this sense.

(2k) Wittgenstein's reductio argument against platonism is at once also an attack on the thesis that meaning is normative. This negative attitude in *PI* towards the thesis contrasts with his middle-period view, in which he implicitly defends the thesis.

(2l) The later Wittgenstein is a radical opponent of the semantic normativity thesis in the sense that he rejects the view that a semantic notion (whether it is the 'meaning', 'semantic rule' or some distinctive 'mental state' that is correlated with a word) can do the work of determining what counts as correctly or incorrectly using a word.

3 Scepticism About Meaning

Wittgenstein's name has been associated with the issue of scepticism about meaning primarily as a result of Saul Kripke's influential 1982 book, *Wittgenstein on Rules and Private Language* (*WRPL*), which depicts the later Wittgenstein as embracing a version of that doctrine. Kripke was aware from the outset that his interpretation was highly unorthodox, and he even included the disclaimer in his introduction that his intention is the relatively modest one of explicating 'Wittgenstein's argument as it struck Kripke, as it presented a problem for him' (1982, 4). Unfortunately, this has only contributed to the near complete consensus that his interpretation is deeply flawed or inaccurate. I will argue in this chapter that despite containing major errors, Kripke's reading is of enormous value and if properly developed it can go further than most other readings in clarifying Wittgenstein's argumentative strategy. And I will show that the consideration of Wittgenstein's views on meaning in relation to the doctrine of scepticism about meaning is extremely useful in getting to grips with what is genuinely radical in Wittgenstein's reflections on language in *Philosophical Investigations* (*PI*) (even though any identification of Wittgenstein with the radical sceptic is misleading).

There are three specific components to Kripke's depiction of Wittgenstein as a type of sceptic about meaning: first, that Wittgenstein developed a *sceptical challenge* to the view that we mean something by the words we use (or that we follow rules); second, that Wittgenstein believed that the challenge could not be met directly or with a 'straight solution', and thus that he accepted a *sceptical conclusion* concerning meaning and rule-following; and third, that he proposed a *sceptical solution* that sought to present an alternative positive picture of the legitimacy of semantic discourse (of making utterances such as 'Jones means addition by "+"') while somehow accommodating this sceptical conclusion. Although all of these features of Kripke's reading have been vigorously opposed by almost all prominent Wittgenstein scholars, one of the major difficulties we face here is that there is significant ambiguity concerning all three of them. I will attempt to clear up these ambiguities in this chapter and thereby prepare the way for a better appreciation of Kripke's reading and of Wittgenstein's relation to scepticism about meaning.

This chapter of the book differs from the others in being concerned far more with recent literature in the philosophy of language – from the 1980s onwards – than with Wittgenstein's writings. This reverses the proportions of the discussion in the other chapters. Nevertheless, at key points in the chapter I will draw upon the reading of Wittgenstein's *PI* that I have defended so far in order to evaluate Kripke's reading. For example, the semantic normativity issue turns out to be central to Kripke's reading, so the topics raised in the previous chapter will be discussed in this new context. The emphasis will thus be on the constructed figure of Kripke's Wittgenstein (henceforth referred to as 'KW'), and on the relation between the views of this figure and the sceptic about meaning. The question of whether or not the historical Wittgenstein coincides with KW and/or the sceptic will be treated subsequently (see section 3.3–3.6).

One of the main claims I will defend is that KW's negative argument is structurally similar to Wittgenstein's anti-platonist argument. More specifically, both of them should be formulated as reductio arguments that target a platonist or classical realist conception of meaning. Therefore, by drawing attention to this parallel I will be able to extend the discussion of the previous chapter and show how Wittgenstein's *PI* connects deeply with the issue of scepticism about meaning. Clarifying the similarities between Wittgenstein's and KW's arguments will also lead to a partial defence of Kripke's reading at the end of the chapter.

3.1 Kripke's Wittgenstein's Argument for Scepticism About Meaning

Kripke begins his analysis of Wittgenstein's discussion of rule-following and meaning by stating that it can be taken as presenting 'a new form of philosophical scepticism' (1982, 7). He interprets Wittgenstein as presenting a sceptical challenge to the view that our thought and behaviour are rule-governed and, moreover, to the view that we mean anything by the words we use. In Chapter 2 of his book, he discusses the details of this sceptical argument, the conclusion of which is the radical sceptical claim that 'There is no such thing as meaning anything by any word' (1982, 55). He distinguishes between a 'straight solution' and a 'sceptical solution' to this sceptical challenge. A straight solution is one that shows 'that on closer examination the scepticism proves to be unwarranted' (1982, 66). The most direct way of doing this would be to identify a class of meaning-constituting facts as an answer to the sceptic, but it is also possible to show that the scepticism is unwarranted by rejecting one or more of the assumptions or terms of the challenge.[1] By contrast, a sceptical solution accepts that the sceptical challenge cannot be answered and therefore seeks

[1] One such way of objecting to the sceptic would be to question the kind of meaning-constituting facts he is demanding we identify (see below), and to instead identify a different kind of

to salvage the notion of meaning while accepting a version of the sceptical conclusion. Kripke argues on Wittgenstein's behalf that none of the straight solutions are adequate and in Chapter 3 of *WRPL* he outlines the structure of a sceptical solution and attributes it to Wittgenstein. We are told that the main features of the sceptical solution are that it rejects the notion of facts about meaning corresponding to meaning ascriptions and replaces the truth-conditional conception of meaning with an assertability-conditional conception. There are many important points of detail concerning each of these types of response; to begin I will consider some of the details of Kripke's characterisation of the sceptical argument itself.

Kripke formulates the sceptical challenge in terms of the example of the meaning of the symbol, '+', but he states that it applies to 'all meaningful uses of language' (1982, 7). The signs 'plus' and '+' are used to denote the mathematical function, *addition*, which is defined for all pairs of positive integers. Kripke writes:

One point is crucial to my 'grasp' of this rule. Although I myself have computed only finitely many sums in the past, the rule determines my answer for indefinitely many new sums that I have never previously considered. This is the whole point of the notion that in learning to add I grasp a rule: my past intentions regarding addition determine a unique answer for indefinitely many new cases in the future. (1982, 7–8)

Given the finitude of my past uses of the symbol for addition, there are an infinite number of possible uses that I have not yet in fact made. The discussion then turns to the consideration of one such new use of the symbol. Kripke, for convenience, takes the example of the use of the symbol in the computation '68 + 57'. Even if we have done this sum before, there are an infinite number of sums that we have not, and this example just stands in for one of them (1982, 8). Carrying out this computation, I obtain the answer '125', and I am confident that it is the correct one.

It is at this point that Kripke introduces 'a bizarre sceptic' who questions whether ' "plus", as I intended to use that word in the past, denoted a function which, when applied to the numbers I called "68" and "57", yields the value "125" ' (1982, 8). Kripke goes on: 'Perhaps, [the sceptic] suggests, as I used the term 'plus' in the past, the answer I intended for "68 + 57" should have been "5"!' (*Ibid.*). The sceptic continues by stating that if, in my past use of '+', I intended '68 + 57' to denote 125, then this cannot be because I gave myself explicit instructions to that effect. By hypothesis, I never previously encountered this particular computation, and so I never explicitly told myself that '125' was the correct answer to it. Because in the past I could have given myself only a finite number of examples instantiating this function, there is

meaning-constituting facts. This, for example, is the strategy adopted in different and competing ways by McDowell (1998) and Wright (2001).

room for scepticism regarding any new use of the sign I believe to denote this function. Kripke's sceptic states:

So perhaps in the past I used 'plus' and '+' to denote a function which I call 'quus' and symbolise by '$\oplus$'. It is defined by:

$$x \oplus y = x + y, \quad \text{if } x, y < 57$$
$$= 5 \quad \text{otherwise.}$$

Who is to say that this is not the function I previously meant by '+'? (1982, 8–9)

The sceptic thus states that it is possible that I always meant *quus* by my use of 'plus' and '+', and challenges me to show that this is incorrect, that I in fact meant *addition* by 'plus' and '+'.

It should be noted that Kripke's original formulation of the sceptical challenge is 'based on questioning a certain nexus from past to future', viz. 'the nexus between past "intention" or "meanings" and present practice: for example, between my past "intentions" with regard to "plus" and my present computation "68 + 57 = 125"' (1982, 62). The force of the challenge is conveyed by the observation that there are an infinite number of binary functions besides addition (for instance, quus or quaddition) that are compatible with my entire past use of the sign '+'. How can I be certain that in the past I grasped the addition function, rather than one of these other functions, when I used '+'? This argument is formulated in such a way that the meaningfulness of my present use of words is not placed in doubt; i.e. my present use is assumed to be legitimate in order to formulate the sceptical argument regarding my past use of a particular term (see 1982, 12). But it is obvious that there is nothing peculiar about my past use, or about the sign '+', and so the argument can eventually be generalised to all terms, and to every person's use of any term at any time.

A few points of clarification should be made. Kripke emphasises that in the sceptical challenge, 'Neither the accuracy of my computation nor of my memory is under dispute' (1982, 11); and neither is the arithmetical truth that '68 + 57 = 125' (see 1982, 13). Hence, 'it ought to be agreed that *if* I meant plus, then unless I wish to change my usage, I am justified in answering (indeed compelled to answer) "125", not "5"' (1982, 11). What *is* challenged is what I *meant* by the sign in question, i.e. it is challenged that I meant addition by '+' in the first place. This is significant because it reveals an important aspect of how the sceptic conceives of what it is to mean something by a term. The sceptic assumes that if I did mean addition by '+', then this entails that the correct application of '+' is determined in a potential infinity of particular cases and that I am compelled to apply it in just these ways. This assumption about meaning is also apparent in what Kripke calls the 'two conditions' that the sceptic puts on an adequate response to his challenge (1982, 11). Firstly, my response must 'give an account of what fact it is (about my mental state) that constitutes my meaning plus, not quus' (*Ibid.*). Secondly, the meaning-constituting fact I identify 'must, in some sense, show how I am justified in giving the answer "125" to "68 + 57"' (*Ibid.*). In the next two sections, I will address the major problem of how to accurately characterise this assumption about meaning-constitution that the sceptic makes when mounting his challenge, as well as the role it plays in the challenge (specifically in determining what counts as a straight solution) and whether it can take different forms. For now, it is important merely to highlight that some such assumption is in play in the sceptical challenge.

Kripke devotes a large part of Chapter 2 of *WRPL* to considering and rejecting various candidates of meaning-constituting facts. Such a fact could, for example, be about my past 'dispositions' to use the sign in a particular way (see 1982, 22–37). The response, then, would state that even though I did not explicitly think of this specific use of '+' when I grasped it, I was disposed to answer in accordance with the addition function in the sense that if I had been asked at the time about the computation, '68 + 57', I would have answered '125'. I will not, though, go into the details of this or other candidates here because I only want to elucidate the form of the sceptical challenge as presented by Kripke. These straight responses can be either reductive in the sense of identifying some non-intentional fact about me (for example, facts about my dispositions) as underlying my meaning, or non-reductive in the sense of positing some primitive act of meaning. The sceptic argues that no such fact – intentional or non-intentional – can be found that could determine or 'constitute' my meaning addition by '+' rather than some other function. And he states that we must conclude that there is no fact as to what I meant by '+' in the past. Generalising to all terms, language users, and times, the sceptic concludes that no-one ever means anything by any term (see 1982, 21).

This is a very broad outline of the sceptical challenge to meaning that Kripke reconstructs from Wittgenstein's later writings. I will turn in the next section to considering some of the most important features of it. There are a number of fundamental questions that arise in the context of this challenge. For example, Kripke tends to give conflicting answers to the questions concerning what the sceptical conclusion is, whether KW accepts it, whether KW thereby rejects the existence of facts about meaning, and whether KW and the sceptic about meaning are really the same character in his dialectic.

3.2   Wilson and Miller on the Form and Scope of the Sceptical Argument

My focus in this section will be on George Wilson's reconstruction of the sceptical argument and Alexander Miller's critical comments concerning its wider-than-anticipated scope. Wilson is usually classified as one of the most significant 'factualist' readers of *WRPL*, which means that he goes against the dominant trend of interpreting the figure of KW as siding with the radical sceptic and rejecting facts about meaning. On Wilson's reading, KW is viewed as emerging from the sceptical challenge by accepting in some highly qualified sense that there are after all facts about what we mean by our words. The details of this will be discussed in due course. Miller is important in this context because he modifies and extends Wilson's analysis to show that the factualist reading of *WRPL* is ultimately unsustainable.

Wilson's Reconstruction of the Sceptical Argument

The most distinctive feature of Wilson's interpretation of Kripke's *WRPL* is that he makes a sharp distinction between KW and the sceptic; and he argues that whereas the latter denies the existence of facts about meaning, the former merely denies the legitimacy of a particular conception of meaning. Wilson's reading is based on two closely related ambiguities in Kripke's text: firstly, concerning whether Kripke takes KW to be a sceptic about meaning (for example, contrast 1982, 60 and 63); and secondly, concerning whether Kripke takes KW to deny the existence of facts about meaning or merely a particular conception of such facts (for example, contrast 1982, 70, 71, and 77, on the one hand, and 1982, 69, on the other).

Addressing the second issue first, Kripke refers to the conception of meaning that KW opposes as 'the classical realist picture' (1982, 73). Wilson formulates it along the following lines (see Wilson 1994, 239):

> **Classical Realism (CR):** If a speaker means something by a term 'Φ', then there are facts about the speaker that establish an extra-linguistic item – out of an indefinite range of alternatives – as the standard of correctness for his use of 'Φ'.[2]

[2] For the sake of a more succinct statement of the sceptical argument, I have made two modifications to Wilson's presentation of its main premises, including this classical realist one. First, while Wilson tends to focus on the particular case of predicates, I have chosen to state them in the more general form pertaining to any term. Second, I shorten Wilson's presentation by one step by combining two premises in his statement of the argument into one premise in mine. Wilson distinguishes the 'classical realist' premise, which states that 'If S means something by a term "Φ", then there is a non-linguistic item that has been established by S as the meaning-constituting standard of correctness for her application of "T"' from what he calls the 'Grounding' premise, which states that 'If there is a non-linguistic item that has been established by S as the meaning-constituting standard of correctness for her application of "Φ", then there must be facts about S that fix the non-linguistic item as the standard S has adopted' (see 1998, 106–7). I combine these into the single premise: 'If S means something by a term "Φ", then there are facts about S that establish a non-linguistic item – out of an indefinite range of alternatives – as the meaning-constituting standard of correctness for her application of "Φ"'. This modification is superficial and merely allows for the shorter presentation I give in this section. The effect is to cut out one

Wilson only formulates CR for the particular case of predicate expressions, but it is designed to be applicable to all types of expression. The above is an attempt to give a general formulation and the expression 'extra-linguistic item' is supposed to stand in for whatever it is that governs the correct application of the linguistic expression in question. For example, such an extra-linguistic item would be a property in the case of a predicate expression or a truth-condition in the case of a sentence. Or to take Kripke's famous example, CR would state that if a speaker means something by '+', then there are facts about the speaker that establish a particular function, viz. *plus* (rather than some other function such as *quus*), as the standard of correctness for his use of '+'. Wilson's claim is that the sceptical challenge presupposes this classical realist conception of meaning and that *KW*, in contrast to the sceptic, ultimately responds to the challenge by rejecting this conception.

To see how this plays out, we need to distinguish two further propositions that Wilson articulates and holds are required to give a complete statement of the sceptical argument (see 1994, 240/1). They are both sceptical claims, one stronger than the other:

> **Basic Sceptical Conclusion (BSC):** There are no facts about the speaker that establish an extra-linguistic item – out of an indefinite range of alternatives – as the standard of correctness for his use of 'Φ'.
>
> **Radical Sceptical Conclusion (RSC):** The speaker does not mean anything by the term 'Φ'.

In order to fully represent the sceptical argument in accordance with Wilson's analysis, with each step transparent, let:

> P = A speaker means something by the term 'Φ'.
> Q = There are facts about the speaker that establish an extra-linguistic item – out of an indefinite range of alternatives – as the standard of correctness for his use of 'Φ'.

Using these, we can represent the three central propositions as follows:

> CR = If P, then Q
> BSC = not Q
> RSC = not P

step, i.e. if we were to follow Wilson's original presentation, then when the 'Basic Sceptical Conclusion' is drawn (see below), we could infer by *modus tollens* the negation of the antecedent of the Grounding premise; and on this basis infer again by *modus tollens* the negation of the antecedent of the classical realist premise, which when generalised gives us the 'Radical Sceptical Conclusion'. But on my presentation, the Basic Sceptical Conclusion allows us to infer in a single step by *modus tollens* the negation of the antecedent of the classical realist premise and to generalise to the Radical Sceptical Conclusion.

The sceptical argument can then be succinctly stated:

(1)	If P, then Q	(i.e. CR)	Assumption
(2)	not Q	(i.e. BSC)	Following the case-by-case analysis of the candidates for such facts

Therefore:

(3)	not P	(i.e. RSC)	*Modus tollens*

The radical sceptical conclusion can then be generalised to all speakers and all terms to give the conclusion that 'no one ever means anything by a term' (Wilson 1994, 241).

This is sufficient as a statement of the steps in *the sceptic's* reasoning and of the conclusion he reaches. Wilson, though, distinguishes KW from the sceptic by arguing that although they both hold that there are no facts about the speaker that show that he has established some particular item (for example, a property or function) as the standard of correctness for his application of the term (i.e. they both accept BSC), KW does not accept the radical sceptical conclusion, RSC. Rather, according to Wilson, KW extends the argument as a *reductio ad absurdum* of the original classical realist assumption (1998, 109). The full KW argument can thus be represented as follows:

(1)	If P, then Q	(i.e. CR)	Assumption
(2)	not Q	(i.e. BSC)	Following the case-by-case analysis of the candidates for such facts

Therefore:

(3)	not P	(i.e. RSC)	*Modus tollens*
(4)	P	(i.e. not RSC)	KW's new premise

Therefore:

(5)	not (if P, then Q)	(i.e. not CR)	Reductio

Wilson's reconstruction of the sceptical challenge to meaning, and of KW's attitude to this challenge, raises a host of questions. Most importantly, it forces us to reconsider whether the character of KW in Kripke's book is really opposed to the existence of facts about meaning, or merely to a particular class of such facts (those corresponding to the classical realist conception). Addressing this enables us to engage with the more substantive question of the nature of the sceptical challenge that Kripke develops and whether it compels us to adopt a non-factualist position regarding semantic discourse. I will now consider a major criticism that has been proposed against such a factualist reading of *WRPL*.

Miller and Wilson on the Scope of the Sceptical Argument

By arguing that KW is not opposed to facts about meaning *per se* but only to a particular conception of meaning, Wilson prepares the way for an interpretation of KW as a type of semantic factualist – specifically, where the semantic facts that are posited are different to those characterised by the classical realist. Miller (2010) develops a series of powerful criticisms of this way of reading Kripke's *WRPL*. His strategy is to argue that the non-classical realist factualism that Wilson attributes to KW is actually *as susceptible* as classical realist factualism to the sceptical challenge (see Miller 2010, 173–6).

He begins by considering Wilson's claim that KW

tries to explain the content of meaning ascriptions in terms of their role and utility in the relevant language games, and the normative conditionals about meaning [for example, 'If Jones means addition by "+", his answer to "68 + 57 =?" should be "125"'], which the Classical Realist misconstrues as describing a super-rigid semantical determination, are explained in terms of the requirements that our use of standard criteria for meaning ascriptions engender and enforce. (Wilson 1994, 258)

Miller focuses on the notion of 'requirements' mentioned in this passage and states that they are that which, for Wilson, 'on the non-Classical Realist view constitute facts about meaning' (2010, 174). Miller then proceeds to construct an analogue of the original sceptical argument (as reconstructed by Wilson), with alternative formulations of its main propositions. These alternative formulations replace the talk of 'standards of correctness' in CR and BSC with talk of the 'requirements' from Wilson's passage.

Miller presents this analogue of the sceptical argument as follows:

(1) NCR: If a speaker S means something by 'Φ', then there are facts about the speaker that constitute requirements – enforced and engendered by the use of standard criteria for ascriptions of meaning in S's speech community – that govern the correct application of 'Φ' for S.

(2) BSC*: There are no facts about the speaker S that constitute any requirements – enforced and engendered by the use of standard criteria for ascriptions of meaning in S's speech community – that govern the correct application of 'Φ' for S.

Therefore:

(3) RSC: The speaker S does not mean anything by 'Φ'.

The original assumption about meaning in this argument – NCR – is distinct from the classical realist assumption. Nevertheless, Miller argues that the requirements that it states to be necessary for meaning something by a term can be challenged by the sceptic along the same lines as he challenges the view that the classical realist criteria can be satisfied. The challenge is to identify a fact about the speaker S that 'constitutes the requirement' R_1, rather than some other requirement R_2, as the requirement that governs S's use of 'Φ'

(see Miller 2010, 175). Miller argues that KW must accept the conclusion –
BSC* – that such a challenge cannot be met; or rather, that there is no greater
possibility of answering the sceptic here than in the original classical realist
case. The same radical sceptical conclusion, RSC, follows.[3]

Aside from the question of the strength of Miller's objections to Wilson, we
should recognise that they provide a good basis from which to consider the
question of the proper *scope* of the sceptical argument. We saw earlier in this
section that Wilson holds that its scope is limited to undermining the classical
realist conception of meaning-constituting facts. Miller's criticism of Wilson
is essentially based on the conviction that the scope of the sceptical argument
is wider than this, i.e. that it undermines not just classical realism but also
all other conceptions of meaning that are of a similar 'strength' to classical
realism. The suggestion is that there is a common core to both classical realism
and Wilson's non-classical realist factualism, and that it is *this* that makes both
of them equally vulnerable to the reductio argument.

However, Miller does not say a great deal about what this common core is.
He does state that the 'source of the problem for Wilson's interpretation' is that
it takes KW to be attempting to 'explain the content of meaning ascriptions in
terms of their role and utility in the relevant language games' (Wilson 1994,
258; see Miller 2010, 180). He argues that this feature of Wilson's interpretation is in direct conflict with a significant passage from Kripke's *WRPL*:

> It is important to realise that we are *not* looking for necessary and sufficient conditions
> (truth conditions), or an analysis of what such rule-following [or meaning] 'consists in'.
> Indeed such conditions would constitute a 'straight' solution to the sceptical problem,
> and have been rejected. (1982, 87)

Miller's main objection here is that:

> Wilson's interpretation ultimately fails because his KW, even though he rejects
> Classical Realist truth-conditions, is still attempting to give a truth-conditional account
> of ascriptions of meaning: precisely the sort of account abjured by KW in the passage
> just quoted [at Kripke 1982, 87]. (2010, 180)

In short, Miller's claim is that Wilson's factualism fails for the same reason as
classical realist factualism, viz. it attempts to state the necessary and sufficient
conditions for meaning anything by a term. This, for him (as for Kripke), is
what the sceptical argument has shown to be impossible and this is the common core between Wilson's factualism and classical realism that makes them
both vulnerable to the sceptic.

If we only take into account Wilson's articles on Kripke's *WRPL* from
1994 to 2006 (as Miller does), then Miller's objections appear well-placed.
However, Wilson's (2011) seems to have a decisive response to it. Apparently

---

[3] Miller notes that this argument is similar to Wright's (Wright 2001, 105).

independent of Miller's (2010), Wilson shows that he is aware of this potential objection to his factualist reading by acknowledging that his non-classical realist factualism cannot provide the necessary and sufficient conditions for meaning (see his 2011, 272, where he alludes to the same passage in support from *WRPL*). But this raises a question about how we are to view Wilson's factualism if it does not have these aspirations.[4] From the perspective of this chapter, the important point is that Miller and Wilson are actually in agreement about the proper scope of the sceptical argument when extended as a reductio in the way outlined in this section, i.e. it is capable of undermining *any* account of meaning that attempts to state the necessary and sufficient conditions for meaning something by a term.

Although the question of its ultimate plausibility is not settled, the argument is obviously of enormous significance in its own right. My focus will now turn to the parallels between it and the argument in Wittgenstein's *PI* that inspired it.

3.3   Kripke's Wittgenstein's Sceptical Argument and Wittgenstein's Anti-Platonist Argument

If we follow Wilson's reading of Kripke's *WRPL*, the sceptical argument that culminates in the claim that no-one ever means anything by any term is only a fragment of an overall reductio argument; specifically, a reductio argument in which KW parts ways with the radical sceptic by rejecting the robust conception of meaning that led to the sceptical paradox. Viewed in this way, the parallels between the argument in Kripke's *WRPL* and what I have called Wittgenstein's anti-platonist argument are striking. The similarities run much deeper than scholars of either Wittgenstein or Kripke have realised, and include the following specific features:

(a) Both arguments operate with a particular conception of meaning that is realist or platonist.

(b) Both arguments show that if such a conception of meaning is presupposed, a sceptical 'paradox' follows directly (and in both cases it is a sceptical paradox because the notion of meaning is undermined).

(c) Both arguments are reductios in the sense that they conclude by rejecting the original conception of meaning that generated the paradox.

There are some notable differences too. The biggest is perhaps that KW's argument seems to be based only on Wittgenstein's gerrymandering argument – for

---

[4] In his most recent article, Wilson characterises KW's factualism as a 'modest dispositionalism' (2011, 281). My approach in this chapter is not to consider the details of this and other elaborations of KW's positive position, but to assess the kinds of constraints that are placed on that position at the outset as a result of the sceptical challenge.

example, Kripke's quus example is partly based on Wittgenstein's example at §185 of *PI* of the pupil instructed to 'Add 2', which is the example around which Wittgenstein presents the gerrymandering considerations. Hence, Wittgenstein's overall anti-platonist argument is more complex because it contains both the regress argument and the gerrymandering argument, as set out in the previous chapter. KW's argument may thus be viewed as an incomplete version of Wittgenstein's anti-platonist argument.

These differences, though, are quite superficial. At a more fundamental level, both arguments are characterised not merely by using a reductio strategy to attack a classical realist or platonist conception of meaning; they both also adopt this strategy by targeting the same vulnerable point of this conception. In the previous chapter, I argued that Wittgenstein's anti-platonist argument involves attacking the semantic normativity thesis that is an essential component of the platonist conception. This, as I will explain, is the same aspect of the classical realist conception that KW's argument undermines. It will thus become apparent that Wittgenstein and KW are united in opposing the thesis that meaning is normative.

What we first have to see is that Kripke's sceptic employs the semantic normativity thesis as a major implicit assumption when presenting his sceptical challenge. Recall that one of the 'conditions' that must be satisfied by an adequate response to the challenge is that the purported meaning-constituting fact 'must, in some sense, show how I am justified in giving the answer "125" to "68 + 57"' (1982, 11). Couple this with the sceptic's insistence that what is challenged is that I mean *plus* by '+' (rather than challenging, say, my memory of what I meant by the sign before or my ability to perform a basic computation (*Ibid.*)), and we can articulate the sceptic's demand as: if I do mean *plus* by '+', then I should answer '125' to '68 + 57'. Hence, the sceptic assumes that attaching meaning to a sign entails obligations for how the sign should be used in particular instances. That is, he assumes the semantic normativity thesis. Kripke did not draw any more attention to the thesis than what we find on p. 11 of his book, and he certainly did not highlight it as a problematic assumption on the sceptic's part. In this regard, his implicit positive attitude to the assumption is in keeping with most other philosophers' view of it around this time. However, in light of Wilson's formal characterisation of the sceptical argument, we can try to go further than Kripke's discussion by making the role of the thesis fully explicit.

Wilson, as we have seen, identifies the classical realist conception of meaning as the main assumption enforced by the sceptic. His formulation of that view has the advantage of making it clear that the normative notion of 'correctness' (of the use of a term) is central to it; the view states that if someone means something by a term, then there are facts about the speaker that determine what it is to use the term correctly or incorrectly in particular instances. This notion is also apparent in Miller's modified version of the view. Following Miller, I mentioned that what is common to classical realism and the modified version of it is that they both provide particular analytical definitions of meaning. This is true, but it is not the whole picture because it must be more precisely articulated what such a definition amounts to. This is where semantic normativity comes in. The sceptic is able to put pressure on the defender of meaning not merely by enforcing a general conception of what meaning is; ultimately, the basis of the sceptic's pressure is a particular conception of meaning in which a word can be said to be genuinely meaningful only if that meaning determines how the word should be correctly used in particular instances. This assumption is the sceptic's most powerful weapon because it is what makes it so difficult for the defender of meaning to provide an adequate response to the sceptical challenge (where the parameters of an adequate response or 'straight solution' are implicitly laid down by the sceptic).

What makes KW's position so different from the radical sceptic's is that they adopt directly opposing attitudes to the semantic normativity thesis. In short, whereas the failure to identify a meaning-constituting fact that satisfies the semantic normativity constraint is interpreted by the radical sceptic as support for his view that there is no such thing as meaning anything by a word, KW interprets the same failure as providing compelling evidence that the semantic normativity constraint itself is flawed. The overall KW reductio argument thus targets the semantic normativity thesis and uses this strategy to undermine the classical realist conception of meaning, of which this thesis is an essential component. In this regard, the KW argument and Wittgenstein's anti-platonist argument are fundamentally the same. They differ only in points of detail.

3.4   The Idea of a Sceptical Solution

The correspondence between KW's argument and Wittgenstein's anti-platonist argument is only one part of the story of Wittgenstein's importance for the issue of scepticism about meaning. The other major part is what Kripke calls, using Humean terminology, a 'sceptical solution'. This label has turned out to be extremely misleading and it is largely responsible for the misunderstanding of KW's position. The biggest problem with the label is that it carries with it the suggestion that KW ends up embracing radical scepticism about meaning, which, following Wilson, I have argued is not the case. A fundamental question in what follows will be that of whether it is KW or the radical sceptic who defends a sceptical solution. First, though, it would be wise to consider in general terms what a sceptical solution to a sceptical problem is supposed to be. This will help to clear away the ambiguities that have stood in the way of a satisfactory assessment of both KW's and Wittgenstein's relation to scepticism about meaning.

In section IV of the *Enquiry Concerning Human Understanding*, Hume formulates 'sceptical doubts' concerning the possibility of giving a rational justification of our judgments about causation and inductive inferences. In section V, he proposes a 'sceptical solution of these doubts' that involves accepting that such judgments and inferences cannot be based on reason. His 'solution' is to state that their legitimacy derives from some other 'principle of human nature', which he calls 'habit' or 'custom' (1975a, 42–3). However, Simon Blackburn states that this is not the part of Hume that matters most for *WRPL*. He writes that:

What matters is [Hume's] reinterpretation of the concept of causation – the topic of section VII of the *Enquiry*. It is here that Hume has a (fairly) pure example of the process I described: a sceptical argument forcing us to revise our conception of a kind of fact. It is here that he parallels KW. But the reinterpretation does not deserve to be called a 'sceptical solution' to anything, nor did Hume so call it. It is at most a proposal prompted by sceptical problems. But in principle it might have been prompted by other considerations altogether. And in fact Hume's reinterpretation of causation is only partly motivated by scepticism. (2002, 30)

This, however, is debatable and it could also be maintained regarding section VII that 'in it a sceptical problem and its solution are compressed into one section' (Buckle 2001, 191). For example, Stephen Buckle interprets the second part of section VII as providing

a sceptical solution to those doubts [concerning the origin of the idea of necessary connection], by tracing the origin of the idea to an internal impression of a very special kind, which arises independently of singular perceptions, and indeed of any operation of the understanding. (*Ibid.*)

Viewed along these lines, Hume's sceptical solution consists of providing an alternative account or 'definition' of causation in terms of the origin of the idea from the internal impression or feeling that arises when one is compelled by habit to expect an event that in the past has always occurred with another.

Aside from the issue of how to correctly interpret Hume's sceptical solution, this brief presentation shares some features with the sceptical solution that Kripke outlines. Most notably, Hume's sceptical solution is not opposed to the concept in question itself, but to a particular dominant account or assumption concerning the source of its legitimacy. Hume argues that its legitimacy cannot consist in reason and his solution is to account for it in terms of a non-rational but equally fundamental principle of human nature. It is an open question whether Hume's sceptical solution amounts to an alternative explanatory account of causation, or merely a description of our actual custom of making certain causal judgments on the basis of certain internal feelings arising from habit. There is no need to address this question here. The point I want to emphasise is that there is a specific sense in which the sceptical solution in Kripke's *WRPL* is similar to Hume's, viz. it is based on accepting some far-reaching negative conclusion and proposing an alternative conception of the notion in question (in Kripke's case, meaning).

Now for the key question: does KW or the radical sceptic about meaning propose a sceptical solution? The answer is that it is actually KW's solution. Although this may be surprising, it makes more sense when we understand both the position of the radical sceptic and the nature of a sceptical solution. The crucial point to appreciate is that the *radical* sceptic does not – indeed could not – propose any type of solution whatsoever to the sceptical challenge. In holding that there is no such thing as meaning anything by any term, there is literally nothing that the radical sceptic can say. His position is better characterised as *eliminativist*; it involves rejecting the entire notion of meaning and much more besides (including the legitimacy of our linguistic practices). What Kripke calls the sceptical solution is obviously not nearly as extreme a position as that.

Neither Hume nor KW are eliminativists; a sceptical solution cannot be coupled with eliminativism. KW's sceptical solution involves describing how our shared practices of using words like 'means' still have a legitimate function, even in light of the results of the sceptical challenge (which, though, are not as destructive as the radical sceptic believes). This is why we should view the sceptical solution as KW's, not as the radical sceptic's. For it is KW who emerges from the sceptical challenge with a positive perspective on the notion of meaning, albeit one that cannot be underpinned by the existence of meaning-constituting facts of any kind.

However, if the sceptical solution is KW's and not the radical sceptic's, does this mean that the label is inappropriate? That is a matter of choice. It should be kept in mind that KW accepts what might be viewed as quite a far-reaching, even moderately sceptical, conclusion. This negative conclusion may be stated as follows:

It is not the case that: A speaker means something by a term only if there is some fact (for example, about the speaker's mental states) that establishes a standard of correctness for the use of the term in particular instances.

It could, as we have seen, also be formulated similarly as the rejection of the thesis that the meaning of a word entails obligations for how we should use the word in particular instances. A negative conclusion of this sort is the basis of KW's 'sceptical' solution. In a sense, then, KW may be viewed as defending a version of scepticism about meaning, but only if this is formulated in the above way and thus as more moderate than the radical scepticism that involves eliminating the concept of meaning.

3.5   A Partial Defence of Kripke's Reading of Wittgenstein

A major concern in this chapter has been to indirectly evaluate Wittgenstein's relation to scepticism about meaning by considering KW's relation to that position, and arguing that there is a strong affinity between KW's reductio argument and Wittgenstein's anti-platonist argument. The primarily positive assessment of Kripke's controversial reading of Wittgenstein that I am pushing comes with some important caveats. What I am most drawn to is the spirit rather than the letter of his reading. That is, I agree that Wittgenstein's discussion of meaning and rule-following in §§138–242 essentially has a negative and a positive strand; that the negative strand consists of a powerful attack on a classical realist or platonist conception of meaning; that this attack can be presented as a complex reductio argument, and thus presented in a way that is more formal than Wittgenstein's own presentation; and that the positive strand involves a series of suggestions or remarks concerning how our ordinary linguistic practices are untouched by the negative conclusions concerning the platonist conception.

Regarding the details of Kripke's reading, there are major shortcomings and errors that have to be acknowledged. The most important to note are:

(i) Kripke does not make a clear distinction between the figures of KW and the radical sceptic about meaning.

(ii) The pivotal role of the classical realist conception of meaning in the sceptical challenge – as well as KW's ultimate rejection of the conception – is only suggested and not emphasised.

(iii) Kripke does not attempt to explain the fact that KW effectively uses the sceptical argument as a tool to attack the classical realist conception of meaning.

(iv) His use of the terminology of 'sceptical challenge' and 'sceptical solution' misleadingly suggests that KW endorses radical scepticism, while other passages imply he could not have endorsed it.

(v) He does not make it sufficiently clear that KW *must* reject the radical sceptical conclusion (thus parting ways with the radical sceptic) in order to propose a sceptical solution.

(vi) He does not explain that the defender of the sceptical solution – i.e. KW – must be a more moderate type of sceptic about meaning (if indeed it is appropriate to label him a sceptic at all).

My reading has built on the work of other philosophers who have responded in a constructive way to Kripke's *WRPL*, and I have sought to eliminate the above defects while preserving what is of genuine value in his interpretation.

In 1984, soon after the publication of *WRPL*, Baker and Hacker published a book-length response to it that was very critical of Kripke's reading of Wittgenstein. Although it may seem that my reading is at odds with theirs, there is in fact a lot of common ground because I acknowledge that Kripke's reading has major shortcomings. I agree with them on many points, but where our readings differ is in seeing something essentially correct at the heart of Kripke's reading. It will be helpful to conclude by noting these points of divergence as a way of indirectly clarifying Wittgenstein's significance for the doctrine of scepticism about meaning.

Baker and Hacker attacked Kripke's *WRPL* on two accounts: first, as an interpretation of Wittgenstein; and second, concerning the common perception that *WRPL* succeeds in highlighting an issue that is of 'profound' philosophical importance in its own right. Concerning the second issue, they argue that it only appears to be of independent importance in light of certain fundamental assumptions about language and understanding that, they maintain, are widespread in contemporary philosophy of language, semantics and linguistics (in the 1980s, but subsequently too). They identify these assumptions as 'conceiv[ing] of a language as a highly complex calculus of rules' and 'of understanding as a hidden process of operating this calculus or depth-grammar' (1984, Preface viii-ix). They continue:

The postulates of cognitive psychology, theoretical linguistics and (on some versions) philosophical semantics seem to be called into doubt [in *WRPL*]. So even though proponents of 'Wittgenstein's rule-scepticism' would not dream of presenting their arguments as attacks on modern linguistic theories, nor consider them as a *reductio ad absurdum* of such theories, they manifestly cast a shadow over the proceedings which are taking place centre-stage. This makes sense of the appeal (or threat!) of a form of philosophical reasoning that would otherwise seem unmotivated and devoid of interest (save as a mistaken interpretation of Wittgenstein). (1984, x)

This shows that Baker and Hacker believe that the considerations raised by Kripke *do* have a direct bearing on certain key assumptions in contemporary theorising about language, and they even suggest that the sceptical considerations may act as a '*reductio ad absurdum* of such theories'.

Interestingly, though, they make this point only with regard to the issue of whether Kripke's discussion is of independent interest, and not with regard to his interpretation of Wittgenstein. Contrary to their separation of these issues, my concern has been with defending two claims: (1) that Kripke's discussion is indeed best read as developing a sort of reductio argument against certain fundamental assumptions about language or meaning; but (2) that this corresponds to a basic strategy in Wittgenstein's later work. Defending these claims has the potential to defuse many of Baker and Hacker's deeper or principled criticisms of Kripke's reading, and by extension a lot of the other criticisms that have become common since they published their study. If Baker and Hacker take Kripke to be interpreting Wittgenstein as endorsing a form of scepticism about the very notion of meaning – rather than about certain theoretical assumptions about meaning – then a lot of their criticisms are misplaced.

Baker and Hacker's most forceful objection is to Kripke assigning the label 'sceptic' to Wittgenstein, as well as the attribution to him of the development of a sceptical paradox concerning meaning and a sceptical solution to this paradox. This objection has been echoed by the vast majority of commentators ever since. Baker and Hacker quote from Wittgenstein's early notebooks from 1914–16 and his last writings, published as *On Certainty* (*OC*), and state that

[i]t would be very surprising to discover that someone who throughout his life found philosophical scepticism *nonsensical*, a subtle violation of the bounds of sense, should actually make a sceptical problem the pivotal point of his work. (1984, 5)

Although this objection seems compelling, it is cast in a different light as soon as we make the distinction between Wittgenstein (and indeed KW) and the radical sceptic about meaning. Their objection is correct if it is taken to claim that Wittgenstein could not have been a radical sceptic. But there is a further question that is not settled about his relation to a more moderate scepticism, one that is defined in terms of the rejection of the kinds of notions that the platonist or classical realist is inclined to posit. And while Wittgenstein would have resisted the sceptical terminology, I have tried to argue that there is a definite sense in which Wittgenstein's reflections on meaning have an affinity with Humean scepticism.

Another important criticism that Baker and Hacker develop is that Kripke's reconstruction of Wittgenstein's argument in §§138–201 of *PI* does not in fact correspond to Wittgenstein's argument properly understood. They summarise Kripke's reconstruction as follows:

The core problem is, according to Kripke, a *normative* version of Goodman's 'new riddle of induction'. No past fact about my mind or behaviour constituted my meaning W by 'W', so nothing in my present use of 'W' can constitute accord (or conflict) with what I meant by 'W' (the meaning I assigned to 'W'). So I cannot know that in my current use I am still using 'W' with the same meaning. But not even God, were He to peer into my mind, could know this. So there is no such thing as using a word in accord with a rule (with the meaning one gave it), no such thing as meaning something by a word, and hence no such thing as a meaningful language. This is the 'paradox'. (1984, 10–11)

Baker and Hacker state that Wittgenstein's main concern is with 'what is involved in a speaker's understanding an expression, knowing what it means, using it in accord with a correct explanation of its meaning', whereas Kripke maintains that the problem is with 'what a speaker means by an expression, of whether he is now using an expression in accord with what he previously meant by it' (1984, 42). The defect in Kripke's reconstruction, according to them, is that he states the problem in essentially *temporal* terms, as the problem about how my present use of a term could accord or conflict with how I previously meant it.

Kripke in effect shifts Wittgenstein's problem of how, in what sense, a rule determines its application, to a problem of the relation between my past and present intentions, my meaning addition by 'plus' (and not a different arithmetical operation christened 'quaddition'). (1984, 27)

This criticism, though, suffers from the same error as Colin McGinn's (1984) in failing to appreciate the full generality of the problem discussed by Kripke. It is correct that in some instances Kripke presents the problem in temporal terms as a problem between 'the nexus between past "intention" or "meanings" and present practice' (Kripke 1982, 62), but it generalises beyond this context to the relation between the meaning of a term and its correct application. Boghossian (1989) highlights this point when criticising McGinn's reading of Kripke. McGinn characterises the sceptic as challenging us to show that what we mean by a word now is 'the *same*' as what we meant or how we intended it to be used at some previous time, such as when we were taught it (McGinn 1984, 146). Boghossian argues that if this were a correct formulation of the challenge, then it could be easily met by practically '*Any* theory of meaning' (1989, 147). For example, the dispositionalist account that Kripke rejects would meet it because 'there are perfectly determinate facts about what dispositions are associated with a given expression at a given time' and 'it is always possible to ask whether an expression has the same or a different meaning' on this account (*Ibid.*). Boghossian holds that this is strong evidence that this temporal characterisation does not adequately capture the nature of the sceptical challenge. Rather, the challenge arises from the fact that 'meaningful expressions possess conditions of *correct use*'; and further (this is where the classical realist or platonist constraint comes in) that any candidate of meaning-constituting fact must show 'what is the correct use of that word' (1989, 148). This explains how the dispositionalist account runs into difficulties, i.e. it must show what the 'correct' use of a word is as opposed to merely what we will be disposed to do with it. The important point here is that this kind of objection raised by Baker and Hacker – and McGinn – fails because it misrepresents the sceptical challenge in *WRPL*.

A big issue that I have not discussed at all yet is Kripke's famous claim that 'the real "private language argument"' is to be found in the sections *preceding* §243' of *PI* (1982, 3), or that the rejection of private language is a 'corollary' of Wittgenstein's discussion of rule-following in general in §§138–242. No analysis of Kripke's reading would be complete without addressing this claim. I will return to it in the next chapter (see section 4.4). What I have argued for here concerning KW and scepticism about meaning will be seen to have major implications for how we interpret Wittgenstein's discussion of private language and the significance of his appeal to communal agreement and practices of use.[5]

3.6   Conclusion

Is it correct, then, to call Wittgenstein a sceptic about meaning? The most succinct answer is that while he was definitely not a radical sceptic about meaning

---

[5] I have also chosen to omit from the present chapter any treatment of the issue of whether KW holds semantic discourse to be factual or non-factual. This is central to Chapter 3 of *WRPL*, but addressing it adequately would lead us too far away from the main discussion of Wittgenstein running through this book.

(in the sense of being eliminativist and rejecting the legitimacy of words such as 'means'), he was a moderate or Humean-type sceptic about meaning. This moderate version is manifested, for example, in his belief that it is misleading to think of meanings as entities of some sort (see section 6.6 of the final chapter), or of meanings as somehow constituted by or reducible to certain mental states. The Humean component is that the use of words like 'means' is held to have a legitimacy that is independent of the characterisations of meanings as entities or as underpinned by distinctive mental states.

Although much of this chapter has been devoted to Kripke's *WRPL*, the intention was to consider a significant example of how Wittgenstein's *PI* can be connected with certain recent debates in the philosophy of language. Contrary to most interpreters of *WRPL* and *PI*, I have argued that Wittgenstein is never very far from the constructed figure of 'Kripkenstein', and by extension his views and arguments are as relevant as *WRPL* to issues such as scepticism about meaning, semantic realism, and semantic factualism. My purpose has been to show that the arguments in §§138–201 of *PI* have wide implications, one of which is to motivate the above moderate sceptical view concerning linguistic meaning. The next chapter will explore how these arguments also impact on the issue of the social dimension of language.

Taking this view of the broader significance of the arguments discussed in Chapter 2 creates challenges for reconciling the different parts of *PI*. For the arguments seem to be leading Wittgenstein in certain definite directions and towards substantial theoretical commitments. I will continue to highlight this tension by laying out what I take to be the main lines of argument concerning language in *PI*, before addressing in the fifth chapter how this tension may be resolved.

Summary of Main Points

(3a) Wittgenstein's relation to the doctrine of scepticism about meaning is best clarified by considering Kripke's reading of Wittgenstein because it brings this doctrine to the fore in a manner that is instructive and unlike any other reading.

(3b) Although Kripke's reading has been harshly criticised by most Wittgenstein scholars, his reconstruction of parts of the discussion in *PI* offers us a unique way of reflecting on what is innovative in Wittgenstein's later remarks on meaning.

(3c) However, Kripke's discussion also contains ambiguities and errors of detail, which have contributed to its negative reception. George Wilson's analysis of Kripke's reading has been one of the most successful in eliminating these shortcomings.

(3d) On Wilson's reading of Kripke, the character of Kripke's Wittgenstein is sharply distinguished from the radical sceptic about meaning. Whereas the radical sceptic attempts to argue for the conclusion that 'There is no such thing as meaning anything by any word', Kripke's Wittgenstein rejects this conclusion.

(3e) The sceptical argument presupposes a 'classical realist' conception of meaning, which amounts to imposing a high standard on what is to count as an adequate response (or 'straight solution') to the sceptic's challenge. The sceptical conclusion is in effect that this standard cannot be met and that there is thus no such thing as meaning anything by a word. Kripke's Wittgenstein, though, takes this radical sceptical conclusion as evidence in favour of rejecting the classical realist conception that led to it.

(3f) This reading of Kripke allows us to appreciate the strong parallels between the views of Kripke's Wittgenstein and Wittgenstein himself. First and foremost, there is a parallel between Kripke's Wittgenstein's argument that the classical realist conception is flawed and Wittgenstein's anti-platonist argument in *PI*. Both arguments are reductios that take the derivation of a sceptical paradox to be grounds for rejecting a realist or platonist conception of meaning.

(3g) Kripke's Wittgenstein's argument and Wittgenstein's anti-platonist argument are also alike in targeting the thesis that meaning is normative. Kripke's Wittgenstein targets it in the classical realist doctrine, while Wittgenstein targets it in the platonist doctrine. The thesis is the vulnerable point in each doctrine.

(3h) Kripke uses the Humean terminology of 'sceptical solution' to characterise the sceptical position he attributes to Wittgenstein. This term is only appropriate if it is emphasised (as Kripke fails to) that the sceptical solution is proposed by the figure of Kripke's Wittgenstein rather than the radical sceptic. The radical sceptic is not capable of providing any solution because he has abandoned the notion of meaning itself; by contrast, it is by virtue of adopting a more moderate standpoint (in which the legitimacy of our linguistic practices is not questioned) that Kripke's Wittgenstein is capable of proposing such a solution.

(3i) Even though he would have resisted the label, Wittgenstein may be called a sceptic about meaning; but his scepticism is strictly of a moderate or Humean kind rather than a radical kind. He is not an eliminitivist about the notion of meaning like the radical sceptic. His standpoint is rather defined by the rejection of the assumption that meaning something by a word must be underpinned by meaning-constituting facts of some sort.

4 The Social Dimension of Language

After discussing §§1–64 of *Philosophical Investigations* (*PI*) in Chapter 1, and §§138–201 in Chapters 2 and 3, I now turn to the two sets of sections of *PI* usually grouped as §§202–242 and §§243–315. While §§202–242 contains many of Wittgenstein's famous remarks concerning the importance of communal agreement in linguistic practices, much of §§243–315 is devoted to the subject of sensations, or more specifically the language we use to talk about sensations (for example, 'pain'). I will be most concerned with the latter set of sections in this chapter, while the former will be addressed across this and the final chapter.

Given the privileged access that each of us seems to have to our own sensations, a question arises concerning the meanings of the words we use to talk about these sensations: If a particular part of language is used to talk about a private domain of entities, must that part of language itself be private, i.e. must the meanings of the words be intelligible only to the person having the sensations and using the words?

§§243–315 in *PI* is most famous for apparently containing Wittgenstein's so-called 'private language argument', the conclusion of which is usually taken to be that a private language is impossible. This has attracted so much attention because if the argument is compelling it will tell us something very important about language in general, viz. that language is essentially social, or that all linguistic meaning is shared (or at least *shareable*) meaning. This conclusion in turn has been taken to have major implications for other areas of philosophy – notably, epistemology and the philosophy of mind – by undercutting all philosophical problems and theories that are developed within a broadly Cartesian framework that presupposes the possibility of private language.

David Stern categorises 'orthodox readings' as those that make the private language argument central to Wittgenstein's discussion in §§243–315 (see Stern 2011, 335–44). Despite the diversity of readings that he groups together under this heading, Stern maintains that they resemble each other in interpreting Wittgenstein as proposing a type of *reductio ad absurdum* argument against private language, and moreover in holding that the argument can be abstracted from his broader discussion (2011, 337). However, what makes them 'orthodox' is not just that they attribute an argument to Wittgenstein, but that they hold that he relies on some theory or thesis to derive its main conclusion. For example, Judith Jarvis Thomson claims that Wittgenstein relies on the principle of verification, while Norman Malcolm holds that the argument invokes the community view of language which is discussed elsewhere in *PI* (see section 4.2). Other orthodox readers, as we shall see, identify other philosophical theses as crucial to the argument.

Stern and other 'unorthodox' or 'Pyrrhonian' readers such as Stephen Mulhall and the later Gordon Baker view this approach as wrong-headed because it ignores two fundamental features of Wittgenstein's later metaphilosophy: firstly, that he was not interested in developing arguments; and secondly, that he was not interested in defending particular philosophical theses or theories. The basic challenge that this more recent trend pose is that of interpreting Wittgenstein's remarks on sensations and private language in a way that does not contradict his general methodological and metaphilosophical convictions (see sections 5.2–5.4 of the next chapter).

In this chapter, I will defend a reading that goes against both the orthodox and unorthodox readings. Against the unorthodox readings, I will argue that Wittgenstein does propose an argument against the possibility of private language; but against the orthodox readings, I will argue that Wittgenstein does not need to rely on any philosophical thesis or theory to establish his conclusion. My reading will thus attempt to show that we can attribute a compelling private language argument to Wittgenstein without disregarding or contradicting his metaphilosophy. My focus throughout the chapter will be on §258 of *PI*, where the private language argument is traditionally located. Essentially, I intend to argue that Wittgenstein's argument against private language does not rest on considerations to do with privacy at all, but rather with more general considerations concerning language that he has treated at length in his discussion of meaning and rules (especially in §§138–201 of *PI*). Therefore, I maintain that Wittgenstein's argument in §258 must be interpreted as being continuous with this preceding discussion, and that doing so will enable us to see how he can present an argument against private language without relying on a particular philosophical thesis or theory.

All the sections will converge on the issue of where Wittgenstein stands with respect to the view that language is essentially social, or to what is often called 'the community view' of language. Sections 4.1–4.4 will address this in terms of the possibility of private language, while sections 4.5–4.7 will address it in terms of the separate issue of the possibility of *solitary* language (defined as the primitive language of a socially isolated individual, and as being 'unshared' rather than strictly speaking 'unshareable' like a private language). I will argue that Wittgenstein provides strong grounds for rejecting the possibility of both private and solitary languages. And while these arguments do not employ substantive philosophical theses, there is the additional troubling question of whether Wittgenstein commits himself to the thesis that language is essentially social.

4.1 Preliminary Analysis of Wittgenstein's Argument Against Private Language

Does Wittgenstein present an argument of any sort in §258 of *PI*? For the purposes of providing a preliminary discussion of §258, temporarily set aside his metaphilosophical statements that suggest he is not interested in making arguments and instead consider whether there is even the semblance of an argument presented there. This is how the interpretation of central passages of *PI* has often proceeded in the decades following its publication. But I will take this approach self-consciously and merely as a starting-point for the discussion. For if there is even the appearance of an argument in §258, this will surely be significant for the subsequent analysis of his overall philosophical method and how passages such as this tally with his metaphilosophical remarks.

It is best to begin, then, by quoting §258 in its entirety:

Let us imagine the following case. I want to keep a diary about the recurrence of a certain sensation. To this end I associate it with the sign 'S' and write this sign in a calendar for every day on which I have the sensation. – I will remark first of all that a definition of the sign cannot be formulated. – But still I can give myself a kind of ostensive definition. – How? Can I point to the sensation? Not in the ordinary sense. But I speak, or write the sign down, and at the same time I concentrate my attention on the sensation – and so, as it were, point to it inwardly. – But what is this ceremony for? For that is all it seems to be! A definition surely serves to establish the meaning of a sign. – Well, that is done precisely by the concentrating of my attention; for in this way I impress on myself the connexion between the sign and the sensation. – But 'I impress it on myself' can only mean: this process brings it about that I remember the connexion *right* in the future. But in the present case I have no criterion of correctness. One would like to say: whatever is going to seem right to me is right. And that only means that here we can't talk about 'right'.

Taking the passage at face value, a chain of reasoning does seem to be presented here. One way of reconstructing the individual steps in the reasoning is as follows:

(1) The diarist resolves to 'keep a diary about the recurrence of a certain sensation'.
(2) To achieve this, the diarist introduces a sign 'S' and attempts to define it or give it meaning by 'a kind of ostensive definition' involving the recurring sensation.
(3) This ostensive definition is provided not by correlating 'S' with his outward manifestations of the sensation, but by impressing on himself a connection between this sign and his private sensation.

(4) The meaning that the diarist will give to the sign will thus be *private* because it is defined in relation to a private sensation.

(5) This sensation functions as a sample, and all other sensations to which 'S' is correctly applied must be similar in a relevant sense to it (i.e. it must *feel* the same or have the same qualitative characteristics).

(6) In this way, the sensation is supposed to provide a standard or norm for how 'S' is to be correctly used. This private semantic norm is, roughly: 'S' applies correctly to a sensation only if it is the same kind of sensation as the one used to define 'S'.

But:

(7) If the semantic norm governing 'S' is private, there will be no distinction between a use of 'S' that *seems correct* and a use that actually *is correct*.

Therefore,

(8) If the semantic norm is private, there will be no genuine distinction between using 'S' correctly and using it incorrectly.

Therefore,

(9) The private semantic norm governing the use of 'S' is not a genuine semantic norm (it does not establish a distinction between correct and incorrect use).

Therefore,

(10) 'S' does not have a meaning.

Therefore,

(11) It is not possible to give a sign a private meaning.

This presentation of the steps is imperfect for two reasons. Firstly, it goes beyond what Wittgenstein actually states in §258. In particular, premises (5) and (6) are formulated based on what he states elsewhere in *PI* concerning ostensive definition in general and on what he implies that it involves (see §§26–32). These premises are formulated on the assumption that the ostensive definition of any sign consists of determining the meaning of that sign by (a) identifying a relevant sample (the thing pointed to) and (b) using this sample to establish a norm or rule for the use of that sign (generally, that the sign should only be applied to objects that are similar in a relevant sense to the sample or thing pointed to). The mention of ostensive definition in the passage necessitates referring back to this discussion because it is the only way that the first part of the passage involving setting up the diary and pointing 'inwardly' to a sensation can be connected in an informative way with the remarks concerning applying the defined sign rightly or wrongly in the second part of the passage.

The other shortcoming of the above presentation of the chain of reasoning is that it is incomplete. Crucially, premise (7) states that if the semantic norm or rule governing the use of 'S' is private, there will be no way of distinguishing uses of 'S' that seem correct from the uses that really are correct. But it is left unexplained what is supposed to be wrong with a norm governing the use of a sign being private. This is the core of the argument against private meaning and hence a more complete presentation of the argument must include additional premises in support of (7). I have deliberately omitted these premises because it is around this issue that most of the debate concerning the strength of Wittgenstein's argument has revolved. However, for the moment it does not matter what extra premises we appeal to in order to complete the argument. The important point is that some such premises are required to attribute to Wittgenstein a private language argument without major missing steps. Hence, the first substantial claim I want to make about §258 of *PI* is that there appears to be a *fragment* of an argument presented there. The next question has to do with whether Wittgenstein himself presents us with the resources to complete the argument. Some have maintained that he does not provide sufficient support for it and instead merely assumes some dubious premise such as scepticism about memory or the principle of verification (see next section). The interpreters who believe that Wittgenstein has provided support for the argument against private language elsewhere in *PI* have always focussed on one of the following set of sections: Wittgenstein's opening discussion of naming and ostensive definition in §§1–38; his remarks on the role of the community or communal agreement in constituting linguistic practices in §§202–242; or the remarks on privacy before and after §258.

Contrary to these readings, I will argue that the argument presented in §258 is best supported by drawing on his discussion of rules and meaning in general, especially in §§138–155 and §§185–201. My defence of this reading will be based on demonstrating two claims: firstly, that the resulting argument is more compelling when it is supported in this way; and secondly, that it renders the presentation of the argument compatible with many of Wittgenstein's key metaphilosophical statements.

4.2   Shortcomings of Prominent Readings of §258
of the *Philosophical Investigations*

Before presenting my own reading of Wittgenstein's argument against private language, I will look at some of the most influential 'orthodox' readings. These readings consist of various attempts at completing or supplementing the argument in §258 of *PI*. It will be instructive to consider them because they represent prominent strategies for articulating Wittgenstein's argument, but that all have the defects of attributing a bad argument to him and depicting his attack on private language as violating his own metaphilosophical convictions. I will attempt to avoid making these errors, but only after discussing how they have been central to the interpretation of this part of *PI*. In the process, the argument in §258 will be brought into greater focus.

The scenario in §258, to reiterate, is introduced with the private diarist resolving to 'keep a diary about the recurrence of a certain sensation' and to do this by writing the sign 'S' into the diary 'every day on which I have the sensation'. The steps in the reasoning that follows can be usefully grouped into two stages (see Candlish 1980):

> **Stage 1:** The private diarist attempts to give himself 'a kind of ostensive definition' of 'S' by 'concentrat[ing] my attention on the sensation' while writing 'S' into the diary, and thus 'as it were, point[ing] to it inwardly' and 'impress[ing] on myself the connexion between the sign and the sensation'.
>
> **Stage 2:** Wittgenstein objects that: ' "I impress it on myself" can only mean: this process brings it about that I remember the connexion *right* in the future. But in the present case I have no criterion of correctness. One would like to say: whatever is going to seem right to me is right. And that only means that here we can't talk about "right".'

Presented in this way, the first stage sets up the scenario in which the conception of private language is supposed to be genuinely applicable, while the second stage is where Wittgenstein explains why it fails.

Although §258 only deals with one attempt to apply this philosophical conception, the conclusion has typically been taken to be far-reaching, i.e. as attempting to establish the impossibility of private language. It could only have this wider significance if the considerations raised against the diary example in the second stage are general enough to undermine any similar attempt to ground the notion of private language. What are these considerations? Wittgenstein says very little in §258 itself. The pivotal point is expressed in the claim: 'But in the present case I have no criterion of correctness.' The point seems to be that when the private diarist defines the sign 'S' by associating it with a particular recurring sensation, a standard or criterion for correctly applying 'S' must thereby be established; but that when the private diarist subsequently goes on to apply 'S' to a new sensation at the later time, there is no such standard or criterion to appeal to. Why, though, is there no criterion of correctness?

Immediately prior to this claim, Wittgenstein seems to suggest that the *memory* of the meaning that has been given to 'S' is crucial. He writes that 'impress[ing] on myself the connection between the sign and the sensation' in the private ostensive definition of 'S' in the first stage must '[bring] it about that I remember the connection *right* in the future'. The claim that there is no criterion of correctness, then, is apparently to be interpreted as stating that there is no criterion for correctly *remembering* the connection between 'S' and the sensation used to define it. Therefore, it appears that the crucial step in Wittgenstein's argument rests on doubting the reliability of our memory of our own sensations. This way of reading §258 was quite common up until the 1980s and it was usually coupled with a negative evaluation of the argument because it proves too much; i.e. the same scepticism about memory could be used to doubt our capacity to use publicly defined words.

Stewart Candlish, though, argues that there is a more plausible way of reading Wittgenstein's remark about memory. He presents it in the context of a discussion of Anthony Kenny's reading, but he attempts to highlight an error that is characteristic of most readings of §258:

> Kenny, along with almost everyone else I know of, has assumed that even in the circumstances of the 'private language' there is actually an application of a sign to a sensation by a private linguist, and that the problem is one of later remembering this earlier application in order that 'S' should have meaning (or possibly, be known to have meaning). The question then seems to be whether our admittedly fallible memory is adequate for the securing or maintenance of (possibly knowledge of) meaning. But why should we assume that a private linguist could even ostensively define his sign to himself in the first place? (1980, 91)

The assumption that Candlish identifies in many readings is that the problems for the private diarist only start to arise in the second stage, i.e. when there is the attempt to apply 'S' to new sensations. It assumes that 'S' is successfully defined at the first stage, but that its meaning or the standard for correctly applying it is lost or cannot be reliably recalled at the second stage (on this point, see also Stern 2011, 347). The alternative reading that Candlish is suggesting is that 'the ceremony' at the first stage is empty and that there is nothing to be remembered; in other words, it is impossible to remember a connection between 'S' and the sensation because no connection has been established. Rather, what occurs at the first stage is as pointless and without consequence as an attempt to 'give' myself money by passing it from my right hand to my left (see *PI*, §268).

It is helpful to examine some of the other dominant ways of reading §258 by considering the role that this assumption plays in them. For example, two further reasons that have often been cited for why there is no criterion for correctly using 'S' at the second stage are:

> **No Verification:** There is no way of verifying that my current sensation is the same kind of sensation as the one used to ostensively define 'S'.

No Public Standard: The sample used to ostensively define a term functions as a standard for determining whether subsequent uses of the term are correct. This standard must be public and hence there can be no such standard in the attempt to use a sensation-sample to ostensively define 'S'.

Judith Jarvis Thomson interprets the argument in §258 as relying on both of these reasons and she uses this assessment to expose its weakness. Although she famously asserts that 'the private language thesis is really a mere restatement of verificationism' (1964, 29), the finer detail of her reading reveals that she holds that the verificationist principle on its own does not establish the conclusion that a private language is impossible. On her reading, the Wittgensteinian argument relies on assuming that 'S' is not a genuine word in a language because it is impossible to 'find out' or verify whether what I am currently experiencing (or the sensation I am currently having) is an instance of the same sensation originally used to define 'S'.[1] But the reason that I cannot find this out is that there is no public standard for determining that my new sensation is an instance of S.

Thomson's reading implies that the key issue is not the assumed verificationism, but rather 'what kinds of ascriptions you [take] to be possible to verify' (*Ibid.*). That is, it is not the principle of verification, but the particular conception of the standards of verification *as public*, that drives the argument in §258. It is the absence of such public standards that, for her, lead Wittgenstein to state that there is no criterion of correctness for using 'S'. The general assumption that Candlish highlights can be easily identified in Thomson's reading. It assumes that the private ostensive definition is successful at the first stage, but that there is no way of finding out or publicly verifying that any subsequent sensation is a sensation of the same kind as that used to define 'S'.

Other reasons have been cited as relevant to Wittgenstein's argument, most notably:

No Public Stage-Setting: The necessary background or stage-setting for ostensively defining any term is public, and hence it is not in place in the attempt to ostensively define 'S'.

No Independent Measure: The sensation-sample used to ostensively define 'S' does not provide a measure or standard that is independent of what it measures (i.e. a measure that is independent of my subsequent sensations).

---

[1] See where she states that 'the denial of the possibility of private languages' hinges on the 'general principle' that 'a sign "K" is not a kind-name in a man's language unless it is possible to find out whether or not a thing is a K. And it is plain that this is nothing more than a revised formulation of something very familiar indeed, namely the Principle of Verification'. (1964, 29)

It is not so clear whether readings that emphasise these reasons make the assumption that Candlish identifies. For example, if we maintain that the background for ostensively defining a term must be public, surely we would have to hold that the attempted private ostensive definition at the first stage cannot succeed. I will conclude this overview of orthodox readings of §258 by considering Kenny's reading because it takes the above two reasons to be central to Wittgenstein's argument. I will argue that Kenny too relies on the problematic assumption because in order to explain why the stage-setting for ostensive definition must be public, other reasons must be introduced that do locate the difficulties exclusively in the second stage of going on to apply 'S' to new sensations.

According to Kenny, the discussion in §258 (and the sections before and after it) is not attempting to deny that a person can give a name to a particular recurring sensation; it is rather claiming that the name must have a shareable meaning because the general requirements on what makes a sign a name are public:

> Wittgenstein is not denying that one can give a name to a sensation; he is merely affirming that giving a name presupposes stage-setting. Such stage-setting, he will go on to argue, is possible in a public language, but not in a private language. Given the stage-setting, the word for a sensation may be ostensively defined no less than the name of a colour or a piece of furniture. (1971, 209)

However, this does not explain why Wittgenstein would insist that the stage-setting – or the background to giving a name to a sensation – must be public. Kenny's explanation invokes what I called the *No Independent Measure*. He takes the decisive principle that Wittgenstein is employing in §258 to be that 'a measure must be independent of what it measures' (1971, 228).[2] In the diary scenario, the measure in question is the sensation-sample that the diarist appeals to in providing an ostensive definition of 'S'. Why, though, would Wittgenstein hold that this measure or standard is not independent (i.e. not independent of the subsequent sensations that are compared with it)? In the following passage, Kenny implies that the reason is that the measure is not public:

> A measure must be independent of what is measured; as we have seen, there is no way of giving 'S' genuine independence of the object it purports to name short of taking it into a public language. (1971, 221)

Hence, it turns out that, for Kenny, the ultimate reason underlying Wittgenstein's objection to the private ostensive definition of 'S' is that there is no *public*

---

[2] See, for example, where Wittgenstein states that 'justification consists in appealing to something independent' (*PI*, §265). Kenny interprets this view as closely connected with, and as having its origins in, 'the *Tractatus* principle that a proposition must be independent of what it records' (1971, 228).

measure or standard to compare current sensations with and to evaluate whether 'S' should be applied to them. This, as we saw, is also the main reason that Thomson holds that Wittgenstein relies on.

The problem with readings such as Thomson's and Kenny's is not just that they assume that the difficulties for the private diarist arise only in the second stage when he goes on to apply 'S' to new sensations; it is that they do not adequately explain why Wittgenstein would hold that the standard or norm used in applying a term must be public.[3] Of course, this gap in their readings is only a problem if we want to be charitable to Wittgenstein, and to not take it for granted that he simply assumed that the standard must be public. There are readings that trace Wittgenstein's public measure demand back to his remarks on communal practices and agreement in §§202–242 of *PI* (for example, Malcolm 1954 and Rhees 1954). But I will argue in the next two sections that it is begging the question against the private diarist (or the defender of a private language) to simply apply this general communal conception to the case in §258.

A similar shortcoming is evident in Candlish's reading in the sense that it leaves us with an unanswered question about Wittgenstein's reasoning in §258, viz.: why is the attempted private ostensive definition of 'S' in the first stage unsuccessful? In answering this, we are potentially led back into the other reasons listed in this section. For example, it could be maintained that the ostensive definition of 'S' is unsuccessful because the shared background or stage-setting for the act of naming is not in place. But then we are back to the same question as to why the stage-setting must be public.

Identifying the shortcomings of these readings is the starting-point for my reading to be developed in the next few sections. I agree with Candlish's claim about the failure of the attempted private ostensive definition in the first stage of §258, but I will provide a reason for the failure that does not force me back into the circle of reasons considered throughout this section. Instead, I will

---

[3] Kenny identifies the problem with a private measure as consisting in the fact that it is comparable to 'a yardstick which grows or shrinks to the length of the object to be measured'. This shows that he takes the point in §258 to be similar to the one that Wittgenstein makes that 'The procedure of putting a lump of cheese on a balance and fixing the price by the turn of the scale would lose its point if it frequently happened for such lumps to suddenly grow or shrink for no obvious reason' (*PI*, §142). The functioning of such ordinary practices depends on certain 'extremely general facts of nature', for example, that objects of this sort do not suddenly change in size (see Wittgenstein's note to §142). The comparison with the attempt in §258 to use a particular occurrence of a sensation as a measure would be legitimate if the sensation is unstable in a similar sense. But is it? The sensation *S*, whatever it is, may be fleeting. And after it has receded, the only thing that can endure is the memory of it. There is no reason to suppose that this memory is unstable. We can doubt whether we have remembered it correctly, but this is different. If the memory of the sensation used to define 'S' persists, it is accessible as a measure to compare with my current sensations. It seems that we need a further reason for holding that a private measure is any less stable or reliable than a public one.

develop the claim that the source of the argument against private language is in Wittgenstein's discussion of rules and meaning in general in §§138–201 of *PI*.

4.3 Semantic Normativity and the Argument Against Private Language

Why, then, does the diarist's attempt at giving a private ostensive definition of a sign fail? The answer I will defend here is that the impossibility of private meaning or private definition rests ultimately in Wittgenstein's rejection of semantic normativity earlier in *PI*. It will take some explanation to see how this is so, but it will reveal the true force of the argument that is adumbrated in §258 of *PI*.

To begin with, it should be remembered that Wittgenstein of course accepts that there are correct and incorrect ways of using words, and that there are obligations to use words in certain ways and not others. For instance, it is correct to call this apple 'green' and incorrect to call it 'black'. What he rejects is the assumption that such correctness conditions and obligations originate in things called *meanings*, whatever they are. This implies that the source of the correctness conditions and obligations must lie elsewhere. But where? This, I argue, is where Wittgenstein's discussion is at immediately after §201 of *PI*. His answer to the question is not straightforward because he does not respond by trying to give an account of meaning or language use. However, he does respond with an appeal to 'practices' and 'agreement' between language users. See, for example:

Disputes do not break out (among mathematicians, say) over the question whether a rule has been obeyed or not. People don't come to blows over it, for example. That is part of the framework on which the working of our language is based (for example, in giving descriptions). (*PI*, §240)

'So you are saying that human agreement decides what is true and what is false?' – It is what human beings say that is true and false; and they agree in the *language* they use. That is not agreement in opinions but in form of life. (*PI*, §241)[4]

Although difficult to interpret in the broader context of his metaphilosophical opposition to theorising, his references to communal agreement, customs and practices of use are significant because they allude to a type of normativity that is not semantic (especially not in the platonist's or classical realist's sense) but social and that may be fundamental to language use. These social norms or standards are customary ways in which we agree over how a word is used. For example, it is a brute fact that we tend to agree over how to use words such as

---

[4] See also Wittgenstein's statement that 'the agreement of ratifications [concerning a mathematical proof or theorem] is the precondition of our language-game, it is not affirmed in it' (*Remarks on the Foundations of Mathematics*, 365).

'green', 'tall', 'five', 'water' etc. Whether there is more to be said about this agreement, specifically something more that would satisfy the platonist or classical realist, is a question that has by this point been abandoned (in light of the arguments leading up to §201). What Wittgenstein does seem to be inviting us to say is that these social norms of use may be, as he puts it, 'part of the framework on which the working of our language is based'.

This appeal to communal agreement and shared practices of use is obviously relevant to Wittgenstein's discussion of privacy and sensation language in §§243–315 of *PI*, and specifically to the argument in §258. The important point that has not been appreciated, though, is that of exactly how he could have made use of this appeal without weakening the argument in §258 and/or contradicting his metaphilosophical opposition to defending theses and theories. That is, it cannot be the case – as many interpreters have assumed – that Wittgenstein adopts a community view of language prior to §243 and then merely applies it in §258 to undermine the diarist's attempt to give a private definition of a sign. That would simply beg the question against the diarist since the diarist clearly does not accept the community view, or the view that language is essentially social or public. This strategy would thus attribute a bad argument to Wittgenstein, as well as making him into a philosopher who defends theses and applies them in arguments whenever he needs to.

On my reading, Wittgenstein's reasoning in §258 is more subtle and not open to these charges. Essentially, the argument hinges on his refusal to give the private diarist what he needs, which is the semantic normativity thesis. The only way that the diarist's attempt at giving a private definition of 'S' can be successful is if the semantic normativity thesis is assumed; i.e. if it is assumed that the correctness conditions and the obligations for applying 'S' somehow follow from the *meaning* that 'S' is supposed to have. In other words, the meaning that is given to 'S' in the original ostensive definition is – by the diarist's own lights – supposed to entail constraints for how that sign is applied subsequently (constraints that must be constituted in the privacy of the diarist's mind alone); and if there were such constraints and the diarist was aware of them, the problem about how to correctly apply 'S' to subsequent sensations would not arise. But since Wittgenstein has provided compelling reasons in his arguments prior to §201 for rejecting the semantic normativity thesis, the private diarist cannot rely on it. And since in line with the private scenario the diarist cannot appeal to other types of norms (such as social norms) to underpin the correct use of 'S', it follows that 'S' has no correctness conditions attached to it. There is no criterion of correctness for the use of 'S'. What the diarist needs for the definition to be successful is not available to him.

This way of looking at the argument in §258, which sets it in the broader context of Wittgenstein's discussion of meaning and rule-following in general, does not make the mistake of interpreting him as adopting a philosophical thesis and using it as a premise in an argument. Recall that Wittgenstein's opposition to semantic normativity and platonism about meaning proceeds by a reductio method. This means that at most he employs assumptions or theses only to demonstrate that they lead to contradictions or absurdities. Hence, when the private diarist implicitly or unknowingly helps himself to a version of the semantic normativity thesis, Wittgenstein has the means to show that it is an unwarranted move; and more generally, to show that the diarist's attempt to give a private meaning to a sign fails.

4.4　The 'Real' Private Language Argument: Evaluating Kripke's Claims

Kripke's *Wittgenstein on Rules and Private Language* (*WRPL*) defends an interpretation of Wittgenstein's private language argument that is radically different to any of those considered in this chapter so far. Although it appears to have more in common with 'orthodox' readings because it explicitly attributes a traditional-style argument to Wittgenstein, it is also at odds with them because Kripke locates the argument in the sections prior to §243 of *PI*. One reason why I wish to consider Kripke's reading in this section is to supplement the analysis of it begun in the previous chapter. More importantly, though, I think his reading of this aspect of *PI* presents an interesting example of how *not* to appeal to the discussion prior to §243 to help elucidate Wittgenstein's opposition to private language. Therefore, by reflecting on this aspect of Kripke's reading, I will attempt to provide additional support for my view of how Wittgenstein's discussion of meaning and rule-following in general should be utilised to clarify his argument against private language.

Kripke makes the following three controversial claims regarding Wittgenstein's private language argument. Each of them concerns the relation between Wittgenstein's discussion of rule-following and meaning in §§138–242, on the one hand, and his discussion of privacy and sensation language in §§243–315, on the other:

THE LOCATION CLAIM: That '*the conclusion* [of the private language argument] *is already stated explicitly*' at §202 of *PI*, where Wittgenstein writes: 'Hence it is not possible to obey a rule "privately": otherwise thinking one was obeying a rule would be the same thing as obeying it' (see Kripke 1982, 3).

THE APPLICATION CLAIM: That §§243–315 of *PI* 'deal with the *application* of the general conclusions about language drawn in §§138–242 to the problem of sensations' (1982, 79; see also 1982, 3).

THE COUNTEREXAMPLE CLAIM: That 'sensations have a crucial role as an (apparently) convincing *counterexample* to the general considerations previously stated' (1982, 3).

While I am opposed to the specific ways in which Kripke tries to defend these interpretive claims, I will argue here that a *version* of all three of the claims can be defended but only by going against or beyond Kripke's discussion. Given that each of the claims concerns §§243–315 of *PI*, an adequate defence of them requires that we provide a close reading of these sections. One of the major problems with Kripke's defence of them is that he provides almost no analysis of these sections.[5] I will thus take the three claims as they stand and defend them by going further than Kripke's *WRPL* and connecting the claims with a close reading of §258 (and related sections).

The Alternative Private Language Argument (Prior to §243): The Kripkean Location Claim

What exactly is the 'real' private language argument that Kripke thinks is presented somewhere in §§138–242 of *PI*? Defending the Kripkean 'location' claim requires us to address the fact that the only explicit mention of the notion of privacy prior to §243 is in §202, which therefore justifies the questioning of the view that there is a private language argument of any sort in these sections. In §202, obeying a rule privately is contrasted with obeying a rule as 'a practice'. Hence, assuming that practice means communal practice (a controversial assumption itself), if there is a notion of privacy implicit in these sections it is perhaps to be correlated with being non-communal. However, even if this is accepted, the definition of a private language as not being shared or communal is different to the definition presented after §243 of a language 'which describes my inner experiences and which only I myself can understand'. This has led many to object to Kripke on the grounds that the relevant notion of privacy is not introduced until after §243, and therefore that the argument against private language could not possibly be presented prior to §243 (see, for example, Goldfarb 1985, 100, and 2011, 82, fn). I will respond to this later in the section. First I will try to characterise the argument prior to §243, before going on to compare it with the argument in §258.

The thrust of the alternative private language argument prior to §243 is to propose a conception of language in general and then show that it follows from it that there can be no such thing as a private language. Insofar as Wittgenstein does operate with an assumption about language in *PI*, it is that if a word is meaningful there must be a standard or norm for correctly applying the word; i.e. he accepts with everyone else that there must be right and wrong ways of

---

[5] The main exception is (1982, 60, footnote 47). But even in this footnote, there is no textual analysis of §§243–315; there is merely a brief discussion of some of the general themes that have been raised in the secondary literature on the private language argument, and specifically of Ayer's formulation of the argument in §258. It does not explain how Wittgenstein's remarks should be read in light of Kripke's main interpretive claims.

using words. This can be construed generally, so that there is no claim made about what kind of standards of correctness they must be or how they are constituted. However, remaining non-committal, we could assert that the standards must be either communal or non-communal (i.e. individualist/mental). For the sake of the initial presentation of the alternative private language argument, I will take it that Wittgenstein operates with these general claims in his discussion of rule-following and meaning in §§138–242. Using these assumptions, the following is how the alternative private language argument might look:

Private Language Argument prior to §243:

(1) If a word is meaningful, there must be a norm or standard
    of correctness for using the word.   Assumption
(2) The norms for correctly using words must be
    either mental/ individualist or communal.   Assumption
(3) The norms cannot be mental.   (From the arguments at §§138–201)
(4) Therefore, the norms must be communal.   (From 2, 3)
(5) A private language consists of terms with
    norms that are non-communal.   Definition
(6) Therefore, a private language is impossible.   (From 4, 5)

The argument thus proceeds in the third step by considering the possibility that the norms for correctly applying words are mental and rejecting it. This leads to the claim that the norms must be communal, which is what rules out the possibility of a private language *in the sense of* a language containing terms with non-communal standards governing their use.

I will take it for granted that this is how the alternative private language argument should be characterised and I will consider the question of its relation to the argument in §258 of *PI*. It is first necessary to respond to the objection that the notions of privacy in both 'private language arguments' are different. If there is a significant disconnection between these two parts of *PI*, it would potentially undermine the Kripkean 'counterexample' and 'application' claims because they both depend on these parts being continuous or dealing with issues that are directly relevant to one another. For example, if the relevant notion of privacy is not introduced until after §243, it threatens the claim that the discussion of privacy is concerned with a counterexample to the general conception of language presented prior to §243 because this general conception makes no claim that is relevant to this notion of privacy.

This objection, though, depends on overstating the discontinuity between the discussion before and after §243. While it is true that the notions of privacy in each stage are different, there are connections between them that should not be overlooked. Their connection consists in the fact that the definition of privacy in terms of words standing for sensations or 'inner experiences' (and that 'only I myself can understand') concerns a particular *instance* of the general notion of privacy in terms of non-communal standards of correctness. The norm or standard of correctness that is supposed to be established by the ostensive definition of 'S' in §258 (by focussing my attention inwardly on a recurring sensation) is merely one example of a non-communal norm. Hence, the conviction that our sensations or inner experiences can establish such non-communal norms for correctly using words does constitute a potential counter-example to the general view that the norms must be communal.

Granted that there is this possible connection between the discussions before and after §243, what can we say more concretely about how the alternative private language argument prior to §243 relates to the discussion of the private diarist in §258? To answer this, we must examine the counterexample and application claims more closely because they directly concern this issue. However, when we reflect on the latter two Kripkean claims together, they look to be in conflict. It appears that the counterexample claim does not fit with the application claim because if there is this potential conflict between the general communal conception of language and the particular scenario of the private diarist in §258, it would be no use to merely *apply* that general conception; for that would merely be to re-assert the general conception and would not resolve the conflict between it and the counterexample. In other words, the counterexample may turn out to not be genuine, but the point is that this cannot be shown to be the case merely by applying the general communal conception of language. Some other means of undermining the counterexample are required. It is, I hold, by attending to what these other means could be that we can grasp the genuine force of Wittgenstein's arguments prior to §243 *and* their applicability to the private diarist case in §258.

These other means are to be found *elsewhere* in the discussion of rule-following and meaning in §§138–242. Kripke himself suggests that the application to the case of sensations would be of the general communal conception of language apparently adopted by Wittgenstein in §§202–242 (in the sense that the impossibility of private language follows from Wittgenstein's communal conception; see 1982, 79). However, I will develop the proposal that an adequate defence of the application claim requires that we take a wider view and allow ourselves to draw on the many different subtle strategies and arguments presented throughout Wittgenstein's discussion of rule-following, but particularly in the earlier discussion at §§138–201.[6] Hence, I will go against

---

[6] This approach has a parallel in Martin Kusch's treatment of how to address the clash between the general communitarian conception of language (in Kripke's Wittgenstein's sceptical solution), on the one hand, and the radical social isolate or 'born Crusoe', on the other. Kusch's writes: 'As ever the individualist begs the question against the sceptical argument. If the behaviour of Crusoe is to indicate rule-following how is that rule-following to be conceived? If the rule-following is to be conceived in terms of a mental state (perhaps reduced to dispositions) then we face all the familiar problems' (2006, 193). The 'familiar problems' have to do with the sceptical considerations that Kripke's Wittgenstein raises against such meaning-constituting mental states. These

Kripke's own way of defending the application claim and give priority to Wittgenstein's discussion at §§138–201; and I will provide additional support for my reading that this discussion is crucial when it comes to the evaluation of the argument at §258.

The Kripkean Application and Counterexample Claims

My defence of the Kripkean application claim – that §§243–315 of *PI* 'deal with the *application* of the general conclusions about language drawn in §§138–242 to the problem of sensations' – will thus be to argue that it is the negative arguments presented in §§138–201 that should be applied in dealing with the private diarist case in §258.

When the diarist identifies an instance of the recurring sensation at the initial stage of providing a private ostensive definition of 'S' it is used, as we have discussed, to establish a norm or rule for correctly using 'S'. The reading I have been proposing is that the failure of the attempt to establish such a rule for correctly using 'S' has nothing to do with the fact that the object or sample (the sensation) is private. Rather, it fails for the same reason that, for example, the attempt to determine the meaning of the word 'cube' through forming a mental picture of a cube fails. The failure is shown by the fact that the mental picture does not in itself succeed in compelling the language user to use it one way or another; it is not able to dictate how *it* should be followed. The crucial thing is the use that we as a matter of fact make of it, for example, in applying it to a box of a certain square shape rather than to a triangular prism. As Wittgenstein states in *RFM*, 'it is *we* that are inexorable' when it comes to using a word or applying a rule (1956, 82). Anything that we might attach to or associate with the signs we use have no more normative force than the words themselves.

The case is the same in the private diarist's attempt to ostensively define 'S' by pointing inwardly to a sensation. This sensation-sample is no better than the mental picture of the cube in dictating or determining the correct way of using 'S'. Wittgenstein's statement that 'in the present case I have no criterion of correctness' means that any instance of writing 'S' into the diary can be construed as correct or incorrect. The only elements we have in this case are a sign and a sensation. The diarist can view himself as using the original sensation as a measure and comparing it with new sensations he has. But the sensation itself

---

considerations are reconstructed by Kripke primarily from §§138–201 of *PI*. Hence, the point I am taking from Kusch's claim is that the Crusoe counterexample can be attacked using these considerations, and the communitarian conception can thus be re-asserted in the face of this counterexample. Kusch's primary focus is on Kripke's reconstruction of Wittgenstein's discussion in §§138–242, and hence he does not apply this strategy to the analysis of the diary case in §258.

cannot force the diarist to use it one way rather than another. He may feel that one application of 'S' is right, but this is a matter of the use he makes of the sensation-sample rather of the use that is prescribed or determined by the sample itself. There is in this case nothing to separate right from 'whatever is going to seem right'. This can be articulated in terms of Wittgenstein's rejection of semantic normativity. Whatever it is that is attached to or correlated with a sign – in this case, a particular recurring sensation – does not have the required normative force; it does not determine what it is to use the sign correctly or entail obligations for how it should be used.

We might wonder, then, how norms for correctly using words and following rules are established if not by certain distinctive mental states. To reiterate, Wittgenstein does seem to want to make an important point about the role of the community in establishing such norms. Broadly speaking, the point is that given that there is nothing (for example, no mental entity or mental state) to determine the correct use or to compel us to apply words or rules in particular ways, the only thing that we can legitimately appeal to is the basic fact that we do apply words, extend arithmetical series, follow rules etc. in these ways and not others (see *PI*, §§217 and 240–2). The only norms we can appeal to are those that are established by these actual patterns of use. Whether we accept this community view (or even whether we accept that Wittgenstein accepted it), I have argued that it does not matter to his argument in §258. That is, the community view itself is not applied in that argument, for doing so would, as I have argued, merely beg the question against the private diarist. Instead, what we get in §258 is a potential counterexample to this community view; and this counterexample can be undermined by applying the method – practiced in §§138–201 – of dealing with candidates of mental states that purport to determine the meanings of terms. Therefore, versions of the Kripkean counterexample and application claims can be simultaneously defended in a close reading of §258.

4.5   Solitary Language and a 'Born Crusoe'

Primarily as a result of the influence of Wittgenstein's discussion in *PI*, the most common way of addressing the issue of whether language is essentially social is to look at the possibility of private language. Put simply, if private language is shown to be impossible, it seems that language must be held to be essentially social.

However, there is a separate topic that is also directly relevant to the issue of the social dimension of language. It concerns the possibility of what may be called *solitary* language, as opposed to private language. A good way of characterising the difference is in terms of the distinction between an *unshareable* language, on the one hand, and an *unshared* language, on the other. A private language, as Wittgenstein defines it, is unshareable, i.e. the meanings of the words in the language (like 'S') cannot be understood by anyone except for the one person using the word. In contrast, a solitary language is merely unshared in the sense that the words or signs of the language are *as a matter of fact* only used by one person, but it is in principle possible for others to understand those words or signs. Another way of clarifying the distinction is in terms of what the signs of each type of language stand for. The signs in a private language are supposed to stand for entities accessible only to the individual language user (for example, the individual's private sensations), while the signs in a solitary language may stand for objects in the person's environment that are observable to others.

In this section and the next, I will address the question of the possibility of a solitary language because doing so will highlight additional aspects to the issue of whether language is essentially social. I will begin in this section by looking at the question in abstraction from Wittgenstein's philosophy, and in the next section I will give a more comprehensive response to it by drawing on the reading of Wittgenstein presented in this chapter so far. The overall goal will be to assess whether he has a compelling argument, or set of arguments, for the view that language is essentially social (which is traditionally associated with him).

The best way of getting to grips with the question of the possibility of a solitary language is to consider the example of a Robinson Crusoe-type figure who is completely isolated from other people. But unlike the original Crusoe in Defoe's novel, the Crusoe in our example is isolated *from birth* and thus has grown up without ever having any contact with another human being. Hence, we should call him a 'born Crusoe' or a 'Super-Crusoe' to distinguish him from the character in Defoe's story (see Bar-On 1992, 27). If this individual could conceivably develop and use a language, he would be the only person who understood the words or signs of the language. Therefore, it would be a solitary language. The person could use the language to, say, depict or describe features of his environment, and thus we may imagine that other people could come to understand his language if they were ever to come in contact with him.

Dorit Bar-On attempts to specify what is involved in inquiring into the possibility of solitary language by reflecting on a Crusoe figure:

I take it that proponents of solitary language are not proposing that someone like Super-Crusoe might up and invent a language the way one of us might up and invent a new game. Rather, the idea is that Super-Crusoe might gradually come to employ signs in such a way that it would make sense to speak of his uses of those signs as being linguistically correct or incorrect. (Bar-On 1992, 31)

As Bar-On formulates it, the issue would seem to be whether a born Crusoe is capable of coming to use certain basic signs that are sufficiently *language-like* in the sense that there are correct and incorrect ways of using the signs. Note that the relevant notion of correctness does not have to be semantic. The point may be the general one that there must be some notion of using the signs correctly and incorrectly (as there is for words of our sophisticated, shared languages), while it is left open what kind of correctness this is or what ultimate source it has.

How exactly would a defender of the possibility of a solitary language proceed? I will continue to focus on Bar-On's discussion because it raises a lot of pertinent questions. She suggests that the defender could argue 'that nature might exert various pressures on Super-Crusoe to mark regularities in his environment' (1992, 31). And she gives an example of how this could lead Super-Crusoe to invent a basic system of signs:

For instance, he might discover a connection between eating a certain kind of berries and suffering a severe skin-rash and then have a reason to mark the poisonous fruits, perhaps by attaching pieces of red string next to the bad berries, blue strings next to the good ones. But then he would have developed techniques involving marks for getting on better in his environment, which could succeed or fail. In time, we are to think, Super-Crusoe could come to possess a mini-science of his environment encoded in a notational system which serves as an instrument for avoiding trouble and gaining better control over his surroundings. (1992, 31–2)

To avoid getting severe skin-rash, then, Super-Crusoe marks the bad berries with red string and the good berries with blue string. This kind of behaviour is potentially significant because from the fact that 'Super-Crusoe's use of this instrument could succeed or fail, it seems that we already have an objective difference between his going right and his going wrong with his use of marks' (Bar-On 1992, 32). That is, it appears that there is a distinction between being correct and merely seeming to be correct in how Super-Crusoe uses these signs. However, is this distinction enough to justify attributing a language of sorts to Super-Crusoe?

To answer this question, we need to look at the kind of distinction between correct and incorrect that is in play in the Crusoe scenario. Bar-On calls the relevant sense of normativity 'teleological normativity':

[C]onsider the following case. Suppose, after various attempts to bring down apples from tall trees in my yard, I arrive at the following routine: I look for a long stick, pick it up, then gently hit the apple near its base, etc. My steps can be evaluated as good or bad, depending on how successful they are. We have here a clear element of what I shall call 'teleological normativity'. (*Ibid.*)

What Bar-On calls teleological normativity pertains to the distinction between correct and incorrect that is relative to some goal or purpose. For example, a method for knocking apples down from high trees will be called 'correct' if it is successful in achieving its purpose. In general, we can say that someone is adopting the right method of doing something if it works in achieving the relevant purpose. Bar-On elaborates on this type of normativity as follows:

Teleological normativity abounds: there is right and wrong about how to build a boat, how to bake a torte, how best to attract someone's attention at some given moment. Teleological normativity is not restricted to intentional purposeful actions: there is right and wrong about how to build a decent nest, which direction to swim in when winter comes (remember poor Humphrey the Californian whale), and so on. (*Ibid.*)

We can think of a norm as a standard by reference to which actions can be judged as ideal, correct or incorrect, required or prohibited – something whose function is to regulate and/or evaluate action or behavior. Legal rights, a carpenter's square, yardsticks, industrial regulations, paint chips, traffic laws, role models, rules of etiquette, are all examples of norms. Teleological norms, then, set standards for purposive behavior and actions; they allow us to evaluate means given a specific, pre-existing end. (1992, 32–3)

From the mere biological fact that Super-Crusoe is a human being, it seems justified to hold that his behaviour could be governed by various teleological norms. In order to characterise his behaviour as guided by and open to evaluation relative to such norms, we need only attribute particular desires and intentions to Crusoe (for example, the desire to avoid being hurt or poisoned).

Even though we may characterise Super-Crusoe's behaviour in terms of teleological norms, it remains an open question whether this warrants us in holding that he is capable of developing and using a language. Is the ability to follow teleological norms sufficient to be a language user? First of all, the notion of 'following' a teleological norm is extremely wide if it is supposed to cover the patterns and regularities of behaviour in non-human animals and insects. The problem for the defender of the possibility of solitary language is that *if* this wide notion is legitimate, it undermines the attempt to use examples of this kind (for example, the use of coloured string to mark good and bad berries) to justify attributing a language to Super-Crusoe. For the defender ends up making it too easy to be a language user; he would be forced to also accept that the behaviour of bees and birds is sufficiently complex to count as language-like.

Bar-On also views the appeal to teleological norms as inadequate in the attempt to defend the possibility of solitary language. Her main point is that although we can characterise Super-Crusoe's behaviour in terms of the attempt to achieve certain goals or purposes – and hence, evaluate his actions as correct or incorrect relative to those teleological norms – this is different to actually attaching *meaning* to signs (see Bar-On 1992, 33–4). Something more is required to be able to hold, for instance, that Super-Crusoe's red string means *poisonous berries*. But this raises the further question of what this 'more' is, i.e. what notion of correctness or incorrectness (in the characterisation of a creature's behaviour as correct or incorrect) is required in order to attribute a language to a creature such as Super-Crusoe.

A possible answer is that his behaviour, specifically his use of signs, must be guided by *semantic* norms. However, as I have interpreted Wittgenstein, it would be inappropriate to appeal to semantic norms to help characterise the criteria for being a language user. Wittgenstein's *PI*, as we shall now see, has a major role to play in this debate over whether a socially isolated individual could develop a language.

4.6   Wittgenstein and the Possibility of Solitary Language

What characteristics must a person have, for example, in terms of their behaviour, to count as having a language? Or to put the question slightly differently, what is it for behaviour to be language-like? Obviously, there must be a basic level of complexity, but the difficulty lies in specifying exactly what kind of complexity is relevant to being a language user (see Williams 1999, 172/3). The discussion in the previous section suggested that it is not sufficient for the individual to have certain goals that follow from having certain desires (such as eating, or avoiding getting sick or injured) and in relation to which the individual's behaviour can be classified as correct or incorrect insofar as it helps or does not help in achieving those goals. In short, it seems that teleological normativity is the wrong kind of normativity when it comes to language. Furthermore, following from my reading of Wittgenstein's arguments in §§138–201 of *PI*, it also appears that having a language or being linguistically competent is not a matter of being guided by *semantic* norms.

This leaves us with some pressing questions. Two of these are uppermost in the present discussion:

(1) What, then, is it for behaviour to be language-like if it is not for the language user to be guided by either teleological norms or semantic norms?
(2) In light of this, how are we to evaluate the possibility of a born Crusoe developing a solitary language?

Obviously, we need to try to get clear on what it is to be a language user or to be linguistically competent before we can evaluate the possibility of a born Crusoe developing a language. Answering the first question thus holds the key to being able to answer the second.

Based on what has already been argued in this chapter, it can be seen that Wittgenstein's answer to the first question involves the appeal to the mundane facts concerning the communal agreement in language use. This appeal, I maintained, stems from his acceptance of the platitudinous point that there are correct and incorrect ways of using words, and his rejection of any view that locates the source of the correctness and incorrectness in mysterious mental states or entities of any kind, such as the platonist is inclined to posit. Wittgenstein looks to the community of language users to support the distinction between correct and incorrect language use. But the result is not an explanatory account to rival the platonist's account, and this is shown by the modesty of Wittgenstein's aims. He does not attempt to identify special powers that the community possesses to *make it the case* that certain uses of language are correct and others incorrect. He merely draws attention to patterns of actual language use, or facts concerning how in practice we agree on, for example, whether a certain animal is called a 'cow', whether this apple is 'green', whether '1002' is the next number after '1000' in the series beginning '2, 4, 6, 8 ...' etc.

The nature and importance of Wittgenstein's appeal to use is the subject of the final chapter; the above is just a brief statement of why use is significant for him. But if I am right about Wittgenstein relying on the community of language users to support the basic distinction between correct and incorrect uses of words, there is the immediate corollary that it is *impossible* for a socially isolated individual like Super-Crusoe to develop and use a language (or for his behaviour to be sufficiently language-like for him to be viewed as using a solitary language).

However, before giving up on the possibility of a solitary language, I will consider another influential example of how a Super-Crusoe may be held to exhibit behaviour that is complex in the relevant sense and that warrants us attributing a primitive language to him. Given what I have just said about Wittgenstein and the impossibility of solitary language, it is interesting that Baker and Hacker argue that Super-Crusoe *can* develop and use a language. Although the case they make in their (1984) is inspired by Wittgenstein and they hold that he did allow for the possibility of solitary language, their most compelling example is their own and not Wittgenstein's (despite being linked to his remarks at *RFM*, 344). Their example is of a situation in which Super-Crusoe follows a particular pattern when decorating a wall. This, for them, is similar enough to following a rule or norm, which is what we do when using language. It is a central feature of their comparison with familiar examples of linguistic behaviour that Super-Crusoe is able to make mistakes or to apply the pattern incorrectly. See where they write:

In the first place, it is quite wrong to suppose that distinctions between appearance and reality are inapplicable to an individual in isolation, or are ones which that individual cannot employ. In the particular case of rule-following, there is no reason why Crusoe should not follow a pattern or paradigm, making occasional mistakes perhaps, and occasionally (but maybe not always) noticing and correcting his mistakes. That he is following a rule will show itself in the manner in which he uses the formulation of the rules as a canon or norm of correctness. Hence, to take a simple example, he might use the pattern $- - - \ldots - - - \ldots$ as a rule or pattern to follow in decorating the walls of his house; when he notices four dots in a sequence he manifests annoyance with himself. He goes back and rubs one out, and perhaps checks carefully adjacent marks, comparing them with his 'master-pattern'. And so on. Of course, he is *not* merely following his 'inclinations', but rather following the rule. And it is his behaviour, including his corrective behaviour, which shows that he is following the rule, and *what he counts as following the rule*. (Baker and Hacker 1984, 39)

What is imperative is that Super-Crusoe is able to correct himself or realise that he has applied the pattern incorrectly in a particular instance. Baker and Hacker's point seems to be that if we are willing to hold that Super-Crusoe can exhibit such 'corrective behaviour', we should also be willing to hold that he is capable of developing and using a language on his own because that would require similar corrective behaviour.

Can we really say, though, that Super-Crusoe has made a mistake in his use of the decorative pattern when he writes four dots in a sequence, i.e. that he has applied the pattern incorrectly? And could Super-Crusoe himself view his behaviour of applying the pattern as either correct or incorrect? A problem with using this example to defend the possibility of solitary language is that there are at least two characterisations of the type of norm in question, and both characterisations raise concerns. On the one hand, to say that the decorative pattern – – – ... – – – ... establishes a rule or norm is to say that the relevant notions of correct and incorrect relate to how applications of the pattern *look* compared with the sample or master pattern. Hence, on this characterisation Crusoe's application of the pattern – which is repeated over and over again – will be called *correct* if it looks the same as the sample pattern (i.e. with three dots and three dashes) and *incorrect* if it does not. This raises difficulties because we can ask the same questions about the capacity of this pattern itself to establish a rule as Wittgenstein asks about a sign-post, i.e. 'Does the sign-post leave no doubt open about the way I have to go?' (*PI*, §85). This is the question that leads to the regress of rules because in the attempt to explain how the sign-post is genuinely normative and action-guiding, we feel the need to posit a rule for the use of the sign-post, which in turn creates the need for an additional rule for its use etc. What is to stop these exact considerations from arising in the example of the decorative pattern? How can the sample itself, which is merely composed of dots and dashes, determine how the pattern should be correctly applied?

On the other hand, it may be that the relevant notion of correct and incorrect in this example has additional components, such as relating to Super-Crusoe's aesthetic preference in how the wall he is decorating should look. His application of the pattern may be called *correct* if it fits with Super-Crusoe's decorative preference and incorrect if it does not fit. But this is not going to get the defender of solitary language any further because if the correct and incorrect use is relative to his preference, what is to prevent this from changing as he covers his wall? For his preference may alter slightly so that when he puts down four dots instead of three, he does not see any conflict because he likes how it looks. Therefore, *any* combination of dots and dashes could be construed as correct relative to his personal preference, which just means that there is no genuine norm in play at all.

Jussi Haukioja makes the following points against Baker and Hacker that bring out both of these objections:

[Can Super-Crusoe] be wrong about what the correct application of the master pattern is in a given instance? Certainly *we* would call it an error if he did four dots in a sequence. But it seems that if Crusoe, for whatever reasons, happens to prefer painting a sequence of four dots at a certain point, nothing will force him to reconsider his decision (even if he sometimes does so in the manner Baker & Hacker describe). There is nothing in the master pattern that will, *all by itself*, force one continuation of the series of dots and lines rather than another. In taking the master pattern to have a single interpretation Baker & Hacker are already supposing Crusoe to be a rule-follower. Without this supposition, the example simply does not work. If we do *not* take the master pattern to have an interpretation, Crusoe will be, at any given point, free to take it to suggest anything he happens to prefer. 'Whatever seems right to him is right', and the Crusoe of this example is not a rule-follower. (Haukioja 2004, 10)

Meredith Williams raises a similar set of objections against Baker and Hacker. She argues that the only way we can characterise Super-Crusoe's behaviour with the decorative pattern as genuinely normative is if we judge him from *our* standards or norms. That is, we cannot hold that Super-Crusoe establishes his own norms and that *he* would consider himself as acting correctly or incorrectly relative to some norm. Rather, it is only by viewing his actions from the point of view of our norms that it makes sense to characterise his behaviour as correct or incorrect. And since our norms are communal or social, the example does not succeed in establishing that Crusoe could adopt and follow solitary norms (see Williams 1999, 172–5). She writes:

Insofar as our isolated individual's behavior counts as being corrective, it is only in virtue of his behaviour being like our own, of assimilating his behavior to our corrective practices. The only standard available for what counts as corrective behavior, and so *is* corrective behavior, are the paradigms of correcting that inform our practices. Behavior wildly different from our own, bearing no discernible similarity to our practices of correcting, is simply not corrective behaviour ...

It is only in virtue of Robinson Crusoe's *notional* membership in our own community that he can be said to follow rules at all. The normativity of Robinson Crusoe's behavior is derivable not from the mere complexity or publicness of his behavior, but from the assimilation of that behavior to the complex practices of what we do, practices that distinguish among correcting, modifying, and terminating an activity. The individuation and identity of Crusoe's practice requires assimilation to our practices. It is only in this way that the requisite background for distinguishing among alternative actions (correcting, rebelling, modifying etc.) can be provided. The community provides the logical space for an array of alternatives in terms of which the caveman's behavior can be understood. A consequence of this is that solitary rule-following is only intelligible as the exception. Not all membership in a community could be notional. (1999, 173)

Reflecting on Baker and Hacker's example, Williams draws the conclusion that 'the very idea of normativity ... cannot get a foothold unless the practice is a social one' (1999, 175). Super-Crusoe, on this view, cannot be held to be using a primitive solitary language. The only way of viewing his behaviour as language-like is to judge him by our standards, which would thus be to characterise his behaviour relative to social norms rather than to solitary norms.

The standpoint that Williams defends is similar to the one I attributed to Wittgenstein. The similarity is particularly strong in her claim that:

The origin of normativity, then, lies in the agreement that creates the place for standards and in the possibility of deviation from the actions of the community that hold the standard in place. (1999, 177)

However, it is hard to make a definitive statement about Wittgenstein's attitude to the possibility of solitary language. Baker and Hacker rightly note that there are passages from his later manuscripts that suggest he believed a Crusoe figure could use a very basic language (see Baker and Hacker 2009, 160–6).

My approach has been to focus on the negative arguments in *PI* and to try to show that they create problems for the defender of solitary language, and indeed problems that are largely the same as those faced by the defender of private language. Most importantly, the defender of solitary language cannot help himself to the notion of a semantic norm. And yet he must say something about there being correct and incorrect ways for Super-Crusoe to use his rudimentary signs. I have gone through some of the other senses of normativity that the defender might draw on, such as correctness/incorrectness relative to a particular goal or visual appearance or preference. None of these could do what the defender of solitary language requires. It looks as though the only way of making a relevant distinction between correct and incorrect use of signs is to follow Wittgenstein and base it on what communities of language users actually do with the signs. This, though, is to give up on the possibility of solitary language.

4.7   The Sceptical Solution and the Social Dimension of Language

To conclude this chapter, I will consider the issue of the social dimension of language from the point of view of Kripke's reading of Wittgenstein and thus connect the discussion back to the previous chapter. The foregoing discussion puts us in a better position to properly assess Kripke's interpretation of Wittgenstein as adopting a 'sceptical solution' to the doubts and difficulties he raises regarding meaning and rule-following. The view I will take is that Kripke's strategy is appropriate, but that – like with so much else in his reading – it requires a more careful and detailed defence. Kripke's outline of KW's sceptical solution is essentially an imperfect attempt to give an account of why Wittgenstein *needed* (hence the word 'solution') to appeal to the community of language users when proposing a rough, positive picture of linguistic practices. In this section, I will examine some of the details of Kripke's presentation and then identify the main ways in which I think it can be improved.

Kripke follows Michael Dummett in interpreting Wittgenstein's *PI* as containing 'implicitly a rejection of the classical (realist) Frege-*Tractatus* view that the general form of explanation of meaning is a statement of the truth conditions' (Dummett 1959, 348; quoted in Kripke 1982, 73); and as replacing it with 'an alternative rough general picture', which is basically an assertability-conditional conception of meaning (*Ibid.*). As Kripke writes:

Wittgenstein replaces the question, 'What must be the case for this sentence to be true?' by two others: first, 'Under what conditions may this form of words be appropriately asserted (or denied)?'; second, given an answer to the first question, 'What is the role, and the utility, in our lives of our practice of asserting (or denying) the form of words under these conditions?' (*Ibid.*)

This shift, according to Kripke, is what defines the attitude of the defender of the sceptical solution. As he understands it, it is essential to KW's sceptical solution that KW adopts a 'rough general' assertability-conditional conception. (Note: I will continue to use 'KW' to refer to the character of Wittgenstein in Kripke's book.) This aspect of Kripke's reading has been greatly distorted by interpreters of *WRPL*. I will here draw on my reading of *WRPL* in the previous chapter to clarify what is involved first in rejecting the truth-conditional conception, and second replacing it with an assertability-conditional conception.

The first thing we must emphasise is that – as the Dummett quotation makes explicit – the truth-conditional conception in Kripke's discussion is another name for the 'classical realist' conception of meaning. The notion of a truth-condition is appealed to by the classical realist to account for the meaning of sentences, just as he appeals to functions to account for the meaning of functional expressions, properties to account for the meaning of predicates etc. For the classical realist, a person will be deemed to mean something by a sentential expression only if there is some fact about him that establishes the relevant truth-condition as the standard of correctness for the use of that expression. The sceptical challenge can be run against the conviction that I mean something by a given sentence, and the result will be the familiar one discussed in the previous chapter in relation to Wilson's and Miller's readings. In other words, the reasons for rejecting the truth-conditional conception are the same as those for rejecting the classical realist conception in general, viz. the conception leads to the sceptical paradox. Hence, the motivation for rejecting the conception is based on a reductio argument.

Regarding the alternative picture that KW replaces it with in the sceptical solution, Kripke states that it is in fact misleading to call it an assertability-conditional conception because 'Wittgenstein does not confine himself to declarative sentences, and hence to assertion and denial' (*Ibid.*). He continues:

Thus, if we speak properly, we should not speak of conditions of 'assertion', but rather, more generally, of the conditions when a move (a form of linguistic expression) is to be made in the 'language game'. If, however, we allow ourselves to adopt an over-simplified terminology more appropriate to a special range of cases, we can say that Wittgenstein proposes a picture of language based, not on *truth conditions*, but on *assertability conditions* or *justifications*. (1982, 73–4)

Hence, the more appropriate expressions are 'justification-conditions' or making 'a move' in a language-game, both of which concern the conditions under which a linguistic expression of any sort may be justifiably used in such-and-such ways. The emphasis in the sceptical solution is on the *use* of linguistic expressions and the situations in which we can say of a language user that he or she is using them correctly or incorrectly. Even more generally, the switch in emphasis is from the facts supposedly underlying or constitutive of linguistic meaning, to the actual uses of linguistic expressions. Viewed in this way, the affinity with Wittgenstein starts to emerge more clearly.

In these broad terms, Kripke's reading is correct that what is truly distinctive about Wittgenstein's approach to language is that it involves this change of focus from looking at constitutive facts to looking closely at how we actually use words. The whole point of this alternative approach to meaning, as Kripke sees it, is that it is supposed to offer a 'solution' to the sceptical paradox by clarifying how our use of terms such as 'means', 'understands' etc. is legitimate. Regarding this, Kripke states that:

All that is needed to legitimize assertions that someone means something is that there be roughly specifiable circumstances under which they are legitimately assertable, and that the game of asserting them under such conditions has a role in our lives. No supposition that 'facts correspond' to those assertions is needed. (1982, 77–8)

The KW solution to the sceptical paradox is thus to show that there are conditions under which these terms can be justifiably used and that they play a role or have a utility in our lives. For many, this could hardly be called a 'solution' at all because it leaves unanswered the questions of the nature of meaning and of what grounds our practices of ascribing meaning. This, though, is the same complaint that can be made against Wittgenstein's anti-theoretical standpoint that rejects the project of offering a constitutive account of meaning (see next chapter).

As emphasised throughout this chapter, Wittgenstein did not merely turn his attention to the actual uses of words. He focused on our *shared* or *communal* uses, or the ways we ordinarily agree in using words. This is also a central feature of KW's sceptical solution. As Kripke puts it:

Wittgenstein finds a useful role in our lives for the 'language game' that licenses, under certain conditions, assertions that someone 'means such-and-such' and that his present application of a word 'accords' with what he 'meant' in the past. It turns out that this role, and these conditions, involve reference to a community. They are inapplicable to a single person considered in isolation. Thus, as we have said, Wittgenstein rejects 'private language' as early as §202. (1982, 79)

The fact that a community view of language is at the centre of the sceptical solution is thus what leads Kripke to make the claim that the real private language argument is merely a corollary of the sceptical solution. I have already highlighted the problems with this latter claim, but it is also important to consider the plausibility of his claim that the community view is intrinsic to the sceptical solution. Kripke's formulations of the assertability-conditions for both first-person and third-person meaning ascriptions contain references to the community of language users:

Jones is entitled, subject to correction by others, provisionally to say, 'I mean addition by "plus"', whenever he has the feeling of confidence – 'now I can go on!' – that he can give 'correct' responses in new cases; and *he* is entitled, again provisionally and subject to correction by others, to judge a new response to be 'correct' simply because it is the response he is inclined to give. (1982, 90)
Smith will judge Jones to mean addition by 'plus' only if he judges that Jones's answers to particular addition problems agree with those *he* is inclined to give, or, if they occasionally disagree, he can interpret Jones as at least following the proper procedure ... If Jones consistently fails to give responses in agreement (in this broad sense) with Smith's, Smith will judge that he does not mean addition by 'plus'. (1982, 91)

However, there are a couple of issues concerning these formulations that need to be distinguished.

The first is whether Kripke's formulations of these assertability-conditions are correct, or more importantly whether there are possible formulations of them that are equally legitimate and yet do not make reference to the community. The second issue is whether the impossibility of private language really does follow from this general picture of meaning even if these assertability-conditions are formulated in this way. For example, Goldfarb has questioned Kripke on the first issue, arguing that the assertability-conditions can be formulated without reference to the community (1985, 102). Boghossian has attacked Kripke on the second issue by arguing that the above formulations can at best capture the assertability-conditions that actually obtain in our community, but they cannot provide support for the impossibility claim that forms the conclusion of the private language argument (1989, 155–6).

My view is that Kripke is vulnerable to both of these objections, but that an adequate response can be provided by departing from his discussion in the way I advocated in section 4.4 of this chapter. That is, I agree with Boghossian that the assertability-conditions for meaning ascriptions presented in *WRPL* can at most capture what those conditions happen to be in a community, and cannot support the stronger modal claim that private language is impossible. But we can reply – again, contrary to Kripke – that the impossibility claim does not rest on any positive picture of language (for example, a community view) but on Wittgenstein's/KW's negative arguments, which concern what *could not* be the case, viz. that it is not possible for there to be meaning-constituting facts of the kind that the private linguist requires. Furthermore, we can also agree with Goldfarb that KW's assertability-conditions can be formulated without necessarily referring to the community. But then the onus is on him to specify what using a word that has no established communal use amounts to. And he must do so without falling victim to Wittgenstein's/KW's negative arguments, i.e. must not presuppose the notion of an entity or state with mysterious properties to determine the correct uses of a word.

The real question we need to ask is whether Kripke's reference to the community in the statement of the assertability-conditions is well motivated. And when we appreciate the full scope of KW's negative or sceptical argument in *WRPL*, we see that he does have a strong motivation. It is grounded in the awareness that the alternative, individualist model relies on assumptions concerning meaning and language that the negative argument has shown to be untenable. *Wittgenstein's* references to communal agreement and shared practices of use in §§202–242 of *PI* are based on a similar critical understanding of the individualist alternative.

4.8   Conclusion: Does Wittgenstein Have an Argument for the Claim that Language is Essentially Social?

Although I have argued that Wittgenstein's *PI* contains powerful arguments that undermine the notions of private language *and* solitary language, a lot more needs to be said about his view of the significance of the community or communal agreement to our ordinary linguistic practices. For instance, as we will see, there are certain versions of the community view that also presuppose the semantic normativity thesis, and that would thus be equally objectionable from Wittgenstein's point of view (see section 5.7 of the next chapter).

It is therefore misleading to simply conclude that his opposition to private and solitary languages translates into a straightforward endorsement of a community view of language. The assumption that he adopts the latter view overlooks the distinctive role that arguments play within *PI*, which is not to defend a particular philosophical thesis of his own but to challenge the presumption in favour of theorising. This is a fundamental aspect of *PI* that I have yet to explore, but that will be treated at length in the next chapter.

As I read *PI* (especially §§202–242), Wittgenstein's modest, non-explanatory goals are not merely stipulated or based on some idiosyncratic aversion to theorising; rather, they are based on his awareness of the wide scope of his negative arguments presented prior to §201 and the knowledge that any proposals made about language (such as those concerning the role of communal agreement) must fall outside their scope. Exactly how this plays out will need to be addressed.

The question of whether Wittgenstein has an argument for the thesis that language is essentially social, then, can only be properly answered by reflecting on his distinctive metaphilosophy and his opposition to theorising. The provisional answer is that his arguments do *not* constitute a defence of this thesis. The analysis of his metaphilosophy in the next chapter will provide the necessary context to allow us to understand why this is so. It will be seen that his groundbreaking reflections on language can only be fully appreciated in the context of this metaphilosophy.

Summary of Main Points

(4a) There are at least two ways that philosophers may argue for the view that language is essentially social. The first is to argue that *private* languages are impossible and the second is to argue that *solitary* languages are impossible.

(4b) A private language is a language with signs that have an *unshareable* meaning; they are understandable only to the person whose language it is. A purported example would be a sign that a person uses to talk about his or her own private sensations. A solitary language, by contrast, contains signs that have an *unshared* meaning. Examples would be the signs that a radically socially isolated individual (a 'born Crusoe') would invent and use; these signs would be unshared but not necessarily unshareable.

(4c) Arguments against the possibility of such languages, it would seem, provide support for the thesis that linguistic meaning is essentially *shareable* or *shared* meaning.

(4d) In §258 of *PI*, Wittgenstein presents a fragment of an argument against the possibility of a private language. Much of the debate concerning it has attempted to explain how the argument is supposed to be completed by relying either on an unargued-for assumption (such as the principle of verification) or a substantive thesis apparently established earlier in the book (such as the view that communal agreement is constitutive of linguistic meaning).

(4e) These attempts at supplementing Wittgenstein's private language argument have one thing in common, viz. they make the argument look weak. This is the case even for those scholars who view themselves as defending Wittgenstein.

(4f) Despite the multitude of interpretations that have intentionally or unintentionally undermined this aspect of *PI*, Wittgenstein does have a strong argument against the possibility of private language. The key to it does not lie in making an unwarranted assumption or applying a philosophical thesis from elsewhere in *PI*. Rather, it lies in recognising that the argument needs to be supplemented by Wittgenstein's anti-platonist argument from §§138–201 of *PI*.

(4g) Specifically, the private diarist in §258 implicitly relies on the assumption that meaning is normative; he needs this assumption to maintain that the meaning that is given to the sign 'S' (by correlating it with a private recurring sensation) engenders *constraints* for how that sign is to be used subsequently. Wittgenstein's argument in §258 hinges on showing that there are no such constraints (there is 'no criterion of correctness'). And the reason there is none is that – like the attempts to determine meaning in terms of distinctive mental states in §§138–201 – the private diarist has provided nothing that could entail how the sign is to be correctly used.

(4h) The attempt to determine the meaning of a sign in the private diary scenario fails for the same reason as the attempts discussed in §§138–201. The private diary example is just one more example of the mistaken assumption that the correct/incorrect ways of using a sign are determined by the 'meaning' of the sign (whatever it is). And since Wittgenstein's main arguments against this assumption are presented in §§138–201, the so-called private language argument must ultimately rely on these arguments.

(4i) The advantage of this reading of the private language argument is that it does not hold that Wittgenstein appealed to some philosophical thesis about language that he applied in the private diary example. Instead, it merely shows that the private diarist requires a certain assumption concerning meaning (i.e. the semantic normativity thesis), and that Wittgenstein has the resources to argue that this assumption is unwarranted.

(4j) The defender of the possibility of *solitary* languages must also rely on the semantic normativity thesis. Although Wittgenstein (in his unpublished manuscripts) was more ambiguous in his attitude to the possibility of solitary languages, his negative arguments in §§138–201 can be used to show the impossibility of such languages.

(4k) While other philosophers would take the conclusions of these arguments
as providing support for the opposing thesis that language is essentially
social or shareable, Wittgenstein does not accept this view. He does not
defend this thesis. To understand how he could have rejected both sides
in this debate, we have to reflect on the distinctive role of arguments in *PI*
and how they provide support for his anti-theoretical standpoint (rather
than for some favoured philosophical thesis).

5 Metaphilosophy and the Philosophy of Language

An essential feature of the reading of the later Wittgenstein defended in this book is that *Philosophical Investigations* (*PI*) contains a number of intricate arguments, and furthermore that these arguments directly concern how we characterise the nature of language or linguistic meaning. Chapters 1, 2, and 4 were devoted primarily to interpreting *PI* with a view to clearly articulating Wittgenstein's arguments. However, it is now time to address a troubling issue that has been in the background up to this point, viz. that Wittgenstein seems to explicitly state that he does not present arguments of any sort. The following two remarks express this view most emphatically:

Philosophy simply puts everything before us, and neither explains nor deduces anything – since everything lies open to view there is nothing to explain. For what is hidden, for example, is of no interest to us.
    One might also give the name 'philosophy' to what is possible *before* all new discoveries and inventions. (*PI*, §126)
    In philosophy we do not draw conclusions. 'But it must be like this!' is not a philosophical proposition. Philosophy only states what everyone admits. (*PI*, §599)

These passages also indicate Wittgenstein's closely related opposition to theorising or providing explanations in philosophy. This is clearly expressed in the following well-known remarks too:

And we may not advance any kind of theory. There must not be anything hypothetical in our considerations. We must do away with all *explanation*, and description alone must take its place ... (*PI*, §109)
    If one tried to advance *theses* in philosophy, it would never be possible to debate them, because everyone would agree to them. (*PI*, §128)

The target of these statements is the view of philosophy as a discipline that is conducted around the defence of particular philosophical theses concerning phenomena such as language, the mind, knowledge etc. (and the discovery of deep truths about these phenomena). These theses are the pillars of the accounts or theories intended to provide an explanation of the phenomena in question. And arguments, on this view, play a fundamental role in the defence of particular philosophical theses, as well as in the criticism of competing theses.

132

Wittgenstein is interested in an alternative model of philosophy that *ultimately* does away with arguments and theorising. Therefore, reading the above remarks in isolation suggests a very different picture of what is going on in *PI* to the one I have presented so far. By attributing arguments to Wittgenstein, it appears as if I have depicted him as the kind of philosopher he explicitly opposes in his metaphilosophical statements.

My goal in this chapter is to address this apparent conflict. I have already provided a partial defence of my view that there are arguments in *PI* by considering some of the most significant examples of them. Here, though, the task is the separate one of demonstrating that the presence of these arguments in Wittgenstein's book is – despite appearances to the contrary – compatible with his metaphilosophy. There are a few key steps to my defence. Firstly, I will argue that there is an implicit distinction in *PI* between what Wittgenstein takes to be the correct philosophical method or methods, on the one hand, and the actual one he adopts for therapeutic or elucidatory purposes, on the other; and that the presence of arguments in the book can be explained in terms of him deliberately engaging in the kind of philosophising he directly opposes (see section 5.2). This strategy is analogous to the one we find in *Tractatus Logico-Philosophicus* (*TLP*), as I will explain. Secondly, I will argue that the later Wittgenstein held that philosophical statements are meaningful (see section 5.3). This is important to establish because it is the only way to make sense of the claim that philosophical statements figure in the kind of reductio arguments I have outlined.

In section 5.4, I will defend my reading against that of the later Baker, who was one of the most prominent philosophers to insist that there are no arguments (and no need for arguments) in *PI*. Sections 5.5 and 5.6 will deal with the separate question of whether Wittgenstein unwittingly committed himself to certain substantial philosophical theses, thereby repeating perhaps the most fundamental error of *TLP*. The point is that Wittgenstein's method of engaging in dialogues with more traditional or theorising philosophers is problematic because, on the reading defended here at least, it requires him to think deeply about their theoretical commitments. And it shouldn't be assumed that it is a straightforward matter for him to emerge from these disputes without picking up or defending theoretical claims of his own. In section 5.7, I will address the question of whether Wittgenstein has done enough to motivate his anti-theoretical standpoint, particularly with regard to the study of language.

What will hopefully come out of this discussion will be a view of Wittgenstein's conception of philosophy that will also make it easier to evaluate the possibility of genuine dialogue with philosophers of language who do not share his metaphilosophy (see section 5.8). Prior to dealing with these issues, I will prepare the way by considering Wittgenstein's later view of how philosophical problems arise as a result of misunderstandings concerning the use of words.

5.1   Wittgenstein, the Linguistic Turn and the Origin of Philosophical Problems

The historical phenomenon of the 'linguistic turn' in the analytic philosophical tradition occurred in the late nineteenth and early twentieth centuries, and it was instrumental in the formation of that tradition. What was genuinely remarkable about it was that the study of language became central to philosophy for the first time in its two-and-a-half thousand-year history, whereas until that point it was either peripheral or more often completely ignored.[1] The impact of this turn still continues in the debates over the nature of various discourses, such as moral and mathematical discourses, and whether or not they should be characterised as representational (factual, truth-apt); and it continues in how questions of this sort are deemed to be at least as important as questions concerning the phenomena themselves, i.e. the practical question of which acts are morally right or wrong, or the question of the nature of numbers, sets etc. Similarly, the legacy of the linguistic turn is also apparent in what could be called the method of conceptual analysis, or of attempting to arrive at adequate definitions of concepts like knowledge rather than inquiring directly into the question of what we know (see Devitt and Sterelny 1999, 280–7).

However, prior to these more recent manifestations, the linguistic turn went through at least two distinct phases that roughly map on to Wittgenstein's philosophical development from *TLP* to *PI*. The first phase, beginning in the writings of Frege and Russell, grew out of the conviction that ordinary language is 'logically imperfect'.[2] The opposition between ordinary language and a logically perfect formal symbolism that emerged in this context is crucial to the explanation of why these figures believed that the study of language should be central to philosophy. It wasn't that they believed language was intrinsically interesting and should accordingly be examined. Rather, it was their belief that the critical study of language would enable them to solve philosophical problems that would otherwise remain unsolvable. On this view, many of the troubling philosophical problems arise because the problems and responses are stated in ordinary language; hence, the logical imperfections of ordinary language are held to perpetuate the philosophical problems and prevent us from solving them. From this comes the optimistic assertion that certain philosophical problems are solvable only by constructing and using a formal logical symbolism as an effective tool. Therefore, it was believed that the linguistic turn must be taken because it is by studying the defects of ordinary language,

---

[1] Two notable exceptions of philosophical texts that are specifically concerned with language are Plato's *Cratylus* and Book III of Locke's *An Essay Concerning Human Understanding*.

[2] The perceived logical imperfections of ordinary language included: containing words that are ambiguous; containing words that do not refer to anything; and the logical form of sentences expressed in the language often being disguised by superficial grammatical form.

and making use of a logically perfect language in its place, that we can make progress in solving these problems.

Wittgenstein's *TLP* expresses many of the convictions that characterise this first phase of the linguistic turn, and it does so in a manner that is even more optimistic than Frege and Russell because he believes at this stage that all philosophical problems can 'in essentials' be solved by the proper development and use of a formal logical symbolism (*TLP*, Preface).[3] I will return later to some of the metaphilosophical assumptions in this work. In this section, though, I will consider how Wittgenstein's later work embodies a different kind – or new phase – of the linguistic turn. In *PI* the study of language is still central to his philosophy, but the reasons are very different and much more complicated. It is no longer a matter of trying to uncover the deeper logical form of sentences in ordinary language, or of using a formal logical symbolism as a tool for drawing the distinction between sentences with and without sense. Instead, Wittgenstein stresses the need to pay much greater attention to how ordinary language is actually used.[4] The motivations behind this and the goals it is supposed to achieve are quite difficult to understand, and I will devote this section to a first attempt at articulating them.

Wittgenstein famously writes that 'Philosophy is a battle against the bewitchment of our intelligence by means of language' (*PI*, §109). And throughout much of *PI*, he expresses the view that many philosophical problems arise because of 'misunderstandings' concerning the language we use every day. In §90 he characterises his investigation as 'grammatical' and explains that it involves eliminating these misunderstandings:

Such an investigation sheds light on our problem by clearing misunderstandings away. Misunderstandings concerning the use of words, caused, among other things, by certain analogies between the forms of expression in different regions of language.

Here Wittgenstein also indicates what kind of misunderstanding is involved by identifying one of its causes, viz. in 'certain analogies' that are made between different areas of discourse. These kinds of misunderstanding arise when, for example, we compare the language we use to talk about physical objects with the language we use to talk about our mental states, on the one hand, and mathematical objects, on the other:

---

[3] The qualification 'in essentials' means that the right method for solving the philosophical problems has been provided but the task of applying it in particular instances remains to be carried out. On this, see Kuusela (2008, 99/101) and Conant (2011, 640/1).

[4] What I am calling the second phase of the linguistic turn also includes so-called ordinary language philosophers like J.L. Austin and others writing in the 1950s and 1960s because – for reasons not identical to the later Wittgenstein's – they too emphasised the centrality of the study of language to philosophy while rejecting many of the earlier assumptions concerning what was achievable using a formal logical symbolism. For example, see Austin (1957, 181/2).

One thinks that learning language consists in giving names to objects. Viz., to human beings, to shapes, to colours, to pains, to moods, to numbers, etc. (*PI*, §26)

If we assume that the forms of expression in these different areas of discourse are similar or perform similar functions, it is easy to see how apparently deep philosophical problems quickly arise. For example, compare the following three sentences:

(i)   Obama is tall.
(ii) My toothache is worse today.
(iii) Seven is prime.

Assuming that the first sentence is descriptive does not seem to raise any serious problems. Its truth requires us to accept that such-and-such a person exists and that he has a certain physical property. But if we characterise the other sentences in analogy with the first, numerous familiar philosophical problems – metaphysical and epistemological – follow, including: What kind of thing is a pain? Is it a mental entity? How is it related to physical entities like parts of the body? How do we know anything about them? What are numbers? Are they non-physical and non-mental entities? How do we know anything about them if they are abstract? Philosophers have the choice of addressing these questions directly by developing sophisticated philosophical theories, but Wittgenstein is suggesting that this is fundamentally the wrong attitude to take to them. Instead, he seems to think that it is better to look at how the problems arise in the first place, and to thereby question the assumption that philosophical theories are called for. His method can be called therapeutic because one of his goals is to show that the presumption in favour of theorising in philosophy (which still exists) is symptomatic of a deep delusion, and that philosophers do not have the appropriate self-awareness about what they are doing when they respond to a philosophical problem.

The other side of this radical view is that a better understanding of the language we use can help us to eliminate philosophical problems, or to make us 'capable of stopping doing philosophy' and 'give philosophy peace' (*PI*, §133). Exactly what, for Wittgenstein, would constitute a better understanding of the workings of our language is hard to say, but one thing that is fairly clear is that it would involve a greater appreciation of the *dissimilarities* between ways of speaking in different language-games.

A different kind of way for philosophical problems to arise can be seen by briefly considering the example of understanding again. As we have seen in Chapter 2, it is customary to speak of the understanding of a word as occurring in the mind and as being distinct from the manifestations of that understanding. For example, whereas calling this apple 'green' manifests my understanding of that word, my understanding itself is something separate from this and all other possible applications. This is innocent enough, but it leads to philosophical problems when we add that the understanding is 'a state which is the source of the correct use' (*PI*, §146) and that it must somehow 'predetermine' or 'antici-pate' what counts as a correct application of the word in a potential infinity of cases (*PI*, §188). This generates major problems because the understanding of a word comes to seem like a very strange process, and the theory we would have to adopt to account for it (such as a platonist or classical realist theory) would accordingly be strange too. An example like this is important to consider because tracing the origin of the relevant philosophical problems is not as sim-ple as in the other examples involving the analogies between different areas of discourse. In this example the process is more subtle but Wittgenstein's point is similar, viz. that the appropriate response to the problems that arise is not to respond directly with a sophisticated philosophical theory but to show that the problems are the result of a distortion or inflation of what we ordinarily tend to say about the phenomenon in question.

Broadly speaking, we could summarise the pertinent metaphilosophi-cal issues in play here by distinguishing the theoretical and anti-theoretical responses to philosophical problems; and whereas most philosophers unreflec-tively adopt the theoretical attitude, Wittgenstein adopts the anti-theoretical attitude. However, this is only the starting point for our discussion of Wittgenstein's metaphilosophy because there are a lot of contentious issues around it. The issue that will be of most concern in this chapter is whether he does enough to motivate his anti-theoretical, therapeutic attitude to philosoph-ical problems. I will try to answer this in the positive; but for reasons that will become clear, it will require me to defend the claim that Wittgenstein can con-sistently employ *arguments* – and complex arguments at that – in the course of motivating his distinctive metaphilosophical stance.

Essentially, I will argue that Wittgenstein does not merely draw attention to the supposed origin of philosophical problems in misunderstandings concern-ing language and then dogmatically adopt the anti-theoretical response. On the contrary, he devotes most of *PI* to thinking through the theoretical responses to these philosophical problems. I hold that in this context he constructs argu-ments to show that the theoretical assumptions that are adopted when dealing with the problems actually lead to absurdity. The above example of linguistic understanding is instructive because we have already seen how Wittgenstein argues at great length to show how the platonist theoretical assumptions gener-ate absurd consequences that undermine the very possibility of understanding any word. Therefore, I will argue that Wittgenstein adopts his anti-theoretical attitude in reaction to the failures of the theoretical attitude (see especially sec-tion 5.7). Before defending this claim, it is first necessary to justify my view that Wittgenstein could employ arguments in the way I have indicated without contradicting his own metaphilosophical remarks. This is the goal of the next three sections.

5.2   The Methods of the *Tractatus* and the *Philosophical Investigations*

It is worth emphasising that it is impossible to fully appreciate *PI* without also taking account of *TLP*. Indeed, Wittgenstein explicitly states in the preface to *PI* that his book 'could be seen in the right light only by contrast with and against the background of my old way of thinking'. This makes the present work, which is devoted almost exclusively to interpreting *PI*, slightly problematic. For although I have considered such 'Tractarian' topics as referentialism, as well as the more specific thesis concerning logically simple names referring to logically simple objects, I did this from the perspective of *PI* rather than *TLP*. I believe, though, that the greatest error that could be made would be to attempt to understand his later *metaphilosophical* remarks in isolation from the analogous remarks in the early work. In this section (and later in section 5.5), I will seek to avoid this particular shortcoming by considering the strong lines of continuity between the two books. Beyond noting the parallels between the goals and conceptions of philosophy in each work, I will argue that the manner in which Wittgenstein goes about attempting to achieve his goal in *TLP* contains an extremely valuable lesson for how we should interpret his strategy or methods in *PI*. Along the way, I will discuss some of the other aspects of *TLP*, including his remarks on language and expressibility; but I will not be able to treat them at the length they require.

The notion of expressibility (and hence also inexpressibility) in language is obviously a central concern of Wittgenstein's in *TLP*. This is apparent from the Preface in which he writes that his goal is to 'draw a limit to thinking, or rather – not to thinking, but to the expression of thoughts'. On the face of it, he appears to implement this project of drawing a limit to language or the expression of thoughts by developing a quite substantial account of the conditions that must be satisfied in order for linguistic expressions to be used to represent the world. For example, included in this account is the conception of propositions as pictures of possible states of affairs, and of every genuinely meaningful proposition as according with a single 'general form of proposition' (see *TLP*, 4.5).[5] Towards the end of the book, Wittgenstein states that 'The right method of philosophy' would be:

To say nothing except what can be said, i.e. the propositions of natural science, i.e. something that has nothing to do with philosophy: and then always, when someone else wished to say something metaphysical, to demonstrate to him that he had given no meaning to certain signs in his propositions. This method would be unsatisfying to the other – he would not have the feeling that we were teaching him philosophy – but it would be the only strictly correct method. (*TLP*, 6.53)

[5] All references to *TLP* are to the numbered propositions.

Although this is his view of the 'strictly correct method' of doing philosophy, it is important to understand why Wittgenstein has *not* employed this method throughout *TLP* (see Kuusela 2008, 101).

The reason is that using the correct method depends on there being a way of distinguishing sense from nonsense, or genuinely meaningful sentences from meaningless ones. Hence, when someone 'wished to say something metaphysical', it would be possible to then demonstrate that they have in fact uttered nonsense. But this distinction between sense and nonsense – or the limits of linguistic expression separating them – is precisely what is not clear and that Wittgenstein needed to clarify throughout the book. Instead of employing the correct method, he was forced to adopt a method which ultimately involved (like other philosophers) uttering nonsense, which he explicitly acknowledges at the end:

My propositions are elucidatory in this way: he who understands me finally recognises them as nonsense, when he has climbed out through them, on them, over them. (He must so to speak throw away the ladder, after he has climbed up on it.) (*TLP*, 6.54)

However, now we are presented with a familiar puzzle. If after all Wittgenstein has been uttering nonsense throughout the book – and we simply did not realise this because we did not have a clear grasp of what a genuinely meaningful proposition is – how has he managed to convey anything at all to the reader? In particular, the imagery of climbing the ladder suggests that when we reach the top we have learnt or realised something that was absent prior to climbing the ladder, viz. an appreciation of the distinction between sense and nonsense. For it is only if we grasp this distinction that we will be able to 'recognise [the sentences of the book] as nonsense'. But this recognition or understanding, and even the means by which it could have been achieved, is not something that can be expressed.

Later in the chapter, I will explore how these points directly bear on the question of the theoretical or doctrinal commitments of *TLP*. First, though, I will consider how the duality of methods in *TLP* – the prescribed 'correct' method and the actual method employed – can shed light on the question of method in *PI*.

Is there perhaps a similar duality at work in *PI*? Could it be that something like the following situation obtains in the book: on the one hand, the explicitly metaphilosophical remarks (many but not all of which are presented in §§89–133) point towards what Wittgenstein takes to be the correct or favoured philosophical method, which is one that opposes theorising, the defence of theses, the construction of arguments etc. (see especially *PI* §§109, 126, 128, and 599); but on the other hand, Wittgenstein is forced to adopt a different kind of method in certain parts of the book, especially when it comes to exposing the confusions generated by general philosophical pictures of language (referentialism, platonism) and the mind (Cartesianism)? The second kind of method could follow a similar approach to *TLP* of engaging in the kind of philosophising that Wittgenstein is seeking ultimately to oppose and whereby the confusions inherent in this more traditional or common form of doing philosophy are supposed to be exposed in the process. Hence, if this were the case, it would not be so surprising to find examples within *PI* of philosophical arguments and perhaps even the apparent defence of philosophical theses.

For the moment, let's focus on the issue of philosophical arguments and whether they are to be found in *PI*. There is at least one major Wittgenstein scholar who has hinted that arguments have the kind of ambiguous place in *PI* suggested above, viz. Anthony Kenny. In his introduction to the 2006 revised edition of his book on Wittgenstein (originally published in 1973), he first states his view 'that Wittgenstein seriously maintains that, strictly speaking, there are no arguments in philosophy, and that philosophical methods lead to no conclusions' (2006, xv). However, Kenny goes on to say:

It is not easy to reconcile Wittgenstein's philosophical practice with this description of the role of philosophy. He frequently makes statements that do not look at all like things that everyone admits, and the *Investigations* contains many passages that anyone else would call an argument. Why, then, does he say that philosophy does not make deductions or draw conclusions? (*Ibid.*)

Kenny answers this question by arguing that there is no 'room for deduction, for the drawing of conclusions from premises in accordance with logical rules' in either 'the negative, therapeutic task' of dissolving philosophical illusions or 'the more positive task of giving us an overview of the actual working of our language'. Focussing on what he calls the negative task, Kenny writes:

The negative philosophical task is the destruction of the castles in the air built by bad philosophers: the turning of latent nonsense into patent nonsense (pi, i, §464). The reason why there is no room for deduction here is that the philosopher's dogma is not a genuine proposition from which other things might follow, but only a piece of nonsense in disguise. As was said in the *Tractatus*, it is impossible to judge a piece of nonsense (5.5422): it is equally impossible to make a piece of nonsense a premise in an argument. (2006, xvi)

Here we get a clear explanation as to why Wittgenstein would have been so strongly opposed to constructing arguments in philosophy: there cannot be arguments because philosophers' statements are not genuine propositions, but nonsense, and therefore cannot function as premises or conclusions. If this is correct, it would be a mistake to even attribute negative or reductio arguments to Wittgenstein because strictly speaking the problematic philosophical assumptions could not be held to entail contradictions or paradoxes (or anything at all).

Kenny, though, states that the matter does not end there because there is more to Wittgenstein's complex attitude to philosophical arguments. He emphasises that words like 'thus', 'so', 'therefore' and 'because' that indicate the presence of a chain of reasoning or logical deduction in Wittgenstein's discussion are 'not mere ornament'. They are to be viewed as 'in accord with the demands of the therapeutic procedure'. This is how Kenny explains it:

The misguided philosopher believes that his dogma is a genuine proposition. To cure him of that illusion we have to humour him: we have to take his pseudo-proposition seriously by treating it as if it was a genuine proposition and drawing consequences from it. Of course, these consequences will themselves be pseudo-propositions and only pseudo-consequences. (*Ibid.*)

According to this reading, then, while Wittgenstein's metaphilosophical assertions in *PI* state that the correct method is to not engage in philosophical arguments, the actual method employed throughout much of the book is to 'humour' other philosophers by doing what they do and present arguments. Hence, what Wittgenstein's therapeutic procedure compels him to do is to treat the philosophers' statements as if they were genuinely meaningful, and to draw consequences from them.

It must be said that this is an extremely strange view and, despite Kenny's intentions, it makes Wittgenstein's method seem confused and untenable. The problem is not only that it links Wittgenstein's later method *too* closely with his method in *TLP*, but that it links it with a particularly implausible conception of the *TLP* method. This latter conception is what we find in so-called 'traditional' readings of *TLP* (or perhaps more accurately, caricatures of traditional readings), as opposed to the 'new' or 'resolute' readings. Some of the details of these readings will be discussed in section 5.5; all I wish to draw attention to now is that according to the traditional readings of the method used in *TLP*, Wittgenstein spends most of the book humouring philosophers (primarily Frege and Russell) in much the way that Kenny indicates, i.e. by engaging with them directly and philosophising in a way that they would recognise as proper despite the obvious stylistic differences. While we learn at the end of the book that the sentences used were actually nonsense, Wittgenstein seems to have been treating them *as if* they expressed genuine propositions, putting forward counter propositions, and drawing consequences from them.[6]

The strangeness and implausibility of this 'therapeutic' approach is most apparent in what it claims we can do with the nonsensical sentences that philosophers apparently are pathologically inclined to utter. Again unintentionally,

---

[6] An important example would be his 'fundamental thought' that logical constant terms do not stand for objects (*TLP*, 4.0312), which directly opposes the thesis that there are logical objects and that logical terms refer to them.

Kenny highlights the deep flaws inherent in it when he writes that although Wittgenstein's therapeutic procedure involves drawing 'pseudo-consequences' from 'pseudo-propositions', the procedure nevertheless

must obey the laws of logic. What 'follows from' the pseudo-proposition must be *what would really follow from it if it were a genuine proposition*. To the non-Wittgensteinian philosopher – and in particular to the philosopher whose intellectual malaise is being treated – it does indeed appear to be an argument. Even if one accepts Wittgenstein's own account of his therapeutic method, it need not be misleading to speak, for example, of 'the private language argument'. (*Ibid.*; emphasis added.)

Not only does Kenny attribute to the later Wittgenstein the view that we can get a grip on the notion of what would be expressed by a nonsensical sentence if it had sense – a view usually associated with traditional readings of the early Wittgenstein; he also adds that we can get a grip on the notion of what *must* follow from these nonsensical sentences if they had sense. While there may be some textual basis for holding that Wittgenstein misguidedly operated with these notions in *TLP*, it is mistaken to suppose that he made the very same errors in his later writings.[7]

What I think is worth preserving from Kenny's reading of Wittgenstein's later metaphilosophy is the acknowledgement that arguments have a peculiar or ambiguous place within *PI*. I also agree that this ambiguity stems ultimately from Wittgenstein proclaiming a methodological preference for doing away with arguments, on the one hand, and presenting numerous arguments of his own, on the other. What I wish to challenge most strongly is the view of what the arguments are doing there in Wittgenstein's discussion. Their place in the book may be *analogous* to the place of arguments in *TLP*, but as we will see the many other features that serve to distinguish the two books make all the difference to the later employment of arguments and render his later practice more plausible.

5.3   Are Philosophical Statements Nonsense?

The major wrong turn in Kenny's reading of the metaphilosophical remarks in *PI* is to assert that Wittgenstein believed that the sentences uttered by philosophers are 'nonsense'. It is from this vital part of his reading that the others stem, most notably that the arguments containing philosophical statements as premises or conclusions are not *genuine* arguments. To reiterate, I accept that Wittgenstein may have held a view like this in *TLP*, but I will devote this section to arguing for the contrary view that in *PI* at least Wittgenstein did not hold

---

[7] Once again, Kenny himself does not view them as errors. On the contrary, in the opening pages of his 2006 introduction he stresses his belief in the strength of Wittgenstein's philosophy and regrets that it has waned in influence since the publication of the first edition of the book.

that philosophical sentences are nonsense. This will naturally open the way to a defence of my view that there are genuine philosophical arguments in *PI*, or, to put it another way, there are genuine consequences shown to follow from genuine philosophical statements.

This much can be demonstrated while acknowledging that, for Wittgenstein, philosophers tend to misuse language in characteristic ways. He does sometimes use the word 'nonsense' to characterise what philosophers say or try to say:

> The results of philosophy are the uncovering of one or another piece of plain nonsense and of bumps that the understanding has got by running its head up against the limits of language. These bumps make us see the value of the discovery. (*PI*, §119; see also §464)

But what does Wittgenstein mean here by 'nonsense'? From the analysis of Kenny's reading, we can make a distinction between two kinds of nonsense: firstly, gibberish on a par with 'All mimsy were the borogoves, and the mome raths outgrabe'; and secondly, the kind of nonsense that Kenny holds is uttered by philosophers, which is distinct from gibberish because it is supposed to be possible to make sense of what the sentences would say or entail *if* they were not nonsense. Neither of these really fit with Wittgenstein's discussion. He does not seem to hold that philosophical sentences are literally gibberish and I think we should at least try to be charitable by not attributing to him the view that the sentences are nonsense of the second, highly problematic kind.

What, then, does he mean by calling the results of philosophy 'plain nonsense' if not either of the above notions? We can answer this by reflecting on other significant ways of misusing words that might also be called uttering nonsense. An example will help to bring this out. Imagine that a child is learning to speak and in a particular situation her father is trying to get her to understand the word 'thirsty'. The father might say things like 'Are you thirsty?' while offering her a cup of water, or saying 'You were thirsty' after she has drunk a lot. The child might then utter similar sentences in similar situations, thus using 'thirsty' correctly. Imagine also that new situations arise, such as when the child observes her father watering a house-plant and she says, 'The plant is thirsty'. In yet another situation, upon witnessing her father pouring water into a funnel in the car engine, the child could also say 'The car is thirsty'.

This final sentence clearly involves a misuse of the word 'thirsty'. We could even say that the sentence is nonsense. It is not, however, gibberish. The word 'thirsty' in this context bears more than a mere visual similarity to its occurrences in the meaningful sentences. It is perhaps better to say that it is *absurd*. The absurdity results from applying the word in a context in which it is not suited; or more precisely, it arises as a result of a mistaken generalisation or assumption that pouring water into something can only have one function, i.e. to quench thirst.

Similarly, philosophical statements and questions are not gibberish. But while in some cases they may be called absurd in roughly the above sense, this cannot be extended to all cases because there is no single sense in which philosophers misuse language. The following examples that have been already discussed involve different ways of misusing particular words:

(i)   Is this object composite?
(ii) Where are pains located?
(iii) The understanding of a word is a mental state which is the source of the correct use of the word.

In the first case, the lack of sense is due to not specifying the sense of the word 'composite' (for example, does it mean 'composed of pieces of wood', 'multi-coloured', or something else?).[8] In the second, it involves being misled by an analogy between discourse about mental phenomena and discourse about physical phenomena. And in the third sentence, the misuse occurs in drawing mistaken conclusions from the observation that the understanding of a word is distinct from its particular applications. However, while the specific kind of misuse of language may be different in each case, I think it is plain to see that none of these questions or sentences are gibberish. For example, there is a definite connection between the statements, 'This chair is composite' and 'This chair is made of pieces of wood'. The first statement, which can be viewed as philosophical, is related to the second in a way that a piece of gibberish could not be.

Philosophical sentences like 'The meaning of a word is the object for which it stands', 'A name ought really to signify a simple object', and 'No-one can know what I mean by the word "pain"', are not gibberish either. Despite the misuse of certain words in these sentences there is nothing to forbid us from employing them as genuine premises in arguments, just as there is nothing to forbid us from employing sentences such as 'The car is thirsty' in an argument. In this regard, there is also an important difference between these sentences and the obscure kind of nonsense indicated in Kenny's reading.

However, it should be noted that the absurdity of a statement or the misuse of a word can be more or less apparent (see *PI*, §464). While the mistake in uttering 'The car is thirsty' is obvious, the misuse of words in a sentence like 'No-one can know what I mean by the word "pain"' can be harder to discern. Likewise, it is certainly not immediately obvious that there is anything wrong with the sentence, 'The understanding of a word is a mental state which is the source of the correct use of the word'. This is where Wittgenstein's therapeutic methods

[8] See Chapter 1, section 1.4 and *PI*, §§47–48.

are required most of all. In cases such as these, it is necessary to construct an argument to demonstrate that the philosophical statement in question does in fact lead to absurdity.

Some scholars will disagree with my claim that the later Wittgenstein held philosophical statements to be meaningful, possibly for reasons similar to Kenny's that see a continuity between the early and later work concerning the status of philosophical statements. To clarify, though, I am not suggesting that when philosophers make statements they are successful in saying what they think they are saying. For instance, Oskari Kuusela notes that when a philosopher states that 'I cannot feel another person's pain' he may take himself to be saying something about pains, or more precisely about the nature or essence of pains. But, for Wittgenstein, such statements are better viewed as indicating the philosopher's adherence to a particular rule for the use of the word 'pain' – a rule that forbids us to say that I can feel someone else's pain. The philosophical statement is thus 'not a statement about anything but expresses commitment to a form of expression and thought, a rule of language' (see Kuusela 2008, 103/4). Not all philosophical statements are disguised expressions of rules for the use of words. But the general point is that the statements are not meaningless, even though more often than not philosophers may be mistaken about what they are saying with them.

I will continue this discussion in the next section by considering Baker's later writings on Wittgenstein's *PI*. Among the claims he defends is that Wittgenstein did not present arguments in *PI*, but he holds this for reasons different to Kenny's and more in line with the 'New Wittgensteinians'. Hence, while Baker accepts that Wittgenstein felt the need to employ various methods to highlight the absurdity of certain philosophical pictures and statements, he rejects the view that the construction of arguments was one of these methods.

5.4 The Role of Arguments in the *Philosophical Investigations*: Baker's Later Reading

Baker's later articles on Wittgenstein were published posthumously in the 2004 collection titled, *Wittgenstein's Method: Neglected Aspects*. As the subtitle indicates, he came to see errors and shortcomings in how *PI* had been traditionally interpreted (including in the first two volumes of the *Analytic Commentary* on *PI* that he co-authored with Peter Hacker). Baker's response in his later writings is to 'try to make visible an aspect which escapes everyone' when they read the metaphilosophical remarks, the discussion of private language, and other parts of the book (2004, 121). He wishes to get us to see that Wittgenstein's primary concern is 'to teach us how to get rid of grammatical illusions which create obstacles for us' and 'to make us sensitive to the pictures and prejudices in the grammar of our language which impede a clear view' (2004, 118). Baker's claim that philosophical pictures stand in the way of 'a clear view of the use of our words' (see *PI*, §122) is not unique and is supported by passages such as §5, where the Augustinian picture is described as 'surround[ing] the working of language with a haze which makes clear vision impossible' (see also *The Blue and Brown Books (BB)*, 17). Making this connection also helps explain why Baker would call them grammatical illusions. For while 'we have constructed [the pictures] in order to orient ourselves' in the study of, for example, language or the mind (2004, 115), they end up preventing us from getting a clear view of the use of our words.[9]

The example that Baker devotes the most attention to is 'the *picture* of the mind as a "secret realm"' which has a 'subtle but catastrophic influence' on the attempt to 'clarify the use of words like "think", "understand", "have toothache", "be afraid", etc.'; and he views the goal of the co-called private language argument to be to 'unveil' the negative impact of that picture or grammatical illusion (*Ibid.*). In a later paper in the collection, Baker stresses the close connection between this picture and the general Augustinian picture, stating that the grammatical illusion concerning the mind 'elaborates' the Augustinian picture 'in respect of the meaning of "pain"' (2004, 132).

It is, though, an essential feature of his reading that Wittgenstein does not (and does not need to) construct *arguments* to demonstrate that these philosophical pictures are flawed. Instead, according to Baker, Wittgenstein develops a multitude of diverse methods to get us to adopt a different perspective on those pictures in the hope that we will see the pictures for what they are, viz. distortions or barriers to reflecting on how language is actually used. What Wittgenstein does could be characterised under the heading of 'describing grammar' provided, Baker insists, we recognise that this is 'given a rather extended and varied sense in order to articulate his practice' (2004, 123). As Baker presents it, Wittgenstein's practice of describing grammar includes describing the use of words like 'red' and 'thinking', describing 'possibilities without claiming to note grammatical facts (§§142, 244, 312; cf. *BB*, 49, 53)', discussing and analysing 'language-games which are completely imaginary (§§2, 5, 258)' and language-games 'which are simpler than those which we ordinarily play' (§§3, 5–7, 19; *BB*, 17, 172–3). Furthermore, the description of grammar can take 'the form of an analogy or metaphor' because he uses objects of comparison and 'describes something else' in relation to it (for example, 'the standard metre *as* a tool of language', and 'arithmetical equations *as* rules of grammar'). 'By means of well-chosen analogies,' Baker writes, Wittgenstein 'tries to show aspects of the use of signs to which we are insensitive, although they are obvious because they are in plain view' (2004, 123).

---

[9] On the notion of 'perspicuous representation' and the goal of achieving 'a clear view of the use of our words' discussed in §122, see section 6.4 of the next chapter.

This positive characterisation of Wittgenstein's methods is coupled with a sustained criticism of the supposition that there are intricate arguments in *PI*. This is an intriguing position for him to take given that, in his collaborations with Hacker in the 1980s, he did more than most Wittgenstein scholars to clearly formulate the highly complex chains of reasoning apparently running through *PI*. Taking the example of the private language argument again, he attempts to show the mistake in the common tendency to interpret it as a *reductio* argument of the Cartesian conception of the mind, or more precisely of the 'hypothesis' that 'each word which signifies something inner (e.g., "pain", "anger", "toothache", "thinking", "imagining") is to be explained by virtue of being associated with something mental (e.g., with a particular sensation or an incorporeal process)' (2004, 119). Baker's reasons for opposing this reading are summed up as follows:

The idea that the PLA is a *reductio* leads to serious difficulties. Undoubtedly it stands in need of supplementary premises in order to effect the *reductio*. Consequently, the proof leaves hostages to fortune; the force of the proof could be annulled through doubting any one of the hidden premises ... How could we *demonstrate* that every ostensive definition must make use of a sample? And why *must* a solipsist agree that the understanding of any word whatever requires public criteria? The *reductio* totters unless each of its supplementary premises is unassailable. It seems that it collapses unless we take the text of the *Investigations* as a collection of grammatical facts, destined to erect complex buildings on the solid ground of what has been established before. If the text were not cumulative, the alleged *reductio* would be extremely feeble. (2004, 126–7)[10]

His criticism amounts to the claim that if the private language argument is a reductio, Wittgenstein must have relied on 'supplementary premises' to establish his negative conclusion. And if we are to view the reductio as compelling, it must be the case that Wittgenstein has provided support for these premises elsewhere in *PI*. Therefore, the traditional interpretation forces us to read the book as 'cumulative', or as building up substantial philosophical theses or principles throughout it that are then employed as major premises in the private language argument. This, of course, directly contradicts Wittgenstein's opposition to presenting theses and arguments.

It looks as though the reading of the private language argument that I defended in the previous chapter commits all of the errors that Baker thinks are detrimental to the understanding of Wittgenstein's discussion of private language. Not only have I presented the argument as a rather long series of steps or premises building up to the conclusion that a private language is impossible; my reconstruction is more intricate than most in the sense that I interpret it as

---

[10] See also where Baker writes: 'Unless [Wittgenstein] distorted the truth in describing his own practice, he *could not* have intended to construct a complicated argument, nor to deduce any general proposition, even a negative one. There is no place here for the traditional activities of philosophers' (2004, 124).

relying on other quite complicated arguments earlier in *PI* (specifically, in the discussion of rule-following and meaning in §§138–201). Can Baker's objections be answered?

I have already defended my rationale for attributing arguments to Wittgenstein in the previous few sections by maintaining that he is mimicking or (to use Kenny's word) 'humouring' traditional philosophers in constructing arguments of his own, and that he engages in this strategy in a problematic way in *TLP* and a more plausible way in *PI*. But what about the objection that we are forced to view *PI* as 'cumulative' in the sense specified by Baker? Can this be dismissed in the same way by claiming that Wittgenstein is doing what philosophers traditionally do but for a different purpose to theirs? To a certain extent it can but it is also worth noting that Wittgenstein's private language argument does not rely on substantial premises in quite the way Baker claims it does. For example, he asks in the above passage: 'why *must* a solipsist agree that the understanding of any word whatever requires public criteria?' I agree with Baker that the solipsist, or whoever the defender of private language is, does not have to accept this and that Wittgenstein's argument must proceed without this premise because otherwise he would be simply begging the question. Similarly, for the 'premise' concerning ostensive definition; Wittgenstein does not have to rely on the premise that 'every ostensive definition must make use of a sample'. Instead, each example of ostensive definition can be considered on its own merits. But if no example – particularly in the private diary case – of an ostensive definition that does not need to make use of a sample is forthcoming, it is reasonable to ask about what the sample would be in this example and how it would function. Finally, it is a peculiar feature of my reading that the private diarist is depicted as requiring the thesis that meaning is normative. Again, it is overly simplistic to hold that Wittgenstein relies on the opposite thesis that meaning is not normative. It is rather the case that he has a separate powerful argument (presented in §§138–201) that can be used to challenge any particular claim that the meaning attached to a certain term – for example, 'S' in the private diary case – predetermines what is to count as a correct or incorrect application of the term in every instance. Therefore, Wittgenstein's practice of presenting arguments in a way that mimics more traditional philosophers does not have to be cumulative in the manner described and criticised by Baker.

There are a few other significant components of Baker's reading that I will briefly consider before concluding. For instance, he argues that the interpretation of the private language argument as a reductio ends up distorting or simplifying the identity of Wittgenstein's interlocutor. It leads us to think of all of Wittgenstein's remarks on private language as directed against a single 'adversary' or 'spokesman for Cartesian dualism', who is 'the cunning philosopher who supports the possibility of a private language' (2004, 127). Instead, Baker encourages us to think of Wittgenstein's interlocutor as changing depending on the context, and as varying from the sophisticated philosopher (like Russell or Ramsey) to the students he lectured to at Cambridge. This, I believe, is a strength of Baker's reading and I do not wish to object to it. Despite what Baker claims, I think the reductio reading is actually consistent with his view of the shifting identity of the interlocutor. The argument against private language can be just as I have argued it is, and the point will remain that anyone who is tempted by the picture of a word possessing a private meaning will face the challenge set out in the argument. It is likely that there are other interlocutors that Wittgenstein is addressing within the discussion of §§243–315 that I have not considered, but that does not affect the interpretation of the one rather complex argument I have discussed (centred on §258).

Baker makes the additional claim that in many of the cases where an argument is supposedly presented in *PI*, it is not actually needed. For example, he states that:

The very idea of a private language is evidently absurd, quite apart from considerations of private ostensive definitions, the inability of mental images to function as samples, the category difference between inner objects and physical objects, etc. (2004, 125)

I would suggest, though, that this absurdity is not as obvious as Baker states it is. He might be maintaining that Wittgenstein's other methods are sufficient to highlight the absurdity, and that this is what makes the use of arguments unnecessary. But if we take another of Wittgenstein's examples, we can see that this is mistaken. In Chapter 1 (section 1.2), I distinguished the different steps in his attack on the Augustinian or referential picture of language. Some of the steps correspond to what Baker would characterise as the different methods that Wittgenstein employs, such as constructing an imaginary language-game (i.e. the builders' language-game) to show that the Augustinian picture may have limited applicability at best, or listing the functions of words other than that of naming objects, or giving examples of words that are meaningful but do not stand for anything etc. But, as I argued in that chapter, these particular steps or methods are relatively weak in the sense that they are not likely to sway a philosopher committed to referentialism as a theory of linguistic meaning. As the responses of Frege, Russell and other philosophers to similar problems show, it is possible to develop quite radical proposals to deal with these kinds of objections; this is illustrated most of all in their respective attempts to accommodate non-referring terms (see section 1.5). The further steps in Wittgenstein's attack are more troubling to the referentialist, and these are the ones that involve the presentation of arguments (including the argument that the referentialist must make use of the problematic notion of 'absolute simplicity'). In this example, at least, it is the arguments that matter the most when it comes to shaking the commitment to a particular philosophical picture. To put it another way, it is only when Wittgenstein adopts the practice of presenting arguments that there is the genuine potential for more traditional philosophers to appreciate the force of his objections.

The discussion in this section provides reasons for qualifying the rather simplistic distinction I made in section 5.2 between Wittgenstein's views on the correct philosophical method, on the one hand, and the actual method he employs in *PI*, on the other. It is important to acknowledge that there is a multitude of methods employed in *PI*, only some of which could be described as mimicking the practice of other philosophers. However, I would emphasise again that from the point of view of his critical dialogue with other real or imagined philosophers, his most important method is that of mimicking them by constructing arguments of his own.

5.5   The Doctrinal Commitments of the *Tractatus*

Even if it is true that an integral part of Wittgenstein's therapeutic method in *PI* was to present arguments and take particular philosophical theses seriously, there is the separate question concerning whether or not he nonetheless ended up committing himself to certain philosophical doctrines or theses. The reading I have been pushing has so far suggested that Wittgenstein engaged in these fairly traditional philosophical activities for purely therapeutic purposes. And this implies that he ultimately distanced himself from any of the doctrines under consideration, i.e. that none of his arguments should be interpreted as simply a matter of him arguing for a particular philosophical position. The contexts of his arguments are more complicated than that, and we should view Wittgenstein himself as always at one remove from what may be established or appeared to be established in the course of the arguments.

This is where the reading is heading. But it would be a mistake to assume that the act of distancing himself from his therapeutic practices is unproblematic. On the contrary, it may turn out that despite his explicit intention to not defend any theory of his own, he ends up committing himself to some rather substantial and controversial theoretical claims. This is a basic lesson we must learn from *TLP*. It is this exact unforeseen consequence of his method that undermines his early work. My approach in this section will be to consider how this failure in his method plays out in *TLP* and I will go on in the next section to address whether in *PI* Wittgenstein genuinely improved upon his earlier method in this regard.

The issue of Wittgenstein's doctrinal commitments – specifically, the commitment to *inexpressible truths* concerning the nature of language and reality – is what separates 'traditional' and 'new' or 'resolute' readings of *TLP*. The difference between these types of readings is best characterised in terms of their opposing views of the ladder imagery in 6.54. Both the traditional and resolute readers view the sentences of *TLP* as the rungs of the ladder, and may also hold that when we reach the top (when we reach the end of the book) we somehow acquire an appreciation of the difference between sense and nonsense. But they have diverging views of exactly what is involved in 'throwing away the ladder' after we have climbed up it. Whereas the traditional readings tend to hold that it is merely the nonsensical sentences of the book that are abandoned, the distinction between sense and nonsense is based on the account of language put forward by Wittgenstein, and so these theoretical commitments are retained in some sense.

However, the resolute readings take a more radical line and strive to take 6.54 more seriously by abandoning not only the sentences of the book, but also the absurd notion that these sentences could have allowed us to grasp a particular account of language or the limits of linguistic expression. Hence, according to resolute readers, we are not only throwing away the sentences of the book but also all of the theoretical commitments concerning language that we may have taken ourselves to have been entertaining while reading it. Included in these theoretical commitments is the distinction between saying and showing; and therefore by abandoning this, resolute readings are also rejecting the notion that there are certain truths (for example, concerning the nature or limits of language) that can be shown but not said or expressed. Traditional readings, by contrast, seem to hold on to this and maintain that Wittgenstein is committed to such inexpressible truths.

In their (2004) article, James Conant and Cora Diamond, who are the two most prominent representatives of the resolute reading, argue that there is no *genuine* doctrine of sense/nonsense put forward in *TLP* (i.e. no genuine doctrine or theory that survives in some sense when we throw away the ladder and which is the basis on which the ladder is thrown away). Rather, they argue that if we properly follow through with throwing away the ladder, while at the same time maintaining that the sentences of *TLP* are actually nonsense, then we must acknowledge that nonsense is identified through an informal or *non-doctrinal* method of attempting-but-failing to clarify a given sentence (Conant and Diamond 2004, 63).

Although Conant and Diamond do, unlike Wittgenstein, make some attempt to outline this method of identifying nonsense, their story about what is going on in *TLP* is seen in a much different light when it comes to assessing the book in the context of Wittgenstein's overall philosophical development.[11] This shift in their account stems from a certain tension in resolute readings. These readings consciously set out to be as sympathetic as possible to the author of *TLP* and to not, if possible, attribute plainly untenable views to him (for example, concerning inexpressible truths). But when it comes to

[11] See the final section of Conant and Diamond (2004).

assessing the book in the context of his later development they must identify some deficiencies in that early work. It is not important in the present context to go into the details of how they interpret the relation of the early and later work, but it is significant how their interpretations of *TLP* come to stand with regard to this issue of the presence or absence of a theory of sense/nonsense in that work. Despite the fact that throughout most of their writings Conant and Diamond emphasise that Wittgenstein did not *intend* to put forward any theory of meaning in *TLP* but instead advocated a non-doctrinal method of exposing philosophical nonsense, when considering the deficiencies in the book in the context of his later development they state that Wittgenstein actually or unwittingly held on to the following 'metaphysical commitments' (along with a number of others):

Through the employment of a [logically absolutely perspicuous] notation, it is possible for propositions to be rewritten in such a way that the logical relations are *all* clearly visible.

By rewriting them in such a notation, *what* propositions our propositions are will become clear.

Through our inability to translate them *into the notation*, despite their resemblance in outward form to genuine propositions, certain strings of signs can be unmasked as nonsense (i.e. as strings in which signs to which no determinate meaning has been given occur).

All philosophical confusions can be clarified in this way.

By demonstrating the significance of this tool and its application in the activity of clarification, the problems of philosophy have *in essentials* been finally solved. (2004, 82–3)[12]

Conant and Diamond thus hold that, on the final assessment of *TLP*, Wittgenstein was in fact committed to a substantial doctrine about what constitutes sense and nonsense, a doctrine in terms of translatability of sentences into a specific truth-functional notation based on the conception of a meaningful proposition as either an elementary proposition or a truth-functional construction from elementary propositions (see also Conant 2006, 174–5 and 2011, 643). Furthermore, Wittgenstein's early conception of the activity of philosophical elucidation was fundamentally shaped by this doctrine; it was not, after all, a non-doctrinal method.

This aspect of Conant and Diamond's resolute interpretation, then, reduces to the claim that the early Wittgenstein intended to abandon all assumptions about what constitutes sense and nonsense and to advocate a purely non-doctrinal method of identifying instances of nonsense (including, especially, philosophical nonsense); but that he ended up unwittingly holding on to a great number of assumptions and thus he did not carry through with his own intended project

---

[12] On the unwitting metaphysical commitments of *TLP*, see also Kuusela (2008, 99–102).

properly.[13] This is where resolute readers see continuity with the later work – viz. the continuity of philosophical purpose and of developing a philosophical method of elucidation as opposed to a specific doctrine of meaning – and where they see the later work as achieving this goal more successfully.

Keeping in mind these apparent basic errors of *TLP*, I will now consider whether the rather complicated strategy employed in *PI* really did allow Wittgenstein to be more successful in avoiding theoretical commitments.

5.6   The Problem of Doctrinal Commitments in the *Philosophical Investigations*: Wittgenstein as a Transcendental Idealist

One obvious way of approaching the question of whether Wittgenstein in *PI* unintentionally committed himself to certain doctrines or theses is to consider whether his emphasis on language use and the practical dimension of language from the beginning of *PI* amounts to a theoretical commitment. Another would be to reflect on the possibility that he was committed to a community view of language, as can seem to be the case in light of his argument against the possibility of private language. However, these particular issues will be addressed later (the use-based theory in Chapter 6 and the possible commitment to a community view in the next section).

For now, I will adopt the different approach of considering Wittgenstein's possible unwitting commitment to the metaphysical doctrine of *transcendental idealism*. This will be seen to be a worthwhile example because it has been argued by a number of influential scholars that this doctrine is what ultimately emerges from Wittgenstein's later picture of language. I will devote the rest of this section to exploring this issue. Doing so will require a short detour from the main discussion of Wittgenstein's metaphilosophy running through this chapter, although it will hopefully provide a vivid illustration of how theoretical commitments can be held to be present in *PI* or entailed by the remarks on language contained in it.

Stephen Mulhall notes that the transcendental idealist reading of the later Wittgenstein is at least as old as Stanley Cavell's 1962 review of David Pole's reading, where Cavell makes a connection between central ideas in the later Wittgenstein and Kant's transcendental philosophy (see Mulhall 2009, 386).[14] One of the first sustained treatments of this topic is in Hacker's (1972). But it is Bernard Williams' 1974 paper, 'Wittgenstein and Idealism', that has been most influential in proposing a transcendental idealist interpretation of the later Wittgenstein. Most of the papers on this topic since then (for example, Lear's

---

[13] When viewed in this way, the distance between traditional and resolute readings of *TLP* does not appear so great. Representatives of both readings hold that Wittgenstein was committed to the doctrines in question and they merely differ over how he became committed to them.

[14] This is not to say that Cavell defended a transcendental idealist reading, only that he alluded to a connection between Kant and Wittgenstein that might lead to such a reading.

(1984) and Moore's (1985)) have been direct responses to Williams. I will narrow my focus to Williams' interpretation and A.W. Moore's (2007), which is sympathetic to Williams while resisting a transcendental idealist reading.

Williams ends (1974)[15] by making the following claim regarding Wittgenstein's later philosophy (note also the affinity with traditional readings in how it attributes a theory of meaning to him):

> The new theory of meaning, like the old, points in the direction of a transcendental idealism, and shares also the problem of our being driven to state it in forms which are required to be understood, if at all, in the wrong way. (1974, 163)

This idea, he writes, echoes Wittgenstein's claim in *TLP* that 'what the solipsist *means* is quite correct; only it cannot be *said* but makes itself manifest' (*TLP*, 5.62). Regardless of the question of how to interpret this early remark, it is Williams' contention that in both the early and later periods Wittgenstein grapples with some version of the problem of 'how to put a supposed philosophical truth which, if it is uttered, must be taken to mean an empirical falsehood, or worse' (1974, 163). When Williams gives a concrete example of such a problematic philosophical truth, he mentions the radical conventionalist notion that decision is involved calculating:

> For of course, if our talk about the numbers has been determined by our decisions, then one result of our decisions is that it must be nonsense to say that anything about a number has been determined by our decisions. The dependence of mathematics on our decisions, in the only sense in which it obtains – for clearly there cannot be meant an empirical dependence on historical decisions – is something which shows itself in what we are and are not prepared to regard as sense and is not to be stated in remarks about decisions; and similarly in other cases. (1974, 163)

This connects with transcendental idealism (and the problem of stating it without uttering a falsehood or nonsense) by the fact that the necessity, for example, of mathematics is conceived to be dependent on 'us' in some sense. In Kant, the reference to 'us' is to our forms of intuition, but Williams clearly has in mind a wider notion of transcendental idealism in which the contingent features of 'our' nature can be formulated in other ways than this. For instance, necessity could be conceived to be dependent on the contingent features of our shared nature or form of life, thus resulting in what Williams calls a 'pluralised idealism' or 'a transcendental idealism of the first-person plural' (1974, 161). This is what he believes we find in the later Wittgenstein, but which cannot be expressed without facing the difficulties mentioned above.

Admittedly, this notion of a transcendental idealist reading is still quite vague. But it helps to note that the issue of how to interpret Wittgenstein's

---

[15] All references to Williams' article will be to the page numbers of the reprinted version in his (1981).

emphasis on our shared form of life is at the centre of this kind of reading. Both Williams and Moore state that Wittgenstein holds that 'philosophy can never be completely *detached*' (Moore 2007, 190), and that the proper philosophical method is to make the 'outlook' or perspective that is shaped by our form of life 'clearer to ourselves, by reflecting on it, as it were self-consciously exercising it' and 'moving around reflectively inside our view of things' (Williams 1974, 153).[16] The goal is thus to 'become conscious of, in so reflecting,... something like: *how we go on*' (*Ibid.*).

However, the commitment to transcendental idealism does not follow immediately from reflecting on our shared outlook or form of life, but on how this outlook relates to 'reality' beyond that outlook. As Moore explains, transcendental idealism seems to inevitably follow when we try to acknowledge the contingency of our standpoint in the widest possible sense (so that it is not the kind of contingency involved in, for example, being speakers of the English language) (2007, 193). It follows because we acknowledge the contingency of our standpoint and the possibility of alternatives in an analogous way to how Kant considers the abstract possibility of beings with different forms of intuition to our own or none at all. In short, by holding that our standpoint is contingent in this way, we end up being committed to a distinction between what is understandable within this perspective, on the one hand, and what is not understandable within this perspective but would be accessible from an external or God's-eye perspective (or a perspective without these limitations), on the other.

As Williams points out, evaluating the question of Wittgenstein's commitment to transcendental idealism is problematic because he would surely object to the label. However, this does not settle the issue because the deeper question is whether he committed himself to it unknowingly; or, less plausibly, whether he embraced it while, as Williams states, recognising that expressing his commitment would result in uttering either an obvious falsehood or nonsense. This is what makes the assessment of the later Wittgenstein's doctrinal commitments such an extremely complicated matter.

Williams and Moore quite rightly state that Wittgenstein's conception of correct philosophical method is one in which our goal should be to reflect on our shared perspective or outlook, and to put this outlook itself 'in focus' (Moore 2007, 191) and become conscious of 'how we go on'. It is from this

---

[16] Moore speaks in a similar way to Barry Stroud (1965) of 'various facts of nature, including facts of human nature' that underlie our outlooks, which had they 'been different from how they are, then all sorts of behaviour might have constituted carrying on in the same way' (Moore 2007, 189). See also where he writes: 'The contingencies of language use include all such facts. In particular, and centrally, they include our shared sensibilities, our shared senses of the natural and the salient: our shared outlooks. Without these, communication would break down.' (*Ibid.*)

relatively neutral territory that the doctrinal commitment seems to emerge. When we follow Wittgenstein and reflect on and describe our practices of taking certain propositions to be necessary and certain applications of a rule to be correct, we are led to inquire further into exactly what it is we become aware of. That is, in becoming conscious of our outlook and of how we go on, what are we really conscious of? Are we merely conscious of what seems to us to be necessary or the correct way of applying a rule, and is this distinct from what really is necessary and what is the correct way of applying the rule? The transcendental idealist reading appears to be maintaining that Wittgenstein is forced into recognising such a distinction, as well as accepting that we can never know what in reality the correct way to go on is.

My view is that the later Wittgenstein is not in fact committed to transcendental idealism because he is not compelled to take a stand on this further philosophical question concerning the relation between our shared outlook and what is really the case beyond this outlook; or more importantly, he is not forced to accept that it is an intelligible distinction. Moore indicates this attitude to the reading by stating how Wittgenstein resists the transcendental idealist doctrine:

So – how can Wittgenstein resist such transcendental idealism? By disallowing the questions that led to it ... Somehow we have to see these questions themselves as pseudo-questions, symptoms of an illness awaiting Wittgensteinian therapy. (2007, 194)

According to Moore, then, Wittgenstein avoids this doctrinal commitment by 'disallowing the questions' that lead to it, specifically those concerning whether 'how we go on' is in reality the correct way to go on, and whether what we take to be necessary is really necessary etc.

This strategy may appear to some to be implausible or unmotivated. It can seem as though Wittgenstein would be taking the easy way out by rejecting the philosophical questions rather than doing the hard work of taking them seriously and deciding what the best account is. We are encountering here the bigger question of Wittgenstein's motivation for adopting a quietist standpoint in his later philosophy, or for rejecting the approach of proposing philosophical theses and explanations. Moore's claim is broadly along the right lines, but it needs to be bolstered by an account of how and why Wittgenstein takes this anti-theoretical route. In the next section, I will try to provide such an account and to thus critically assess whether Wittgenstein really is capable of side-stepping the seemingly unavoidable theoretical commitments in *PI*.

5.7   Grounds for Wittgenstein's Anti-Theoretical Attitude

I stated at the beginning of this book that the most striking feature of Wittgenstein's metaphilosophy is his opposition to theorising in philosophy, or to proposing and defending particular theoretical philosophical claims. This is rightly viewed by the majority of Wittgenstein scholars as the central aspect of his distinctive conception of philosophy. Commentators like Baker have understandably used this recognition to help interpret the other aspects of his metaphilosophy, such as his attitude to the use of arguments in philosophy. Wittgenstein must have been opposed to employing arguments in philosophy because – so that reading goes – arguments employ theoretical claims as premises and lead to theoretical claims as conclusions; and hence presenting arguments is intrinsically bound up with theorising. It has thus seemed to many that Wittgenstein's clear opposition to theorising gives us an equally clear rationale for his opposition to constructing philosophical arguments. I have tried to show that this is mistaken because there are uses that can be made of arguments other than the rather straightforward one of defending particular philosophical theses. Most notably, arguments can be used to show how certain general assumptions about linguistic meaning lead to absurdity.

But what about the deeper issue of Wittgenstein's opposition to theorising in philosophy, i.e. aside from how it impacts on his attitude to arguments? Since this is such a radical view (at least when compared with other philosophers' views of their discipline), we should stop and ask why he is so opposed to it. Despite its obvious importance, though, it is remarkably difficult to give a satisfactory response to it. As Baker states, Wittgenstein in *PI* is often more concerned with describing his own methods rather than with presenting us with a compelling case for why these methods are the correct ones and for why the more traditional methods that involve theorising are incorrect (2004, 121–2). This may be true of Wittgenstein's remarks on philosophy and method. However, I want to suggest that he does provide a rather strong case for what is wrong with philosophical theorising in his other remarks, specifically when reflecting on the general pictures of language and the mind that he sees as problematic.

Among the only occasions in which Wittgenstein comes close to directly giving reasons for his anti-theoretical attitude is when he contrasts philosophy with the natural sciences, and states that a great deal of confusion in philosophy results from philosophy trying to imitate the sciences in their methods and the kind of results they attempt to arrive at. This is expressed most clearly in the *Blue Book*, where he states:

Philosophers constantly see the method of science before their eyes, and are irresistibly tempted to ask and answer questions in the way science does. This tendency is the real source of metaphysics, and leads the philosopher into complete darkness. I want to say here that it can never be our job to reduce anything to anything, or to explain anything. Philosophy really *is* 'purely descriptive'. (*BB*, 18)

It is illuminating to consider a remark such as this that pre-dates the composition of *PI* because it is a reminder that a constant throughout Wittgenstein's philosophical development is the insistence on the distinction between philosophy and the natural sciences. It is present in his early period as well as the middle and later period writings (see *TLP*, 6.53). The above passage states that philosophers are led 'into complete darkness' when they are 'irresistibly tempted to ask and answer questions in the way science does'. And Wittgenstein uses this point to highlight the distinction between the theoretical and explanatory method appropriate to the sciences, on the one hand, and the anti-theoretical and descriptive method appropriate to philosophy, on the other.

But these general statements, wherever they appear in Wittgenstein's writings, are unsatisfactory on their own because they do not try to justify the assertion that philosophy falls into error when it imitates the sciences. There is no shortage of philosophers in the analytic tradition especially who hold the opposite view; so why should they take notice of these passages unless Wittgenstein has something to say to back them up? For some, this would appear to be a shortcoming and perhaps a dogmatic feature of Wittgenstein's thought. Its presence in all stages of his career – even when much else changed – may also be seen as further evidence that he adopted this unshakeable anti-theoretical attitude independently of legitimate grounds for doing so.

This, though, would be mistaken. Wittgenstein does, as a matter of fact, provide compelling reasons for his opposition to theorising in philosophy. It is just that these reasons are not presented in a general form; he does not, for example, attempt to provide detailed characterisations of the nature of philosophy and the natural sciences and then make prescriptions for how the practice of philosophy ought to be conducted in a manner that is different to that of the sciences. Instead, his approach is piecemeal. He proceeds on a case-by-case basis by looking at particular examples of how some philosophical issue is treated in accordance with a theoretical or quasi-scientific attitude and demonstrating the difficulties or confusions that arise as a result. This in any case is how I will propose to interpret his later approach. The question of what justification, if any, he provides for his anti-theoretical attitude in the early and middle period writings will not be considered here (although I believe that there is little to be found compared to the later writings).

It follows, then, that in order to properly evaluate the later Wittgenstein's distinctive opposition to theorising in philosophy, we have to reflect on his attacks on particular examples of theorising. We have already done this to a certain extent in the previous chapters, although the discussion was not framed in terms of this metaphilosophical issue. To cite the two examples most prominent throughout §§1–202 of *PI*, the referential and platonist pictures are two theoretical frameworks for thinking about the nature of language. To be influenced by these pictures is to operate (explicitly or implicitly) with certain *general* theoretical assumptions about language, such as that the meaning of a word is the object for which it stands. The word 'influence' is appropriate here because much of what counts as practicing philosophy in this traditional way consists of developing complex theories that propose more specific theoretical claims that are nevertheless in line with the general philosophical picture in question.

Let's assume for a moment that Wittgenstein's arguments that seek – as I have argued – to highlight the absurdity of the general philosophical pictures are successful. How much of a defence of his anti-theoretical attitude can they provide? It is a feature of his piecemeal approach that these arguments can at best provide only a partial support for his attitude. They do this by weakening the hold of this or that philosophical picture, but of course it is always possible to propose an alternative picture, i.e. to propose an alternative theoretical framework for thinking about language (or some other issue) rather than giving up on theorising in philosophy altogether. The option of continuing to theorise in philosophy still appears to be a violable one, even in light of the results of Wittgenstein's arguments.

This is potentially a major worry for Wittgenstein because his arguments typically conclude with a negative theoretical claim, which presumably can be viewed as an indirect argument in favour of the opposite theoretical claim. The clearest example is the argument that concludes with the claim that it is impossible for a word to have a private (i.e. unshareable) meaning. Isn't this a fairly unambiguous indirect argument for the opposing theoretical claim that linguistic meanings must be shareable (or alternatively, that language is essentially social)? If so, certain of Wittgenstein's own arguments would *support* the practice of continuing to theorise in philosophy, rather than abandoning theorising. For these arguments actually – or so it seems – provide substantial support for particular theoretical claims.

What all of this overlooks, though, is that Wittgenstein does not employ arguments in the straightforward way with the simple intention of defending particular claims. As I have tried to show, he remains at one remove from the arguments, which means that his goal is merely to show other philosophers the absurdities that follow from their theoretical commitments. That this strategy cannot be reconfigured into a defence of some other theoretical claim is shown by the fact that his arguments can also be run against these alternative claims. Take once again the example of the claim that language is essentially social. It appears as though Wittgenstein has done a lot to motivate the acceptance of this claim. Not only has he proposed a powerful argument against the possibility of a private language, he has also given us the resources to argue against the possibility of a *solitary* language (see section 4.6).

However, in my interpretation of these arguments, I stressed that the fundamental problem with the notions of private language and solitary language did not strictly speaking have to do with the private or solitary scenarios; rather, it had to do with the fact that the defenders of private language and solitary language had to help themselves to the notion of semantic normativity, which Wittgenstein had shown to be problematic. For the very same reason, a fully fledged theory of language as essentially social would be unacceptable to Wittgenstein if it relied on the same notion. That is, the community view of language is unlikely to limit itself to the description of how *in fact* language is used in this or that community, or to hold that the most we can say about the correct and incorrect use of words is that the members of a particular community tend to use the words in such-and-such ways. To be an explanatory account or theory it will most likely have to say something about how words *ought* to be used given the (shared) meanings that the words have. And Wittgenstein would object to this theory of language as much as he does to the theory that allows for private meanings.

The scenario I have depicted is reminiscent of Kant's antinomies with the crucial difference that whereas Kant considered certain metaphysical theses and antitheses each having arguments to support them, I have tried to show that some of Wittgenstein's arguments are powerful enough to undermine both the thesis and antithesis in question. If we are faced with this paradoxical scenario of both thesis and antithesis being refuted, there are possible ways out. The options are best formulated in terms of a dilemma: either we persist in the theoretical attitude and go in search of yet another theoretical picture but that cannot be undermined by the Wittgensteinian arguments; or we follow Wittgenstein in embracing the anti-theoretical attitude. The second response involves accepting that our philosophical reflections on language or any other topic can never legitimately result in a theory, and that it is misguided to expect that they should.

It is, though, one thing to attribute a theoretical claim to Wittgenstein based on some argument that he develops and quite another to hold that what he does say about language commits him unwittingly to certain theoretical claims. The latter issue appears to be the most troubling because, unlike the first, it cannot be decided by simply showing that Wittgenstein's arguments do not conclude (not even indirectly) with a particular philosophical claim that he then adopts. The issue of his unintentional theoretical commitments was explored in the previous section in relation to the commitment specifically to transcendental idealism. The provisional conclusion was that although, following A.W. Moore, the commitment to this doctrine seemed inevitable (because of the irreducible distinction between how things appear to us given our contingent form of life and how things really are), Wittgenstein's way out was to adopt the quietist standpoint or 'disallow the questions' that lead to the theoretical commitment.

However, can this quietist response be of much help here? That is, even if Wittgenstein has good reasons for adopting his quietist standpoint, can this do any more than merely support the reading that his extensive employment of arguments does not lead to an explicit or intentional defence of a particular philosophical thesis (as the conclusion of one or other of his arguments)? It is not so clear if the quietist response can be used to defend him against the claim that he unknowingly committed himself to a doctrine of some sort.

Despite being a more complicated issue, this response *is* actually helpful. For in order to be committed to a certain theoretical claim – whether that claim concerns transcendental idealism or something else – Wittgenstein would have to be committed to some other theoretical claim in the first instance. There must be something for the apparently unwitting commitment to follow from. But in Wittgenstein's case, there is no original theoretical claim or set of claims that serve as the basis for the implication. The appearance that there is such an implication is based on the assumption that Wittgenstein has his own alternative theory of the nature of language that emphasises its embeddedness in concrete contexts of practical use and its being underpinned by contingent biological and social facts about us (our shared form of life). That this could be mistaken for an alternative theoretical picture is understandable. It is the task of the final chapter to show that this is not the case and hence to show that Wittgenstein could draw attention to these features of language without implicitly adopting the theoretical attitude. If successful, this would also show that there is no basis for attributing even unintentional theoretical commitments to the later Wittgenstein. It would thus be shown that *PI* does not commit the same basic error as *TLP*.

5.8   Conclusion: The Nature of the Gulf Between Wittgenstein and Contemporary Debates Concerning Language

This book is guided by the conviction that within the separate fields of Wittgenstein studies and contemporary philosophy of language there have been major advances concerning the nature of language and linguistic meaning and that the connection between these fields on this topic is greater than usually perceived. Perhaps the greatest barrier preventing genuine dialogue between the fields of research is Wittgenstein's distinctive metaphilosophy, which on a number of points seems to be directly at odds with more traditional and still widely held views of the nature of philosophy. This difference in metaphilosophy can appear more or less extreme depending on the reading of Wittgenstein that is adopted. The reading I have defended leads to a less pessimistic view of the possibility of dialogue between the separate fields concerning language.

On my interpretation, Wittgenstein engages in constructing arguments but he does so for reasons that are different to traditional philosophers. Rather than attempting to provide grounds for adopting one or another theory of language, his arguments have the function of demonstrating the confusions inherent in certain theoretical assumptions concerning language. These arguments are of significance to philosophers who do not share his metaphilosophy because they highlight the problems with the kinds of theories they may be drawn to, such as referential theories.

I am thus suggesting that there are two competing perspectives we can take on Wittgenstein's arguments regarding language. These opposing perspectives are manifestations of a sharp divide, viz. between theoretical and anti-theoretical perspectives on language. I have defended the reading that much of Wittgenstein's *PI* is concerned with challenging the presumption in favour of theorising in philosophy and with showing that it is symptomatic of a fundamental delusion. According to this reading, then, the arguments in question (those against referentialism, platonism etc.) are used by Wittgenstein to provide cumulative support for his anti-theoretical attitude towards the study of language. But, as I have indicated in the previous section, his method is piecemeal in the sense that he can motivate his anti-theoretical stance only by attacking particular theoretical assumptions concerning language on a case-by-case basis. Strictly speaking, then, it is possible to accept the force of Wittgenstein's arguments and to use them for a separate purpose – not as evidence in favour of an anti-theoretical style of philosophising but as providing guidance in the project of arriving at a better theoretical model of the nature of language.

It is up to each philosopher to decide whether the appropriate response to Wittgenstein's arguments is to persist in the theoretical attitude or to follow him in embracing the anti-theoretical attitude. But this just shows that in addition to the interest that other philosophers may take in Wittgenstein's negative arguments concerning language, his discussion also invites philosophers to think deeply about the conception of philosophy they are operating with or presupposing *and* whether such a conception can withstand the repeated failures of philosophers' attempts to theorise about language.

Summary of Main Points

(5a) There is an apparent conflict in *PI* between Wittgenstein's explicit claims opposing the use of arguments in philosophy, on the one hand, and his practice of seemingly developing numerous arguments of his own, on the other.

(5b) This conflict only appears to be genuine if we fail to acknowledge the basic distinction between the *actual* methods Wittgenstein employs throughout much of *PI* and what he views as the *correct* philosophical methods. The actual methods that he employs in *PI* tend to mimic those of more traditional philosophers and thus involve the extensive use of arguments.

(5c) Wittgenstein does not employ arguments in the traditional manner of attempting to prove particular philosophical theses. They cannot even be viewed as indirect arguments for opposing philosophical theses, such as that language is essentially social; this is shown by the fact that in some cases his arguments can similarly be used against these alternative theses.

(5d) It is an important upshot of Wittgenstein's method that he accepts that philosophical statements can be meaningful. For it is only insofar as they are meaningful that they can be shown to entail anything at all and thus figure as premises in reductio arguments.

(5e) Regarding Wittgenstein's dialogue with other philosophers (more traditional in their conception of philosophy than him), his method of presenting arguments is the most important because it is the method most likely to persuade his philosophical interlocutors. His other methods may contribute to loosening the grip or influence of a particular philosophical picture of language, but it is the arguments that are more decisive in convincing opponents.

(5f) Aside from the role of arguments within *PI*, there is the separate question of whether Wittgenstein was committed (even unwittingly) to some substantial philosophical theses. And since one of the most fundamental defects of *TLP* – as many 'traditional' and 'new' readers tend to agree – is that it operates with various theoretical assumptions about language while also opposing theorising in philosophy, we should consider whether there is a similar defect or tension in *PI*.

(5g) Interpreters who hold that there are theoretical commitments in *PI* always defend their views by holding that the commitments either concern Wittgenstein's conception of language (for example, as essentially practical or social) or are entailed by this conception (for example, that it entails a version of transcendental idealism).

(5h) There are no theoretical commitments in *PI* – either explicitly adopted or unwittingly presupposed – because Wittgenstein does not have a theory of the nature of language. The view that he does is based on a misunderstanding of the role of arguments within the book and of the way they provide support for his anti-theoretical attitude.

(5i) Wittgenstein's rejection of theorising in philosophy is not dogmatic. His numerous arguments against misconceptions of the nature of language provide cumulative support for his anti-theoretical attitude. After a certain amount of theoretical assumptions concerning language have been shown to be deeply flawed, the tide slowly turns so that the presumption in favour of the theoretical attitude is weakened. In this way, the anti-theoretical attitude towards language is motivated.

(5j) It remains possible – although not necessarily very plausible – to accept the conclusions of Wittgenstein's negative arguments and yet to part ways with him by insisting on the legitimacy of the theoretical attitude in philosophy. For such a philosopher, the goal would continue to be to arrive at a better theoretical picture of language.

6   Meaning and Use

Most philosophers, including those with a particular interest in language, associate the later Wittgenstein with the thesis or slogan that 'meaning is use'. Exactly what the content of this thesis is supposed to be remains contentious. It is better to approach this issue by first considering the thesis itself and reflecting on why any philosopher might be motivated to defend it, particularly a philosopher who, unlike Wittgenstein, is driven to advance an adequate theory of meaning.

Despite its generality, we can get some sense of what is distinctive about a philosophical theory of meaning that places the thesis at its centre. Call such a theory a *use theory of meaning*. We would expect a theory of this kind to attempt to take account of the practical dimension of language, or the activity of using words in various contexts. And this could be seen as a major advantage over other theories because it would acknowledge rather than ignore the inherent fluidity and dynamic nature of language, as opposed to viewing words statically as having semantic properties ('meanings', 'senses' etc.) attached to them. It would also contrast with the referential theorist's tendency to prioritise the rigid relation of reference or denotation between words and objects. A use theory, unlike most other theories of meaning, would perhaps emphasise the fact that language is used and embedded in concrete practices, and is not merely an abstract structure or system to be examined in isolation from our lives. There are other potential strengths too that begin to emerge when we contrast it with other theories. For example, whereas the referential theory focuses only on the use of words to name and talk about things, the use theory sees this as only one (and not even necessarily the most important) among very many kinds of uses of words. Many of the problems that arise for referentialism stem from its difficulties in accommodating non-referring terms, but it would seem that these problems are avoided by simply acknowledging that non-referring terms can have meanings by having established or definite uses that have nothing to do with referring to objects.

What I have for convenience called 'the use theory' is, of course, an abstraction designed to draw out some of the consequences that may follow from defending the thesis that meaning is use. These consequences do appear to have an affinity with certain passages from *Philosophical Investigations* (*PI*), especially those that stress the diversity of uses of language and their practical settings (see *PI*, §23 where Wittgenstein reminds us of how we commonly use language to ask questions, make promises, sing songs, tell jokes, issue warnings etc.). Wittgenstein also frequently gives the reader or his interlocutor the instruction to pay attention to how words are actually used (see, for example, *PI*, §116). The attribution of the thesis is based on this and the following famous passage where he appears to explicitly endorse it:

> For a *large* class of cases – though not for all – in which we employ the word 'meaning' it can be defined thus: the meaning of a word is its use in the language.
> And the *meaning* of a name is sometimes explained by pointing to its *bearer*. (*PI*, §43)

Given this, it may seem reasonable to hold that Wittgenstein's perspective on language or linguistic meaning has more in common with a use theory than with any other theory of meaning. We should thus ask ourselves whether, even if he has successfully shown the referentialist, platonist etc. conceptions of meaning to be flawed, it is still possible for him to adopt a use theory of meaning as an alternative rather than adopting the more radical, anti-theoretical response.

However, Wittgenstein's opposition to adopting the definition in a theoretical context is already signalled in the above passage by the qualification that the definition does not hold 'for all' cases. The goal of this concluding chapter is to shed light on this and similar passages concerning meaning and use by placing them in the broader context of the arguments presented throughout *PI*. I have postponed the analysis of these remarks until now because I believe that Wittgenstein's attitude to the use of words can only be properly appreciated in light of the negative arguments considered in the previous chapters. There is a danger of misunderstanding the importance of use for Wittgenstein (not dissimilar to the possible misunderstanding of his emphasis on the communal or social aspects of language), and the best of way of guarding against it is to address the issue only after some of the major arguments of *PI* have been discussed. Broadly speaking my goal here is to demonstrate that, from the point of view of his negative arguments, the use theory is just as problematic as the other theories of meaning we have discussed; and that his interest in the actual use of words, and his claim that in most cases the meaning of a word is to be grasped by attending to how it is used, are very far from the concerns of the use theorist.

This difference will be directly addressed throughout sections 6.5–6.7, and I will focus on the example of Paul Horwich's use theory in order to make the discussion more concrete. This example is an appropriate reference point because Horwich sees significant continuities between his use theory and Wittgenstein's later remarks on use. I will attempt to show that these continuities do not exist and that they could not exist in other examples of use theories either. Sections 6.1–6.4

will introduce the main features of Wittgenstein's reflections on use and will connect them with the major themes that have been explored in the previous chapter. The key topics that will be addressed in these opening sections include: how Wittgenstein's interest in use is a central aspect of his anti-theoretical standpoint and his opposition to inflating the concept of meaning (section 6.1); whether he defends a general 'criteria view' of the use of words (sections 6.2 and 6.3); and the importance of the game analogy in highlighting the philosophical points he makes concerning the relation between meaning and use (section 6.4).

My overall aim here is to go beyond the mere recognition that Wittgenstein was opposed to theorising – and therefore opposed to defending a use theory of meaning – and to clarify the precise sense in which his rejection of theorising concerning language also extended to his highly distinctive reflections on the use of words.

6.1   Deflating Meaning by Appealing to Use: The Beetle Example

A good place to begin reflecting on Wittgenstein's view of the relation between meaning and use is to revisit his discussion of the use of sensation words like 'pain'. Based on the discussion of privacy and sensation language in Chapter 4, are we any clearer on how the meaning of a word like 'pain' is determined? Can we at least assert that the meaning is not determined by some private entity or mental state like an individual's sensations of pain? And can we add that it must be determined by something public, shared, communal etc.?

We have to be careful how we answer these questions because when we use expressions such as 'meaning' and 'the determination of meaning' in a philosophical context, we have a tendency to think we know what we are talking about. What the discussion in the first four chapters has shown is that if we are queried on what we mean by these expressions, it is highly likely that any response we give is going to be problematic and laden with deep-seated confusion. For example, we might make the seemingly innocuous claim that the meaning of a word is a property of that word. It is the kind of property possessed by the sign 'table' but not by the sign 'elbat'. It is a *semantic* property. But, of course, this tells us nothing at all about what meaning is or about what we are getting at when we talk about the meaning of a word being determined. In the attempt to be informative, we might characterise meanings in ways similar to the referentialist, platonist, semantic normativist or private linguist – all of which have their attractions, but all of which are vulnerable to the Wittgensteinian arguments we discussed.

The appeal to use makes better sense in this context. It is not an alternative answer to the same question of what meanings really are; it is more like a replacement of the original question with an alternative programme for inquiry that involves paying attention to how words are used in particular contexts. And this is where the possibility of misunderstanding Wittgenstein's appeal to use arises. Turning it into a slogan like 'meaning = use' gives the impression that he is advocating an account of what meaning is that would rival the referentialist or platonist. The task here is to show how this is not the case and to give a sense of how different Wittgenstein's proposals are to anything suggested by other philosophers of language.

To illustrate the issue at stake more concretely, consider again the negative claim that the meanings of sensation words cannot be determined by private mental states or private entities. This has struck many interpreters as a major lesson of Wittgenstein's remarks on private language. The point appears to be that sensations are like *idle wheels* in a mechanism i.e. present and turning but not actually having an impact on the functioning of the overall mechanism. This is brought out in the following passage concerning colour sensations:

> The essential thing about private experience is ... that nobody knows whether other people also have *this* or something else. The assumption would thus be possible – though unverifiable – that one section of mankind had one sensation of red and another section another. (*PI*, §272)

Here Wittgenstein is drawing attention to the assumption much discussed in modern philosophy (going back at least to Locke) that it is conceivable that some people would respond perceptually to an object by, for example, having sensations of red, while other people would response perceptually to the same object by having sensations of green. The assumption is that there could conceivably be an *inversion* in the speakers' sensations of colours. Hence, the person with colour sensation inversion would see red things as green, and green things as red.

Severin Schroeder calls the argument that he believes emerges from Wittgenstein's discussion of this example 'the idle-wheel argument' (see Schroeder 2006, 206–8). According to Schroeder, Wittgenstein argues that even if a colour inversion of this sort were to be the case it would not have any impact on what the language users called 'red'. Neither speaker would be aware of the differences in their colour sensations because everything that one speaker sees as red the other speaker sees as green, and vice versa. Hence, there is a consistency in each of their colour sensations; it just so happens that, for example, when they each call fire-engines 'red', the first speaker has sensations of red and the other speaker has sensations of green. The crucial question is: if speakers agree in their use of the word 'red' despite having different private sensations, do these sensations really matter to the *meaning* of the word? The implication is that they are like idle wheels in relation to a mechanism – that the private sensations that a speaker happens to have are independent of the meanings of the sensations words that the speaker uses.

Wittgenstein pursues this point further with his famous beetle example in §293 of *PI*. In the example, he turns from the consideration of the meaning of colour words to the meaning of the word 'pain', and he compares how the meanings of the words 'pain' and 'beetle' are formed if the objects they stand for are private.

> If I say of myself that it is only from my own case that I know what the word 'pain' means – must I not say the same of other people too? And how can I generalize the *one* case so irresponsibly?
>
>   Now someone tells me that *he* knows what pain is only from his own case! – Suppose everyone had a box with something in it: we call it a 'beetle'. No one can look into anyone else's box, and everyone says he knows what a beetle is only by looking at *his* beetle. – Here it would be quite possible for everyone to have something different in his box. One might even imagine such a thing constantly changing. – But suppose the word 'beetle' had a use in these people's language? – If so it would not be used as the name of a thing. The thing in the box has no place in the language-game at all; not even as a *something*: for the box might even be empty. – No, one can 'divide through' by the thing in the box; it cancels out, whatever it is.
>
>   That is to say: if we construe the grammar of the expression of sensation on the model of 'object and name' the object drops out of consideration as irrelevant. (*PI*, §293)

Under the influence of a Cartesian view or private box model of the mind, it is tempting to suppose that pains are private objects in each mind and that a speaker learns the meaning of the word 'pain' by looking inward and reflecting on his/her own pains. In this passage, Wittgenstein asks us to imagine that the word 'beetle' is learnt in the same way. Hence, each person has a box with something in it that nobody else can see; it is a private object for that person. And we are asked to suppose that each of us learns the meaning of the word 'beetle' from looking into his/her own box and correlating the word with the private object in there.

But then Wittgenstein writes: 'But suppose the word "beetle" had a *use* in these people's language' (my emphasis). The claim he seems to be making is that if the word has a use in the language, it would be a shared use.[1] And if that is the case, whatever meaning it has would be independent of the objects that are in each individual's box. For if the meaning was based on the private objects, there would not be a shared meaning or a shared use of the word. As Wittgenstein states, since the objects in the boxes are private to individual

---

[1] This follows from the sentence that comes after it ('If so it would not be used as the name of a thing'), although it takes some reflection to see why. Essentially, if there were a plurality of individual uses by individual speakers, whereby each speaker uses 'beetle' in a way that is tied to whatever is in their respective box, then each person would presumably be using the word as the name of a thing (but different things for different users). Therefore, the fact that Wittgenstein states that the word could *not* be used as the name of a thing implies that he is asking us to imagine that the word has a *shared* use rather than a plurality of individual uses that may diverge from one another.

speakers, it is 'quite possible for everyone to have something different in his box' and for whatever is in the box to be 'constantly changing'. Hence, on the assumption that the word 'beetle' has a shared use, the conclusion appears unavoidable that the meaning of the word must not be shaped or determined by the private objects in the boxes. Therefore, if this is correct, the point is similar to the one mentioned above, namely that the private object (in this case, the object in the box) is irrelevant to the meaning of the word (in this case, the word 'beetle'). Likewise, following Wittgenstein's comparison, the meaning of the word 'pain' would not be determined by the person's private sensations of pain. As he concludes, 'the object drops out of consideration as irrelevant'.

However, it must be recognised that there are at least two problematic theoretical notions that are targeted in the passage and that constitute the interlocutor's assumptions. One is the notion that a private object can determine the meaning of a word. But another is the referential picture of meaning, or what Wittgenstein here calls 'the model of "object and name"'. When these are combined, they comprise the view that the meaning of a word like 'pain' is determined by its reference to a private object. The more complete statement of his concluding remark is a conditional; it states not simply that the private object is 'irrelevant' like an idle wheel, but that *if* we presuppose the referentialist model then the private object is irrelevant.

What is Wittgenstein's point here? The answer, I think, can be grasped when we recall (as discussed in Chapter 1) that his typical method of attacking referentialism or the Augustinian picture in the opening sections of *PI* involves drawing our attention to how a word is or would be used. Wittgenstein obviously implements the same method in §293 because the crucial step is when he asks us – or the interlocutor – to suppose that the word 'beetle' has a use. His main argumentative point follows from this in the sense that it is precisely this supposition that the word has a use that puts the referential model under pressure. And equally, it is this that highlights that the private object is irrelevant to the meaning of the word. In the first chapter, I identified his apparent reliance on a non-referential characterisation of meaning (in terms of use) when attacking referentialism in order to address the question of whether this weakens his attack. The same question must be asked about his reliance on it in §293, although we are now in a much better position to understand exactly what kind of reliance is in play.

When Wittgenstein asks us to suppose that 'beetle' has 'a use in these people's language', the implication is that such use is something that has to be recognised and accommodated. It is similar to recognising that the word 'pain' has a use in our language. It acts as a starting-point and any conception of meaning must be able to address it. What is shown in §293 is that the referential picture – which in this case must be coupled with the notion of meaning as determined by reference to private objects – cannot accommodate the simple fact that 'beetle' and 'pain' have uses.

A possible response would be for the referentialist to question Wittgenstein's assumption that the shared use of these words must be accounted for. Wittgenstein does not say anything in this passage to deal with this response, but it is open to debate whether he really has to. For we could look at his appeal to use as a sort of deflationary move, i.e. drawing attention to a phenomenon – namely, the actual use of this or that word – as something that we are all inclined to accept. It is deflationary in the sense that there is nothing *yet* built into the notion of the use of a word; it is not a philosophically robust notion of use. For example, it is not dependent on accepting an identification of meaning with use, or an account of the nature of meaning as constituted by use. The inflation of the concepts of meaning and use occur elsewhere, in the accounts provided by other philosophers, and not in Wittgenstein's claim that a word has a use. One such inflation occurs in referential accounts, and hence §293 can be read as showing that this particular way of inflating the notion of meaning is flawed. But, as we shall see later in this chapter, the use theory of meaning represents another significant way of inflating the notion of meaning and one that is especially important to consider because of Wittgenstein's association with such a theory. When addressing this, the gulf separating Wittgenstein and use theories will become much clearer.

The point I want to emphasise early in this chapter is that Wittgenstein's method of bringing the discussion of meaning back to a reflection on the use of a word is a deflationary move. It is a way of putting pressure on any attempt to inflate the notion of meaning because such attempts end up being incapable of accommodating or accounting for the use. §293 of *PI* provides a succinct illustration of how this occurs in relation to the referential picture. The rest of this chapter will clarify how Wittgenstein's method also puts pressure on other theories of meaning, most notably the use theory.

6.2   Criteria and Use

Articulating Wittgenstein's views on the relation between the meaning of a word and the use of that word must take account of his remarks on 'criteria'. These remarks concern all areas of discourse, but because of the interest in his private language argument the emphasis in the literature has been on the importance of what he says regarding the words we use to talk about mental phenomena in particular.

Insofar as there is anything resembling a point of consensus concerning his later remarks on mental phenomena, it is that he opposes a Cartesian dualist metaphysical conception of the mind in which its contents are private and known with certainty only to the person whose mind it is. Accordingly, he is held to oppose a view of mental words like 'pain', 'belief', 'anger' etc., whereby these are taken to be names of entities or states in a private and enclosed domain of the mind. However, characterising what he is opposed to is at most only one aspect of his treatment of the meaning of mental terms. Within the vast secondary literature on the private language argument, there is a tradition of attributing to Wittgenstein an alternative anti-Cartesian, *positive* view of the mind and its relation to the body and behaviour. For reasons that will be discussed in a moment, this may be called his 'criteria view'.

As I have indicated, this view concerns the use of all types of words, including words for physical and abstract phenomena as well as mental phenomena. On certain formulations in the secondary literature it can seem like a proto-theory of the use of words, or an elaboration of what is involved in claiming that the meaning of a word is its use. But, of course, the presence of such a theory or proto-theory in the secondary literature is one thing and the justification for attributing it to Wittgenstein is quite another. Both issues will be considered in this section.

Perhaps the best way of characterising the criteria view is as an account of how we *think* and *talk* about phenomena. Very broadly, it is a view of the *concepts* and *words* we use. Wittgenstein's interest in criteria is intimately connected with his emphasis on the actual use we make of words (see Hacker 1990, 552 and Goodman 2002, 113). Generally, criteria may be thought of as guides for how a word or concept is to be used. For example, the criteria for being fire include the visual and tactile appearances it has. We normally call something fire if it has a certain bright colour and flickering appearance and generates heat etc. (see Witherspoon 2011, 484). These criteria are central to our concept of fire, for it is obvious that our concept and how we talk about fire would change if fire ceased to have these appearances. Therefore, the notion of a criterion allows us – and Wittgenstein, assuming for the moment it is his view – to give a more substantive description of our particular language-games or practices of using words.

At the heart of the account, then, is the 'criterial relation', which in the most abstract terms is between a criterion and what it is a criterion for. Other examples would be: clutching one's jaw being a criterion for having a toothache; and calling this apple 'green' being a criterion for understanding the word 'green'. Most of the disputes in the literature have concerned how Wittgenstein views these criterial relations, as well as how this view can somehow be taken to contain a solution to certain philosophical problems (especially those regarding the relation between the mind and the body that arise in the context of Cartesianism).

To give a brief sense of the disputes involved, some philosophers have argued that the criterial relation is a special evidential relation in which the presence of criteria provides 'non-inductive' or 'necessary' evidence for the presence of what they are criteria for (see Shoemaker 1963 and Lycan 1971). If this were correct, it would be significant because it would, for example, potentially offer a response to a sceptic who doubted the existence of other minds. The response would be something like: since behaviour like clutching one's cheek and wincing are criteria for having a toothache, it follows that if someone exhibits these behavioural criteria in the appropriate circumstances there will be a special sort of evidence that the person actually has the mental state of having a toothache (and therefore has a mind). There is a competing type of reading that goes back to Albritton (1966), Canfield (1974), and Cavell (1979) (and defended more recently in Witherspoon 2011), which sees Wittgenstein's primary concern to be with explicating the patterns for using words or concepts. For example, the *point* of stating that certain visual impressions are criteria for the presence of fire is that it helps to clarify our use of the word 'fire' or the concept of fire, rather than that these impressions provide some special certainty or evidence for our belief that there is fire (see Cavell 1979, 45). The same would go for the toothache example and any other mental example that a philosopher would use to try to provide a response to a Cartesian sceptic.

The latter kind of reading has more to recommend it – especially when it comes to connecting the criteria view back to Wittgenstein's writings – because it provides a more compelling case for why Wittgenstein would be interested in criteria. Regarding the specific cases of mental phenomena, his interest in criteria on this reading would be indicative of his methodological concern with mental concepts and the meanings of mental terms, rather than with a metaphysical programme of determining what mental states (and processes etc.) really are. This tallies with his method of continually opting to return to a reflection on the language we use to talk about mental phenomena and more specifically with his belief that the deepest philosophical confusions concerning the mind (like other areas) originate in misunderstandings of that language. Attending to how we actually use words for mental phenomena, and highlighting the criteria for them, is how he attempts to expose the errors in philosophical accounts concerning the mind. That, though, is merely a general observation concerning how this reading connects with his philosophical method. It is necessary to back it up by considering what he states about criteria.

In *The Blue Book*, Wittgenstein refers to criteria as 'defining criteria' and makes the important distinction between them and 'symptoms'.

Let us introduce two antithetical terms in order to avoid certain elementary confusions: To the question 'How do you know that so-and-so is the case?', we sometimes answer by giving '*criteria*' and sometimes by giving '*symptoms*'. If medical science calls angina an inflammation caused by a particular bacillus, and we ask in a particular case 'why do you say this man has got angina?' then the answer 'I have found the bacillus so-and-so in his blood' gives us the criterion, or what we may call the defining criterion of angina. If on the other hand the answer was, 'His throat is inflamed', this might give us a symptom of angina. I call 'symptom' a phenomenon of which experience has taught us that it coincided, in some way or other, with the phenomenon which is our defining criterion. Then to say 'A man has angina if this bacillus is found in him' is a tautology or it is a loose way of stating the definition of 'angina'. But to say, 'A man has angina whenever he has an inflamed throat' is to make a hypothesis. (*BB*, 24–5)

If something, A, is a criterion of something else, B, then A is a 'defining' characteristic of B. The example he gives is of the presence of the bacillus in the blood as being 'the defining criterion of angina'. It is established by convention in the medical community that this is what the defining criterion of angina is. This contrasts with a symptom such as having an inflamed throat, which is merely 'a phenomenon which experience has taught us that it coincided ... with our defining criterion'. The criteria thus determine the concept in question (and equivalently how we are to apply the word 'angina'), while the symptoms do not. The accompanying symptoms could change and the concept of angina would remain the same.

Transferring this distinction to the most divisive case of mental states, the behaviour of wincing would be a criterion for being in pain while presumably something like complaining to someone else about the pain would merely be a symptom of it. This is because the connection between the typical expressive behaviour and the sensation is so strong that it shapes our concept of pain. If our expressive behaviour was different or changed somehow, it is reasonable to hold that our concept of what a pain is would change; but it is not so clear that if our propensity to complain about our pains changed that our concept would thereby change. It is similar in the case of other kinds of mental phenomena such as emotions. The criteria for being sad includes weeping, the criteria for being angry includes having a flushed face and raising one's voice etc. In general, the typical expressive behaviours for the emotions are the defining criteria for the emotions and, likewise, this means that the ways we ordinarily manifest our emotions shape our concepts of those emotions and what we mean by the words, 'joy', 'grief', 'fear' etc.

When we think of criteria in this way, it becomes clearer why Wittgenstein was interested in them and how it is closely connected with his interest in use. Talking about criteria allows him to say more than the rather vague claim that (in most cases) 'the meaning of a word is its use in the language'. It allows him to say more about particular examples of words and the specific ways in which the uses of those words can be clarified in terms of certain criterial relations. Simply put, the criterial relation between weeping and being sad shapes how we use the word 'sad' (and equally what we mean by the word). The same goes for the criterial relation between, for example, having visual impressions of flickering light and tactile impressions of heat, on the one hand, and the presence of fire, on the other.

Wittgenstein briefly elaborates on the distinction between criteria and symptoms in *PI* in a way that can easily generate misunderstanding of his view. Not only does he still find it useful to draw this distinction in his later work, he seems to believe it is imperative to there being an established use of any word or concept that there are defining criteria for the phenomenon being talked about and not merely contingent symptoms associated with it. In the following passage he makes this point using another non-mental example, this time with the example of rain:

The fluctuation in grammar between criteria and symptoms makes it look as if there were nothing at all but symptoms. We say, for example: 'Experience teaches that there is rain when the barometer falls, but it also teaches that there is rain when we have certain sensations of wet and cold, or such-and-such visual impressions.' In defence of this one says that these sense-impressions can deceive us. But here one fails to reflect that the fact that the false appearance is precisely one of rain is founded on a definition. (*PI*, §354)

In this case, the criteria for it raining are having 'certain sensations of wet and cold, or such-and-such visual impressions', while a symptom would be the barometer falling. Although it may be supposed that there is no genuine distinction between them (i.e. that they are all symptoms contingently associated with rain), what makes the visual impressions defining criteria for rain is that these experiences fundamentally shape how we think and talk about rain. The point is made by considering the example of being deceived that it is raining, where he states that even the possible deception is based on there being defining criteria for being rain in the first place.

The danger here is that it is tempting to extract a general theoretical claim or thesis from Wittgenstein's discussion such as the following: that contingent symptoms alone are not sufficient to shape our concepts or the use of words, i.e. that defining criteria are required. And while the above passage suggests that he endorses such a claim, I want to argue that this is mistaken. My approach in the next section will be to look closer at the remarks on criteria by considering a few more problematic examples of words for emotions. I choose to focus on these examples because they concern mental phenomena more complex than sensations like pain, and as such present greater challenges for the criteria view. The discussion of these examples will also help to further clarify the appropriateness or inappropriateness of calling it a 'view' or theory or proto-theory at all.

6.3   Examples: The Use of Words for Complex Emotions

Although the secondary literature on Wittgenstein's remarks on criteria is enormous, the vast majority of it is limited to the relatively simple examples of sensations like pains. Once again, this is due in large part to the interest in his private language argument, which requires us to engage with the issue of the relation between pain and pain-behaviour. When other examples of mental phenomena are discussed, they are almost always to do with the criteria for linguistic understanding, propositional attitudes or *simple* emotions like fear, grief and anger. I want to draw attention to the additional challenges that arise for the criteria view when we reflect on examples of more complex emotions like hope and love. I will argue that one of the benefits of discussing the criteria of complex emotions is that it allows us to achieve a more nuanced appreciation of Wittgenstein's remarks on the criteria of mental phenomena and, by extension, on criteria generally.

Emotions such as love are more complex in the sense that they have a more complicated relation to the expressive behaviours that are supposedly criteria for the emotions. Wittgenstein's awareness of the difficulties that arise when reflecting on these emotions is shown by his numerous references to the different kinds of behavioural criteria that there are for them. For example, he writes:[2]

How do we compare the behaviour of anger, joy, hope, expectation, belief, love and understanding? – Act like an angry person! That's easy. Like a joyful one – here it would depend on what the joy was about. The joy of seeing someone again, or the joy of listening to a piece of music ...? – Hope? That would be hard. Why? There are no gestures of hope. How does hoping that someone will return express itself? (*RPP* II, §357)

It's easy to imagine an animal angry, frightened, unhappy, happy, startled. But hopeful? (*RPP* II, §358; see also *PI* II, 148)

Here the emotion of hope is singled out as a difficult case in the sense that the expressive behaviour that would indicate that a person – or animal – has this emotion are 'hard' to identify. Wittgenstein makes the claim that 'There are no gestures of hope', which suggests that it is not just hard but impossible to state the behaviour that is expressive of hope. However, he might be over-stating here because there do seem to be examples of expressive behaviour that indicate hope, such as placing a bet and being careful to hold on to the ticket as expressing the hope that it will result in winning money. It is just that behaviour of this sort has a more complicated relation with hope than, for example, smiling has to the emotion of joy. On the other hand, it may be that holding on to the ticket is no more than a symptom of hope, contingently associated with it, rather than a genuine criterion of hope. If that is true, then hope could be an exceptional case in the sense that the word 'hope' is meaningful and has an established use without there being identifiable criteria of hope.

These considerations concerning hope also apply to love. In fact, there are so many different types of love that it makes the question of the typical expression

---

[2] Note that these quotations concerning emotions are taken from the second volume of his relatively neglected *Remarks on the Philosophy of Psychology* (*RPP*), which consists of the manuscripts that Wittgenstein wrote between 1946 and 1948 after 'completing' Part I of *PI*. One of his main concerns in these manuscripts is emotion. For a more detailed discussion of this issue, see McNally (2016b).

of love a much more problematic case. As a sample, consider the following different kinds of love that correspond to the different kinds of objects of love:

Love *for people*: parent, child, friend, spouse, oneself etc.

Love *for other living creatures*: pet, a species of animal, for example, dogs etc.

Love *for things*: food, drink, possessions, movies, books, pieces of music, works of art etc.

Love *for less concrete things*: humanity, one's country, a football team, nature, rainy days, travelling etc.

In light of this diversity, can we plausibly maintain that there is any basic unity in the concept of love? What, for example, is there to connect the love of one's child with the love of rainy days? We might be tempted to posit some agreeable or pleasant bodily feeling or sensation that may accompany the love. But even a little reflection reveals this to be an inadequate response because both examples of love could just as easily be imagined to involve unpleasant bodily feelings or sensations (for example, nervousness regarding the child's well-being or feeling cold and wet from being out in the rain).

The multitude of examples of love invites the question of whether there are genuinely defining criteria of love, as opposed to a wide variety of symptoms that accompany what we call 'love'. Furthermore, can we reasonably expect that such defining criteria, if they exist, would be external or behavioural? To answer these questions, we need to reflect on the examples of love. In some of the examples, the typical expressive behaviour is as obvious and immediate as with the expressive behaviour of joy, sadness or anger. The love of a particular food is expressed by eating it regularly; the love of a football team is expressed by supporting them at football matches, being upset if they lose etc. But there are also examples of love where there is little or no outward expression of the emotion. For example, when a loved one dies, it is plausible to hold that I continue to love them (I still experience the same strong emotion towards them etc.). Here the emotion may be present and yet I may never express it because, for example, the grief that accompanies the loss of the loved one is too great.

To address these complications it helps to consider a comparison with the understanding of language, as discussed in Chapter 2. If I have learnt the meaning of a word at a certain time but a long time passes without my using it, it is still plausible to hold that I understand it unless I go on to misuse it on a number of occasions. Similarly, in the problematic cases of love, the criteria could be that I loved the person in the past and I showed it in typical ways and that there is no reason to believe that the love is gone unless there is behaviour to contradict it. Love is analogous to linguistic understanding, but there are added complications because exhibiting love is less straightforward than exhibiting linguistic understanding. Whereas the criteria for understanding any word would include applying it in appropriate circumstances and being able to give a rough explanation of its meaning, the criteria for loving another person would involve engaging in a complicated set of behaviours such as caring for them, protecting them, acting in their interests etc. (all of which can be manifested in a wide variety of ways).

Arguably, what the examples of complex emotions show is that despite passages like §354 of *PI*, Wittgenstein is not – indeed could not be – defending the general thesis that all concepts must have defining criteria. He does appear to hold the more modest view that as a matter of fact many concepts (including concepts of simpler emotions) have defining criteria. But there are examples where the line between defining criteria and symptoms is too blurred. As he highlights in a related context in §79 of *PI*, 'the bounds of the incidental' are not always clear. The example of love is interesting because there may be some kinds of love that have defining criteria, while other kinds do not. And it looks as though the *deeper* the love, the harder it is to specify the criteria as opposed to the vast array of behaviour that is merely symptomatic of the love. Wittgenstein recognises that there may be lots of such examples as far back as his original discussion of the criteria/symptoms distinction in *The Blue Book*, where he also states that if the line between them is blurred it does not necessarily impact on the usefulness of the concept in question (see *BB*, 25).

For the present discussion, the most important question is how this affects how we view the distinction between the complex emotion and its behavioural expression. While Wittgenstein's answer to the analogous question concerning sensations and simple emotions was that their relation to their expressive behaviour is criterial, it does not seem like he can say the same in cases like love and hope. But if the relation between complex emotions and their outward expression is not criterial, how can we characterise it? Although it is not clear how Wittgenstein would answer this (or indeed that he has to answer it given that – as I maintain – he was not concerned with developing a unified and comprehensive theory of the use of words), I think he has done enough to persuade us from reverting to one of the following alternative accounts of complex emotions: the behaviourist account (there is no emotion aside from its behavioural manifestations); the Jamesian account (the emotion is nothing more than the consciousness of its behavioural/bodily manifestations);[3] or the Cartesian dualist account (the emotion is a mental entity that is metaphysically distinct from any and all of its behavioural manifestations).

As with the cases of simpler mental phenomena, Wittgenstein would ask us to pay attention to how we use words like 'love'. We will undoubtedly find many instances where it is difficult to say exactly what outward manifestations

---

[3] See James (2007, 451–2). See also Goodman (2002) and McNally (2016b).

permit us to attribute the emotion to a person. But such difficulties do not provide support for any of the above alternative accounts. If anything, it is a strength of Wittgenstein's approach that it can acknowledge the genuine complexity of these cases (unlike the behavioural and Jamesian accounts, which demand definite behavioural and bodily phenomena to encapsulate even the most complex emotions) and without positing a mysterious mental entity to impose an artificial uniformity on the particular emotion (as in a Cartesian dualist account). The vagueness and the complexity are in the phenomena – the many kinds of love, the open-ended meaning of 'love' – and the standpoint we adopt should accommodate it rather than seeking to reduce it by using a model of simpler emotions and other mental states.

The point I take from reflecting on these problematic cases is that it is mistaken and overly simplistic to attribute 'the criteria view' to Wittgenstein. He is undoubtedly interested in criteria in the sense of the general conditions under which we typically use words and apply concepts. But this does not mean that he holds that every concept or word must have specifiable defining criteria. To put it rather bluntly, use can outstrip criteria. As Wittgenstein recognises, it is tempting to suppose that the use of words must be rule-governed and one way of articulating this is by stating that there must be criteria for correctly applying every word. This would be to insist that criteria come before use. But, as the discussion in the previous chapters has shown, it is central to Wittgenstein's later reflections on language that it is use that has primacy over anything (such as a rule or mental entity) that could be assumed to do the job of strictly regulating or predetermining the use.

It is difficult to explain exactly what this amounts to; one attempt at explaining it is to say that the use is open-ended. I will explore this more in the rest of the chapter, but the provisional conclusion to take from the discussion so far is that none of the attempted formulations of the criteria view map neatly on to Wittgenstein's discussion. Most importantly, they do not adequately clarify the significance of his appeal to use.

6.4   The Game Analogy

So far very little has been said about what use is. It helps to recognise that Wittgenstein's interest in criteria extends naturally from his interest in the use of words. It allows us to appreciate that his concern is with redirecting our attention to the innumerable mundane facts regarding how we actually use words. For example, we call this furry, four-legged animal a 'dog', but not this other furry, four-legged animal which we instead call a 'cat'. Wittgenstein shifts our focus back to this 'everyday use' (as he puts it in §116 of *PI*) because it affords us an illuminating perspective on how philosophers tend to use words (so-called 'metaphysical' use), and how the ordinary notion of meaning can appear strange as a result. The philosophical discourse comes to seem disconnected when viewed from this perspective.

Another way in which the discussion of use can be opened up is by reflecting on Wittgenstein's analogy between using a language and playing a game. His frequent use of the term 'language-game' expresses his conviction that the analogy is important to what he has to say about the use of words. But how are we supposed to understand the analogy? The analogy is instructive primarily because it allows Wittgenstein to reflect on concrete instances of language use in much the same way as we can reflect on the activity of playing a game like chess. Many of his constructed examples – such as the builders' language-game – are simple and primitive; the rules of the language-game are easily stated, and the exchanges between the individuals engaged in it are comprehensible in light of those rules.[4] It also allows him to consider how the notion of meaning can be closely connected with how a word is used. This is displayed most vividly in the examples where complications arise within the language-game. For example, in §41 of *PI* Wittgenstein discusses a case in which 'the tool with the name "N" is broken'. The builder A gives his assistant B a piece of paper with the sign 'N', thus requesting the tool it is a name for, but he does so without knowing that the tool is broken. Wittgenstein asks:

Has this sign meaning now or not? – What is B to do when he is given it? – We have not settled anything about this. One might ask: what *will* he do? Well, perhaps he will stand there at a loss, or show A the pieces. Here one *might* say: 'N' has become meaningless; and this expression would mean that the sign 'N' no longer had a use in our language-game (unless we gave it a new one).

He then imagines that the builder and his assistant develop 'a convention whereby B has to shake his head in reply if A gives him the sign belonging to a tool that is broken', the point being that the sign 'N' might continue to have 'a place in the language-game even when the tool no longer exists' or is broken. In other words, there is good reason for holding that the sign has meaning if it has a use or a place in the language-game (see also the example in §42).

The appropriateness of the analogy between using words and playing games is indicated explicitly in the following section:

We are talking about the spatial and temporal phenomenon of language, not about some non-spatial, non-temporal phantasm. [Note in margin: Only it is possible to be interested in a phenomenon in a variety of ways]. But we talk about it as we do about the pieces in chess when we are stating the rules of the game, not describing their physical properties.

The question 'What is a word really?' is analogous to 'What is a piece in chess?' (*PI*, §108)

---

[4] See *AWL*, 47: 'What we are doing [when considering primitive language-games] is like taking chess and making a simpler game involving simpler operations and a smaller number of pawns.'

Here Wittgenstein is attempting to clarify the distinctive manner in which he reflects on language. On the one hand, he treats language as concrete or a 'spatial and temporal phenomenon'. And on the other hand, this does not mean that he is 'describing [the] physical properties' of words. The game analogy helps here because the study of the use of words in concrete settings can be viewed as like the study of chess pieces in relation to the rules that govern them. Wittgenstein's interest in the analogy seems to be that it provides him with a way of elucidating the notion of meaning by linking it to the actual uses that are made of words, which is similar to how chess pieces acquire certain powers within a game that are not merely a matter of them possessing certain physical properties (and have to do instead with what we can do with the pieces in accordance with the rules of chess). The comparison has the potential to get us to see that a word having a meaning is no more mysterious than a bishop having a certain role in chess. This, of course, is what the comparison *could* reveal or shed light on, but we will see that confusion can easily arise by over-stretching or misapplying the analogy.

At a more general level, the analogy between using language and playing games can be broken down to a number of different analogies between features of each.[5] The most important of these are the analogies between:

(a) The rules for the use of words and the rules of a game.
(b) Using a word and making a move in a game.
(c) Words and items/pieces in a game (for example, chess pieces).
(d) The meanings of words and the 'powers' of pieces in games (or what we are permitted to do with the pieces, such as being permitted to move the bishop diagonally in chess).
(e) Correctness/obligations in the context of using words and in the context of playing a game.

Although the overall analogy makes sense and has been helpful in interpreting Wittgenstein's concern with use and the practical dimension of language, it also raises a lot of troubling questions such as: How are the rules of games grasped? And what are the 'powers' that chess pieces possess by virtue of being rule-governed? By drawing attention to the analogy, the implication is that these notions in the context of playing games are more intelligible than the corresponding notions in the context of using words. Presumably, the analogy is supposed to function by borrowing some of the greater intelligibility from the simpler case of playing chess. But do the same problems merely recur in this context?

One thing that the analogy does help to emphasise is that the identification of meaning and use is too general to be informative. If we were to deal in slogans,

---

[5] See Baker and Hacker (2005a, 53–4) on a similar and more comprehensive breakdown of the different analogies.

something like the following would be more appropriate: meaning = use *in a rule-governed practice*. For as the analogy highlights, if using a word is like making a move in a game of chess, then we must also attend to the rules that permit and prescribe certain uses of words. But this brings us straight back into the difficult and murky domain of normativity, which thus requires us to say something about being correct or incorrect in our uses of words, or using words as we should or should not etc. Hence, the analogy between using language and playing games is only genuinely enlightening if it is supplemented with a fairly subtle appreciation of the arguments concerning normativity that Wittgenstein presents in his discussion of rule-following (as outlined here in Chapter 2).

Furthermore, we have to be careful not to over-stretch the analogy to the point where it becomes misleading. For example, as Baker and Hacker note, speaking a language is not literally playing a game; also, translating from one language into another does not have a straightforward analogue in playing games, and the notions of winning and losing in games do not have a straightforward analogue in speaking a language (see Baker and Hacker 2005a, 53/4). Another fundamental difference that can easily get overlooked in the analogy is the greater complexity in using language compared to the activity of playing a game like chess. One way of thinking about this complexity – or lack of complexity – is as follows. Although the concept of a game may be called a family resemblance concept, this is understood to mean that there is no fixed set of essential characteristics shared by all instances of games and that it is thus open-ended or undetermined exactly what is to count as a game. But this open-endedness concerns the general concept of game, not necessarily what takes place within a specific game like chess. In fact, it seems as though chess itself is not open-ended – what counts as playing chess is not indeterminate in the same way. Rather, because the rules in question belong to a relatively small set and can be articulated quite easily ('the rook can only move straight, never diagonally' etc.), the activity of playing chess is accordingly limited and circumscribed. This is not to suggest that rules operate in a special way in games, for example platonistically predetermining all possible moves; it is merely that the *people* playing the game can more straightforwardly object or reprimand one another if a move is made that is taken to be in violation of the rules ('it is *we* that are inexorable' (*Remarks on the Foundations of Mathematics* (*RFM*), 82)).

This lack of complexity also exists in many of the primitive language-games that Wittgenstein asks us or his interlocutors to imagine. However, his discussion of language does not end with these examples; it also takes in the much more complex examples of using language that occur in our everyday lives. This increase in complexity in language use compared to playing games makes a significant difference. At least part of this additional complexity has to do with the fact that using words has a variety of functions that do not coalesce around a singular goal like winning (or for that matter, speaking truthfully), and that there is a greater multitude of social contexts in which words can be used. This additional complexity is what leads Wittgenstein to state that:

A main source of our failure to understand is that we do not *command a clear view* of the use of our words. – Our grammar is lacking in this sort of perspicuity. A perspicuous representation produces just that understanding which consists in 'seeing connexions'. Hence the importance of finding and inventing *intermediate cases*. (*PI*, §122)

By contrast, we *do* command a clear view of the moves that can be made in a game like chess. And likewise, we do command a clear view of the use of words in the primitive language-games that Wittgenstein discusses. Where 'this sort of perspicuity' is lacking is in the more complex cases of language use, which are common in everyday life. The mention in the passage of 'the importance of finding and inventing *intermediate cases*' indicates the true value of the game analogy. It is to *start* with the simple examples of language use – examples that are as simple as what we do in certain games or even simpler – and consider ever more complex examples that take us closer to the kind of complicated language use we engage in regularly. In this way, we can as it were borrow or extend the intelligibility of these simpler cases to the more complex cases.[6]

The complexity of our use of words is strikingly evoked in Wittgenstein's comparison of language with a physical landscape such as a city:

Our language can be seen as an ancient city: a maze of little streets and squares, of old and new houses, and of houses with additions from various periods; and this surrounded by a multitude of new boroughs with straight regular streets and uniform houses. (*PI*, §18)

He introduces this analogy because he believes it is genuinely helpful not only in understanding the nature of languages as historically constituted (containing a complicated mixture of old and new elements), but also in highlighting the difficult task of reflecting philosophically on language. In the Preface to *PI*, he famously compares his philosophical remarks to 'a number of sketches

---

[6] The following important passage from *The Blue Book* helps to clarify this point further: 'I shall in the future again and again draw your attention to what I shall call language-games. *These are ways of using signs simpler than those in which we use the signs of our highly complicated everyday language*. Language games are the forms of language with which a child begins to make use of words. The study of language games is the study of primitive forms of language or primitive languages. If we want to study the problems of truth and falsehood, of the agreement and disagreement of propositions with reality, of the nature of assertion, assumption, and question, we shall with great advantage look at primitive forms of language in which these forms of thinking appear without the confusing background of highly complicated processes of thought. When we look at such simple forms of language the mental mist which seems to enshroud our ordinary use of language disappears. We see activities, reactions, which are clear-cut and transparent. *On the other hand we recognize in these simple processes forms of language not separated by a break from our more complicated ones. We see that we can build up the complicated forms from the primitive ones by gradually adding new forms.*' (*BB*, 17; emphases added.)

of landscapes which were made in the course of these long and involved journeyings'. The result of his reflections, then, would be to provide 'a picture of the landscape', or 'an album' of pictures. The above remarks in §122 can be interpreted as elaborating this comparison by stating that he is attempting to provide an 'overview' of 'the use of our words'. Using words without having such an overview would thus be rather like travelling in a city or across a landscape without a map. Using words in this way is something we all do daily, and that philosophers do too, but Wittgenstein sees it as his task to reflect on it in a more effective way and make some sort of record of it. The goal of his investigations is to help us find our way around by providing such a map. In his view, philosophical problems arise because we lack such a map or overview of the use of words. As he puts it, drawing on his landscape analogy: 'A philosophical problem has the form: "I don't know my way about"' (*PI*, §123).

The over-arching point that I want to emphasise is that the much greater complexity that exists in language use compared to playing games is indicative of the priority of use over rules.[7] This priority was illustrated in the previous section with the example of the use of the word 'love', but we could equally reflect on the use of a word for any complicated phenomenon in our life to see how use often outstrips the rules or criteria (in the psychological sphere alone we could list the examples of 'jealousy', 'lust', 'hate', 'pride' etc.). The danger in relying too heavily on the game analogy is that it can easily suggest the opposite priority, i.e. that rules have priority in the sense that the activity or behaviour in question only counts as playing a game if the rules are already laid down and accessible to the player or players.[8]

Hence, if the analogy between using language and playing games is stretched too far, it can easily lead to the mistaken belief that rules or criteria for the use of words must precede (both temporally and logically) the actual use of words. To see the error in this, it helps to consider how the job of compiling dictionary definitions for newly formed and used words is often to reflect the diversity of actual uses of a word and to extract a fairly coherent definition of the word after the use has become established. Typically, then, the rule or definition is formulated after the word has been in use for some time; and there is no contradiction or incoherence in a word having a use before a rule is articulated. There may not even be clear guidelines for what counts as correctly or incorrectly

---

[7] This is not to deny that there are numerous examples of games with complicated sets of rules. Wittgenstein deliberately focuses on the relatively simple examples like chess because it is easier to use them as objects of comparison to shed light on what we do when we use words.

[8] Regarding games, it is not always the case that the rules must be in place beforehand. There are many examples of playing games where the rules are not clearly laid down, such as children's games that are invented as they go along. The point is that it is more tempting to suppose that rules have this priority in the case of games because the most famous and widely played games have clear and explicit sets of rules. Hence, the game analogy can be misleading if this supposition is extended to language use.

using the word in each situation. This can be the case for new words as well as old words like 'love'.

Another reason why it would be mistaken to follow the suggestion that rules have priority over use is that it makes it seem as if there is a simple route to arriving at an overview of our use of words, viz. by articulating the rules for the use of words in much the same way as we would articulate the rules of a game. It makes it seem that what is required is a system of rules that can be overlaid like a grid on our language use, supposedly giving us a clear view of our use of words. But this – to employ Wittgenstein's metaphor – would be like constructing a map of a city that is not fit for purpose because it is overly simplistic and blind to the finer details. This illusory route to perspicuity is precisely the one taken in *TLP* in the statement of the 'general form of proposition', and the one that Wittgenstein in *PI* consciously strives to avoid.

As we shall soon see, this is the same mistake that is made in use theories of meaning. Despite the label, these theories fail to acknowledge the primacy of use or the brute facts of the use that we make of words in all their complexity. Instead, they give primacy to the general rules that supposedly govern the use and that constitute the meanings of the words we use. In the next two sections, I will explore the fundamental differences between how language use is viewed in use theories of meaning, on the one hand, and in Wittgenstein's *PI*, on the other.

6.5   Horwich's Use Theory of Meaning

The distinctiveness of Wittgenstein's reflections on meaning and use can be brought out by contrasting them with a very different approach, viz. one that identifies meaning with use in a fully worked-out use theory. For the present purposes I will focus on the example of Paul Horwich's use theory in his 2005 book, *Reflections on Meaning*, because there is a considerable amount of detail to his version. However, another reason for choosing it is that Horwich followed up this book with a book on Wittgenstein in 2012 and what Horwich takes to be the Wittgensteinian qualities of his use theory are made more explicit there. In the next section, I will reflect on the distinct attitudes to use discussed in each work. My goal is to indicate in the strongest terms that not only does Wittgenstein not propose a use theory of meaning (or proto-theory), but that such a theory goes against what he says about use and meaning. This will require me to depart significantly from Horwich's reading. In this section, though, I will merely present some of the features of Horwich's own use theory, which will subsequently be illuminating as an object of comparison.

A fundamental question that any use theory must be able to adequately address is: *what is use?* However, doing so turns out to be surprisingly difficult.

Two possible answers to the question immediately present themselves, both of which raise problems:

(a) The uses of words are physical events (including – but perhaps not merely – making marks on paper etc.).
(b) The uses of words are more than mere physical events.

A use theory could attempt to adopt either of these responses and they could be roughly characterised as 'semantic reductionist' and 'semantic primitivist', respectively. Generally, the problem with the first characterisation is that mere noises and marks are – so it would seem – not sufficient to constitute meaning, and the challenge is thus to identify other phenomena of a similar kind that somehow explain how we do more than merely make noise when we speak. The problem with the second characterisation is that the 'more than' threatens to introduce an alternative conception of meaning (a non-use-based conception), which undermines the claim that meaning is use. Horwich adopts the first response; but let's briefly look at the second, 'primitivist' response before getting into some of the details of his theory.

The non-reductionist or primitivist response characterises use as intrinsically semantic rather than as reducible to non-semantic phenomena, and it faces the compelling objection that it simply presupposes the notion of meaning rather than providing an explanation of it. The defender of this response must tell us what notion of meaning is involved in calling the use of words meaningful. Again, the defender cannot appeal to a non-use-based conception (for example, a referential conception) because that would amount to accepting that the use theory is inadequate. But how else is the defender supposed to explain how the words that are used are meaningful, i.e. have genuinely semantic properties?

Horwich is aware of these problems, which is presumably why he favours a reductionist version of the use theory (see 2005, 36). He writes that 'The meaning of a word, w, is engendered by the non-semantic feature of w that explains w's overall deployment' (2005, 28). His presentation of his theory is devoted to characterising the 'non-semantic feature' or features that the meaning of a word reduces to, and that 'explains' the word's overall deployment or use. For Horwich, the relevant non-semantic feature of a word is

an acceptance-property of the following form: – 'that such-and-such w-sentences are regularly accepted in such-and-such circumstances' is the idealized law governing w's use (by the relevant 'experts', given certain meanings attached to various other words). (*Ibid.*)

Hence, the relevant non-semantic features of a word are the properties of certain sentences containing the words being 'regularly accepted in such-and-such circumstances'. For example, the word 'red' has the non-semantic feature that we have a propensity to accept sentences containing the word, such as 'This table is red' in response to 'the sort of visual experience normally provoked by observing a clearly red surface' (2005, 49). Horwich's use theory takes its starting point from the view that our propensity to accept certain sentences is governed by particular 'laws', and it proceeds to state that these laws are ultimately what constitute the meanings of words and explain our overall use of the words. As he puts it:

> in order that a word, w, be meaningful (according to [this theory]) it suffices that there be *basic* regularities governing the acceptance of sentences containing it (which will presumably exist whenever there is an acceptance practice involving w). (2005, 30)

Very generally, then, his theory holds that a word has meaning by virtue of a law that governs our propensity to accept sentences containing the word in certain circumstances. As indicated, this law-governed acceptance-property is claimed to be a non-semantic feature of the word, which makes the theory an account of how semantic properties reduce to use properties (or more simply, how meaning reduces to use):

> A word means what it does, according to [this theory], *in virtue of* its basic use; a word's use is *responsible* for its meaning what it does. Thus, not only does a meaning-property *supervene* on a basic acceptance property, but possession of the former is *immediately explained* by possession of the latter. (2005, 32)
>
> For each meaning-property, [this theory] tells us how to find a particular non-semantic use-property such that anything's possession of the former is grounded in its possession of the latter. Thus [this theory] is a form of reductionism. (2005, 36)

After presenting the outline of his use theory of meaning in the second chapter of his book, Horwich devotes most of the rest of the book to developing it and addressing objections to it.

My present concern, though, is with the form that the use theory takes and how it differs radically from Wittgenstein's approach to use. The differences are hopefully already becoming clear. I will conclude by noting one more important feature of Horwich's use theory, viz. that it characterises meanings as entities of some sort. This emerges in the comparison he makes between physical properties and semantic properties:

> Accordingly, just as we sometimes say that being water *is* being made of H_2O, we might, in the same sense, *identify* thick meaning-properties with certain use-properties.
>   But now consider facts of the form
>   w means k to S,
>   where w is a word, k is a meaning, and S is a person (or a community). One might wish to know not merely how such *facts* are constituted, which is the question we have just addressed. In addition one might well wonder how the *components* of these facts are constituted. Specifically, (Q1) what kinds of things are the meaning-*entities*, k? And (Q2) what is the nature of the triadic meaning-*relation*, 'w means k to S'?
>   The answers that I would suggest to these two further questions are

(A1) Meaning-entities are universals – in particular, they are *use*-properties.

(A2) w means k to S $\equiv$ S's w exemplifies k.

Thus [this use theory's] claim, that to have a certain meaning is to exemplify a certain use-property, might be factored into an analysis of 'means' as 'exemplifies', and an analysis of meanings as use-properties. The idea is that just as a flower has a colour and a stick has a length, so a sound has a meaning; just as colours and lengths are properties, meanings are also properties. Therefore the logical form of a simple meaning-fact is '$M(w_s)$', which entails 'S's w has (or exemplifies) the property of M-ness'. And each such property, M-ness, reduces to a use-property. (2005, 33–4)

The characterisation of meanings as entities provides a good illustration of how this use theory prioritises the rule (or 'law') governing the use of a word over the use itself. This, as we have seen, is challenged by Wittgenstein. I will consider this further in the next section, and also discuss how Wittgenstein is opposed to the related claim that meanings are entities.

6.6   Instructive Contrasts: Horwich, Horwich's Wittgenstein and Wittgenstein on Use

Horwich's reading of Wittgenstein on use has a number of features that conflict when considered together. As I noted in the first chapter, he maintains that Wittgenstein takes the definition of meaning as use 'for granted from the very outset of his book and relies on it throughout' (Horwich 2012, 106). Horwich's Wittgenstein holds that when it comes to understanding a language, 'knowing how and when to *use* a term' is more fundamental than knowing what a term stands for. While there are many instances – such as colour words – where we are taught the meaning of a word by someone pointing to an object, even in those cases what is most important is that the person goes on to use the word as others do. Attending to how they use a word is how we tell if they understand it. Like many other interpreters, Horwich stresses that Wittgenstein's definition of meaning as use 'does not qualify as a theory' (2012, 115). However, we will see that the details of the view Horwich attributes to Wittgenstein strongly suggest the opposite conclusion. In fact, Horwich's Wittgenstein's view turns out to have significant similarities to Horwich's own use theory.

The first clear marker that Horwich's Wittgenstein is defending a theory is given in the following passage:

[Wittgenstein's definition of meaning as use in §43 of *PI*] is concerned rather with the facts in virtue of which *any* given word (whether defined or indefinable) has the meaning it does – with the underlying characteristics that are responsible for its possessing that particular meaning. Thus Wittgenstein is addressing a problem about the constitution of a certain range of properties: namely, the various 'meaning-properties' that words can have. Just as one might ask what it is for something to be red, or to be magnetic, or to be true, and so on, in a similar spirit one can ask what it is for a word to mean RED, or for it to mean AND, or for it to mean ELECTRON. These are the questions that his remark is intended to answer – or at least to put us in a position to be able to answer. He is suggesting that each word's meaning what it does consists in certain facts about its use. (Horwich 2012, 109)

Hence, Horwich's Wittgenstein is concerned with addressing 'a problem about the *constitution of* ... "meaning-properties" ', and is guided by the conviction that 'each word's meaning what it does *consists in* certain facts about its use' (my emphasis). This sounds from the beginning very much like an explanatory project, where the goal is to explain how words acquire their meanings by virtue of being used in certain ways. Horwich even employs similar formulations to those he employed to outline his own use theory in his (2005), such as by comparing meaning-properties with physical properties like being magnetic.

This aspect of Horwich's Wittgenstein's view is reinforced on the subsequent page when Horwich writes (alluding to pp. 4–6 of *The Blue Book*) that Wittgenstein wants to 'explain how "life" is given to signs that are otherwise "dead" '. The point of this explanatory project is ultimately to '*fully* demystify the concept of meaning' (2012, 110). Horwich argues that Wittgenstein attempts to do this by offering a characterisation of the use of words 'in behavioural terms', or more specifically without needing to appeal to '*semantic* concepts' like reference or '*intentional* concepts' like intention or belief. Therefore, Horwich's Wittgenstein is similar to Horwich in offering a non-semantic characterisation of use.

Horwich is right about Wittgenstein on the point about demystifying the concept of meaning, and he makes a good case for why this must be so. It comes down to the question of the correct order of explanation. As Horwich states, Wittgenstein's commitment to a '*deflationary* view of truth-theoretic notions' compels him to explain the notion of truth in terms of that of proposition; and the notion of proposition will 'on pain of circularity have to be explained *independently* of truth'. Therefore, Wittgenstein 'cannot be supposing that the notion of proposition be analysed in terms of the notion of *truth* condition' (2012, 110). Horwich thus concludes:

So, given Wittgenstein's commitments and aspirations, it would be incongruous for him to include within the 'use' of a word such properties as 'used to refer to so-and-so' or 'used to express such-and-such beliefs'. Rather, the meaning-giving uses of words must be restricted to *non*-semantic forms of use, including physical, behavioural, and certain psychological forms – for example, the internal acceptance of sentences. (2012, 111)

The big question is then that of how Wittgenstein characterises use in non-semantic terms. And as Horwich indicates in the last sentence, he answers this question along the lines of his own 2005 use theory. Wittgenstein thus comes out looking like a proto-Horwichian.[9]

---

[9] For more on Horwich's attempted defence of this non-semantic reading, see where he writes: 'This interpretation is vindicated by Wittgenstein's *fairly* behaviouristic illustrations. In

However, Horwich's Wittgenstein is not capable of demystifying the notion of meaning in the way that Horwich tries to suggest. This becomes clearer when he discusses the issue of the normativity of meaning and language use (see 2012, 117–21). As he states, the normativity issue concerns explicitly how the meaning is constituted from the use; it asks the question of 'the normative or evaluative status of the features of use that, according to Wittgenstein, issue in the meanings of the words' (2012, 117). Horwich considers a few proposals as to how Wittgenstein addresses this question, and on some of these (specifically the first two he mentions) meaning is viewed as normative in the sense that meaning can only be said to be constituted from use if norms are thereby established for how to use the words. For example, Horwich asks:

is [Wittgenstein] saying that a word's meaning is constituted by how it *should* be used – some fact of the form, 'We ought to use w in such-and-such a way'? (*Ibid.*)

Although he states that there is no single answer to how Wittgenstein characterises the norms governing the use of words, the proposal he favours is articulated as follows:

[M]aybe his idea is that meaning a given thing by a word is a matter of *following imperatival rules* for its use ('Accept such-and-such sentences containing w!')? (2012, 118)

It is perhaps not surprising that Horwich is drawn to this reading since it is the one that fits most comfortably with his own theory that places '*acceptance-conditions*' at its centre.

Horwich elaborates on what he takes to be Wittgenstein's views on the normativity issue by explicitly attributing to him a version of the rule-based conception of meaning, or the view that the meaning of a word is constituted by a rule for its use. See where he writes:

Thus, someone's meaning a certain thing by a word might consist in his following a certain rule for its use, which might in turn be constituted (in large part) by his being disposed to operate with it in a certain law-like way. (2012, 119).

This is Horwich's Wittgenstein's answer to the question of how use constitutes meaning; it does so by virtue of a rule governing the use. And this, then, is ultimately how Horwich's Wittgenstein is proposing to demystify the concept of meaning.

the first paragraph of the *Investigations* he asks us to consider "the following use of language", and he tells us what is *done* with the word "five" – how it is *acted on*, how people *behave* with it (such as when counting out apples in a shop). And then he says "It is in this and similar ways that one operates with words", explaining that he has specified how the word "five" is used. Similarly, for all the primitive language games that he goes on to present – such as the one (described in paragraphs 2 and 8) in which a builder calls out "slab" (or "block", or "beam") then someone brings him a slab (or a block, or a beam). His examples of the meaning-constituting uses of words are never couched in semantic or intentional terms.' (2012, 112)

That it cannot achieve this, not even on Horwich's own terms, soon becomes apparent. When Horwich attempts to specify 'the *normative* import' of this conception (i.e. what kind of normative constraints are involved when we are bound by a rule for the use of a word), the account he attributes to Wittgenstein runs into trouble. He writes:

[A] person's following a rule incorporates his propensity to correct himself, based (presumably) on his immediate reactions of satisfaction or dissatisfaction to his initial inclination. Thus we might well suppose that he manifests an 'implicit *desire*' to obey the rule – in which case it is natural for us to recognize a self-interestedly pragmatic *reason* for him to do so. He *ought* (other things being equal) to conform. (*Ibid.*)

This shows that the account cannot do without mentalistic/intentional notions after all. It is thus not a matter of use constituting meaning, where use is characterised in purely non-semantic and non-intentional terms. Rather, he must rely firstly on *rules* governing the use (whatever they are) and mental states like 'implicit *desire*' to explain how we follow those rules. But, of course, the familiar problems of how any mental phenomena could be constitutive of rule-following (discussed in Chapter 2 especially) arise again. Horwich's Wittgenstein, in short, gives a middle Wittgenstein response rather than a later Wittgenstein response to the issues concerning rule-following, and he accordingly inherits the same difficulties faced by the middle Wittgenstein.

Horwich concludes by formulating the following picture of how meaning is constituted, and attributes it to Wittgenstein:

At the bottom there are propensities to operate with words in one way or another; these help constitute our implicitly following the rules of our language game; and this activity of rule-following constitutes our words' meanings. (2012, 120–1)

Horwich, it should be acknowledged, is correct about two important features of Wittgenstein on use: (a) that a non-semantic, non-intentional characterisation of the use of words is required; and (b) that such a characterisation is central to demystifying the notion of meaning. At its heart, this is the whole point of Wittgenstein's appeal to use. But Horwich's reading fails to give an adequate picture of either. His account of the first ends up depicting Wittgenstein as relying on intentional concepts after all. And regarding the second, on his interpretation of Wittgenstein as engaged in the project of explaining how meanings (and the corresponding norms or 'evaluative implications')[10] are constituted from the use of words, the notion of meaning comes out seeming as mysterious as it is in Horwich's own use theory. The demystifying process is supposed to proceed as follows: meaning is explained in terms of rules (which are assumed to

---

[10] See (2012, 121) on the normativity issue: 'according to this picture, meaning is not *intrinsically* normative – a word's meaning what it does is not *itself* an evaluative fact – but it does have a variety of evaluative implications.'

be less mysterious than 'meaning'); and rules are explained in terms of certain mental phenomena. However, as we have seen, this process does not work. On his reading, there is a lot that 'meaning' has to be. The concept is over-inflated in a way not dissimilar to how it is in other theories of meaning.

The true philosophical significance of Wittgenstein's interest in the use of words can only be appreciated by keeping in mind the power and scope of the negative arguments presented in *PI*. These are the arguments that expose the absurdity of dominant conceptions or pictures of meaning (or those that we are most tempted to think about meaning in terms of), notably the referentialist and platonist conceptions. These are the conceptions that are most responsible for mystifying the notion of meaning. To say that Wittgenstein is striving for a non-semantic, non-intentional characterisation of the use of words is to say that his characterisation of use must not incorporate or rely on any semantic or intentional notion that has been shown by his negative arguments to be flawed. It is only if these semantic and intentional notions are abandoned that he can genuinely move towards a demystification of the concept of meaning by reflecting on the use of words. This is precisely what Horwich's Wittgenstein evidently does not achieve.

Wittgenstein's distinctive attitude to use could also be clarified by viewing it in terms of his opposition to the claim that meanings are entities of some sort.[11] This claim has a long tradition and has taken different forms depending on which kinds of entities meanings were said to be. For example, Locke held that meanings are mental entities or 'ideas' (see Locke 1975, 405), while Frege held that at least one category of meanings – 'senses' – are abstract entities (see Frege 1918, 336–7)). The referential conception also assumes that meanings are entities, although which type depends on which entity a word refers to. Versions of the claim are also clearly incorporated into the platonist picture and the private language picture. Perhaps more surprising, though, is that use theories too hold that meanings are entities; as we have seen in the case of Horwich's version, the entities are rules governing the use of the words.[12]

Wittgenstein departs from all of these theoretical attitudes to meaning by rejecting the frameworks that presuppose particular versions of the claim that meanings are entities, as well as by reflecting on use in such a way that does not obligate him to hold that meanings are entities. Concerning the latter point, he pays more attention to how we actually use words than to the rules that are supposedly constitutive of the meanings of the words and that underpin the

---

[11] See *PI*, §120: 'You say: the point isn't the word, but its meaning, and you think of the meaning as a thing of the same kind as the word, though also different from the word. Here the word, there the meaning. The money, and the cow that you can buy with it. (But contrast: money, and its use.)'

[12] Horwich rather misleadingly calls the entities in question 'use-properties', when it is really the rules for the use of words that are decisive in constituting the meanings rather than the use itself.

use. This is what allows him to depart from use theorists and to avoid being compelled to hold that meanings are entities of some sort. This fundamentally is how Wittgenstein sought to deflate the concept of meaning by appealing to use. It has been shown to be particularly striking because even other philosophers who focus on use or the practical dimension of language tend to continue to build too much into the concept; and there is no greater symptom of this than insisting that meanings are entities (with natures that can be explicated in a theory).

6.7   Conclusion

I stated at a couple of points in this chapter that Wittgenstein attempts to deflate the concept of meaning by appealing to how we actually use words. This helps to explain his interest in use and why he so frequently instructs us to 'look' at how we use words. He believes that many of the philosophical problems that arise around meaning can be dissolved by drawing attention to how we actually use language. However, most of the rest of this book has shown that this way of dealing with the problems is not simple or straightforward, especially when the interlocutor involved is someone in the grip of a certain philosophical picture of meaning. For instance, as we saw in the first chapter in relation to the referential picture, drawing the interlocutor's attention to how words are used had to also be supplemented with particular arguments designed to highlight the problems that are perpetuated by the referentialist theoretical claims.

According to the reading defended here, the theoretical attitude to language is dominated by a multitude of ways of inflating the concept of meaning. And this chapter has added the use theory to the other theories of meaning as representative of yet another attempt to provide an explanatory account of the nature of meaning – in the case of the use theory, meanings are explained not so much in terms of actual use but in terms of the rules for the use of words. It is important to see that Wittgenstein's anti-theoretical attitude sets him in opposition to the use theory as much as to the other theories of meaning we have discussed. His deflationary approach is manifested in the object of his study – how words are actually used rather than how they should be used – and the modesty of his goals in his reflections on language.

I have tried a few approaches to bringing out the distinctiveness of Wittgenstein's reflections on language use. By contrasting him with the use theorist, I have sought to show how his approach could be characterised as (i) deflationist in the above sense, (ii) anti-theoretical, (iii) prioritising the complexity of actual use over rules governing the use and (iv) opposed to the assumption that meanings are entities. These are, of course, closely related. Wittgenstein shows us how the concept of linguistic meaning is easily distorted or misconstrued in philosophy; and this is often due to overlooking how words are actually used. Insofar as we talk about meaning at all, his advice is that in many cases we should talk about it as the use we make of a word because this can help us avoid making the same errors. However, we have seen throughout this chapter that thinking of meaning in terms of use still faces many pitfalls. The more specific advice we end up with is thus not merely to think of meaning in terms of use, but to do so outside the misguided project of proposing a theory of the nature of meaning.

Summary of Main Points

(6a) Broadly speaking, the 'use theory' states that the meaning of a word is identifiable with how the word is used. It can be viewed as a theory that competes with other theories (such as referentialism) that attempt to provide an adequate explanation of what meaning is and how it is constituted.

(6b) Wittgenstein's numerous remarks concerning the close connection between the meaning of a word and its use have undoubtedly inspired the development of use theories of meaning.

(6c) However, Wittgenstein is just as strongly opposed to use theories as he is to all other theories of meaning. This is indicated not only by his general opposition to theorising in philosophy, but even more emphatically by the fact that his own negative arguments – employed against referentialism, platonism about meaning etc. – can in many cases also be shown to undermine the use theorist's attempted explanatory account of meaning.

(6d) Wittgenstein's interest in the use of words is thus distinctive and needs to be appreciated in the context of his anti-theoretical conception of philosophy.

(6e) Rather than seeking to provide an alternative answer to the same question concerning the nature of meaning, his reflections on the use we make of words are central to a different kind of philosophical programme. The goal of his investigation is to demystify or deflate the concept of meaning. This contrasts with the various theoretical approaches to language, which are inflationary in the sense of viewing meaning as a robust property or entity with a nature we need to account for or explain.

(6f) Wittgenstein holds that philosophers have to be able to acknowledge or accommodate the simple fact that words are used. In examples such as that of the beetle in §293 of *PI*, this helps to demonstrate the inability of referentialism and other theories to account for meaning on their own terms (because the mere notion of using the word in question comes to seem problematic or impossible).

(6g) By considering Wittgenstein's remarks on words like 'hope' and 'love', where the use is complicated, we can come to understand how he gives priority to the actual use we make of words. That is, he gives priority to the sheer complexity and open-endedness of use over anything like a rule or mental entity that could be held to determine that use in advance.

(6h) Giving priority to the actual uses of words (in all their diversity and complexity) over rules and criteria is ultimately what is distinctive about Wittgenstein's reflections on use, compared with those of the use theorist.

(6i) Horwich's use theory, by contrast, clearly prioritises the rules for the use of words over the use itself. In this regard, there is a fundamental divide between Wittgenstein's remarks on use and use theories of meaning.

(6j) All of the theoretical characterisations of meaning (including those provided by use theorists) view meanings as entities of some sort. Wittgenstein's rejection of these theoretical approaches accords with his rejection of the assumption that meanings are entities.

Conclusion

> In philosophising we may not *terminate* a disease of thought. It must run its natural course, and *slow* cure is all important. – Wittgenstein, *RPP* II, §641

The most important interpretive claim I have defended in this book is that Wittgenstein presents numerous arguments in *Philosophical Investigations* (*PI*). The purpose of each of the chapters (with the exception of Chapter 5) was to develop this general claim, and provide support for it, by clarifying the different arguments concerning language in *PI*. These include: anti-referentialist arguments; an anti-platonist argument (itself consisting of the regress and gerrymandering arguments); and a private language argument. In each case, I found problems with attempts by other Wittgenstein scholars to formulate these arguments; the most common defect was that they usually presented the arguments as being weak or as contradicting his metaphilosophical remarks. Where possible, I have tried to formulate Wittgenstein's arguments in a way that shows them to be compelling and genuinely troubling to any philosopher who defends referentialism, platonism about meaning or one of the other doctrines under attack.

It was equally important in this study of his arguments to address the question of what they are doing in *PI* and how they fit with his overall anti-theoretical conception of philosophy. I defended the view that Wittgenstein's arguments, when taken together, provide support for his anti-theoretical attitude. Each argument can be seen as targeting one set of general theoretical assumptions about the nature of language. Hence, if these arguments are successful, they provide a step-by-step demonstration of how philosophers' attempts to theorise about language fail. Nevertheless, a consequence of this reading is that it remains possible for a philosopher to accept the conclusions of Wittgenstein's arguments and yet not follow him in embracing the anti-theoretical standpoint. A philosopher may take the overarching lesson to be that a better theoretical picture of language is called for, i.e. one that is not vulnerable to Wittgenstein's arguments. Therefore, even those who reject his distinctive conception of philosophy can make extensive use of his arguments.

Concerning the possibility of contemporary philosophers of language constructively engaging with Wittgenstein, my reading emphasises that in addition to addressing the specific issue of the nature of meaning philosophers are also compelled to confront their own assumptions about what philosophy is and what its goals should be. *At very least*, the method of theorising in philosophy can no longer be assumed to be legitimate or assumed to be the default philosophical method. Wittgenstein extends the discussion beyond the questions of 'what is language?' and 'what is meaning?' And rather than simply asking ourselves the narrow question of whether the referential theory, the use theory or some other theory is the correct theory of meaning, we are forced to consider whether our metaphilosophical assumptions prevent us from seeing language in the right light. It may be that our conception of philosophy blinds us to the complexity and richness of language, and makes us overlook the possibility of an alternative method of reflecting on language that acknowledges rather than reduces these features.

I will conclude by drawing attention to a couple of ways in which Wittgenstein's philosophical standpoint finds parallels in that of David Hume. These parallels were hinted at in Chapter 3, and in light of what has been discussed in the subsequent chapters it will be illuminating to reflect on them once more. What I have said about Wittgenstein's anti-theoretical standpoint will hopefully be clarified further when viewed in the context of these parallels.

Although Hume explicitly states that there is a central part of his philosophy (what he calls a science of human nature) that is explanatory, this amounts to identifying the fundamental laws that will allow him to explain how the mind works (how certain ideas are formed etc.). But since this explanatory project is supposed to pay close attention to the actual facts of our nature and cannot go beyond what is given in experience, Hume also recognises that there is a limit to what it can explain (see Hume 1975b, 13). For example, there is no explaining the fact that we naturally associate ideas according to certain principles (such as resemblance); the explanations that we can hope for involve arriving at the correct set of principles of the association of ideas rather than explaining why our minds operate with these principles and not others. Explanation thus reaches a limit and at this point it becomes imperative to acknowledge certain natural facts about ourselves. As Hume puts it, we must 'restrain the intemperate desire' to search for explanations where they cannot be provided, and thus avoid being led into 'obscure and uncertain speculations' (*Ibid.*).

There is, of course, plenty in Hume's scientific project that is foreign to Wittgenstein's concerns. But where a parallel certainly exists is in this final issue regarding the end of explanation and the acceptance of brute facts. In Wittgenstein's case, the facts concern how we happen to use language, including the fact that we tend to agree in how to apply everyday words like 'table' and 'cat'. If we try to explain why we use words the way we do, we eventually run out of reasons and all there is left to say is that this is merely what we do with words. We run up against mundane facts, such as that we call this object a 'table' because it looks like this and has this function and we call this creature a 'cat' because it looks like this, behaves a certain way etc. While Wittgenstein does not propose a theory of what linguistic meaning is or must be, the numerous negative arguments presented throughout *PI* do make strong claims about what linguistic meaning could *not* be. Or to put it another way, the arguments show the errors in attempting to provide philosophical explanations where no explanations are possible. His claims about what meaning could not be are motivated by the perceived failure of the philosophical pictures of language to account for or take due notice of the complexity of language as it is actually used in diverse contexts of human interaction.

One other significant parallel with Hume concerns the issue of scepticism. In Chapter 3, I tried to characterise the distinction between a radical sceptical position concerning some notion and the Humean alternative to it. Regarding the basis of causal inferences, for example, the radical sceptic would view the argument that they are not grounded in reason as supporting the radical position that such inferences have no basis; the Humean alternative is more moderate and identifies a different source underpinning the inferences (viz. custom or habit, or more generally the principles of association). Similarly, in the case of linguistic meaning, Wittgenstein's anti-platonist argument can be interpreted narrowly as sceptical in the sense that it contains a chain of reasoning leading to a contradiction; and if this is taken as the endpoint of the argument, it seems to undermine the very notion that there is such a thing as correctly or incorrectly using a word. The radical sceptic would thus advocate that we abandon the notion of linguistic meaning altogether. The Humean response, which Wittgenstein favours (without calling it Humean), is more moderate and sees the problem as lying not with the notion of linguistic meaning but somewhere else.

The difference between these two responses is quite subtle – especially in the Wittgensteinian case – and it is crucial to understanding the nature of Wittgenstein's response and his overall attitude to linguistic meaning. The Humean response is essentially the one that frees Wittgenstein from theoretical commitments. To see how, consider the radical sceptical response. To choose it would be to remain wedded to the legitimacy of the substantive theoretical picture of meaning (i.e. platonism or classical realism) that leads to the sceptical paradox. This is because it is only by assuming such a theoretical picture that the paradox can be generated. Therefore, to embrace the sceptical paradox is to assume that the theoretical assumptions leading to it are legitimate. Wittgenstein's response, as we have seen, is to reject these assumptions and thereby eliminate the paradox that seemed unavoidable when the assumptions were in place. (The ultimate value of Kripke's reading of Wittgenstein is that it hints at this while regrettably not being as clear or unambiguous about it as it needs to be.) The Humean alternative that

Wittgenstein takes is thus a further illustration of his anti-theoretical stand-point and of exactly what this involves. It is the standpoint that Wittgenstein adopts to sidestep *radical* scepticism about meaning and to uphold the legitimacy of our actual human linguistic practices.

All of this serves to emphasise that the historical phenomenon of the 'linguistic turn' took a highly distinctive form in Wittgenstein's later phil-osophy. He placed the study of language centre stage because he believed that philosophical problems arise as a result of misunderstandings of our use of language. On this point, there are affinities with other philosophers who took the linguistic turn, such as Frege and Russell. But the uniqueness of Wittgenstein's position is that in the face of conflict – including the threat of radical scepticism – between the results of philosophy, on the one hand, and our ordinary linguistic practices, on the other, the fault is held to lie in the assumptions and methods of philosophers rather than in some defect (such as 'logical imperfection') in our language or linguistic practices. Again, this view is not asserted dogmatically. Much of *PI* is devoted to carefully tracing out the details of the ways that philosophising falls into error. *Slow* cure is all important.

The flipside of this view of philosophy and of the origin of philosoph-ical problems is that when a greater understanding of our use of language is achieved – in large part by removing the obstacles that general philo-sophical pictures of language create – the philosophical problems that con-front us will supposedly disappear. They will be seen as a function of the philosophical or theoretical assumptions about language that have now been abandoned. However, as Wittgenstein's own life shows, particularly his con-tinuing preoccupation with philosophical problems up until he died, things do not end so neatly. Philosophical problems do not disappear in this way, not even when a compelling case has been made regarding their origins in certain confusions or mistaken theoretical assumptions. The theoretical assumptions or pictures continue to exert an influence; the temptation to the-orise does not go away. In this sense, Wittgenstein's anti-theoretical stand-point might be better characterised as an ideal rather than something to be achieved by merely changing one's attitude. The ideal is to give absolute priority to the richness of linguistic practices and the seemingly endless forms they may take in our lives. It is to look at these practices without feeling lost – like looking at a vast landscape with a sense of how to find one's way around – and to not fool oneself into believing that the best way of getting one's bearings is to construct a general model that can replace the need to keep looking.

Reading *PI* leads us to this point, but only if we appreciate the significance of his anti-theoretical standpoint and thereby grasp the full import of his instruc-tion: 'don't think, but look!' (*PI*, §66).

References

Ahmed, A. ed. 2010. *Wittgenstein's Philosophical Investigations: A Critical Guide.* Cambridge: Cambridge University Press.
2010. *Wittgenstein's Philosophical Investigations. A Reader's Guide.* London & New York: Continuum.
Albritton, R. 1966. "Postscript to 'On Wittgenstein's Use of the Term "Criterion"'." In *Wittgenstein: Philosophical Investigations*, edited by G. Pitcher, 247–50. New York: Doubleday.
Anscombe, G.E.M. 1971. *An Introduction to Wittgenstein's Tractatus.* London: Hutchinson.
Augustine. 1992. *Confessions.* Translated by H. Chadwick. Oxford: Oxford University Press.
Austin, J.L. 1957. 'A Plea for Excuses.' Reprinted in *Austin's Collected Papers*, edited by J.O. Urmson & G.J. Warnock, 175–204. Oxford: Oxford University Press.
Baker, G.P. & Hacker, P.M.S. 1984. *Scepticism, Rules and Language.* Oxford: Blackwell.
1985. *Wittgenstein: Rules, Grammar and Necessity: Volume 2 of An Analytical Commentary on the Philosophical Investigations.* Oxford: Blackwell.
2005a. *Wittgenstein: Understanding and Meaning. Volume 1 of An Analytical Commentary on the Philosophical Investigations.* 2nd Edition. Oxford: Blackwell.
2005b. *Wittgenstein: Understanding and Meaning. Volume 1 of An Analytical Commentary on the Philosophical Investigations. Part II: Exegesis §§1–184.* Oxford: Blackwell.
2009. *Wittgenstein: Rules, Grammar and Necessity. Volume 2 of An Analytical Commentary on the Philosophical Investigations. 2nd Edition.* Oxford: Blackwell.
Baker, G.P. 2004. *Wittgenstein's Method: Neglected Aspects.* Edited by K.J. Morris. Oxford: Blackwell.
Bar-On, D. 1992. 'On the Possibility of a Solitary Language.' *Nous* 26 (1): 27–45.
Beaney, M. ed. 1997. *The Frege Reader.* Oxford: Blackwell.
Beckerman, A. & Nimtz, C. eds. 2005. *Philosophy – Science – Scientific Philosophy.* Paderborn: Mentis.
Berger, A. ed. 2011. *The Cambridge Companion to Kripke.* Cambridge: Cambridge University Press.
Blackburn, S. 1984. 'The Individual Strikes Back.' Reprinted in *Rule-Following and Meaning*, edited by A. Miller & C. Wright, 28–44. Chesham: Acumen.
Boghossian, P. 1989. 'The Rule-Following Considerations.' *Mind* 98: 507–49.
2005. 'Is Meaning Normative?' In *Philosophy – Science – Scientific Philosophy*, edited by A. Beckerman & C. Nimtz, 205–18. Paderborn: Mentis.

Brandom, R. 1994. *Making It Explicit.* Cambridge, MA: Harvard University Press.

Buckle, S. 2001. *Hume's Enlightenment Tract: The Unity and Purpose of An Enquiry Concerning Human Understanding.* Oxford: Clarendon Press.

Byrne, A. 1996. 'On Misinterpreting Kripke's Wittgenstein.' *Philosophy and Phenomenological Research* 56 (2): 339–43.

Candlish, S. 1980. 'The Real Private Language Argument.' *Philosophy* 55 (211): 85–94.

Canfield, J.V. 1974. 'Criteria and Rules of Language.' *The Philosophical Review* 83 (1): 70–87.

———. 1986. *The Philosophy of Wittgenstein: The Private Language Argument.* New York & London: Garland Publishing.

———. 1996. 'The Community View.' *The Philosophical Review* 105 (4): 469–88.

Cavell, S. 1979. *The Claim of Reason.* Oxford: Oxford University Press.

Charles, D. & Child, W. eds. 2001. *Wittgensteinian Themes: Essays in Honour of David Pears.* Oxford: Oxford University Press.

Child, W. 2001. 'Pears' Wittgenstein: Rule-Following, Platonism, and Naturalism.' In *Wittgensteinian Themes: Essays in Honour of David Pears,* edited by D. Charles & W. Child, 81–114. Oxford: Oxford University Press.

Conant, J. & Diamond, C. 2004. 'On Reading the *Tractatus* Resolutely: Reply to Meredith Williams & Peter Sullivan.' In *Wittgenstein's Lasting Significance,* edited by M. Kölbel & B. Weiss, 46–99. London and New York: Routledge.

Conant, J. 2006. 'Wittgenstein's Later Criticism of the *Tractatus.*' In *Wittgenstein: The Philosopher and his Works,* edited by A. Pichler & S. Säätelä, 172–204. Frankfurt: Ontos Verlag.

Conant, J. 2011. 'Wittgenstein's Methods.' In *The Oxford Handbook of Wittgenstein,* edited by O. Kuusela & M. McGinn, 620–45. Oxford: Oxford University Press.

Cooper, J.M. ed. 1997. *Plato, Complete Works.* Indianapolis & Cambridge: Hackett.

Crary, A. & Read, R. eds. 2000. *The New Wittgenstein.* London & New York: Routledge.

Crary, A. ed. 2007. *Wittgenstein and the Moral Life: Essays in Honor of Cora Diamond.* Cambridge, MA: MIT Press.

Davies, D. 1998. 'How Sceptical is Kripke's "Sceptical Solution"?' *Philosophia* 26 (1): 119–40.

Devitt, M. & Sterelny, K. 1999. *Language and Reality: An Introduction to the Philosophy of Language.* 2nd Edition. Oxford: Blackwell.

Devitt, M. & Hanley, R. eds. 2006. *The Blackwell Guide to the Philosophy of Language.* Oxford: Blackwell

Dummett, M. 1959. 'Wittgenstein's Philosophy of Mathematics.' *The Philosophical Review* 68 (3): 324–48.

Ellis, J. & Guevara, D. eds. 2012. *Wittgenstein and the Philosophy of Mind.* Oxford: Oxford University Press.

Fogelin, R.J. 1976. *Wittgenstein.* London: Routledge.

Frege, G. 1918. 'Thought.' Reprinted in *The Frege Reader,* edited by M. Beaney, 325–45. Oxford: Blackwell.

Glock. H.-J. 1996. *A Wittgenstein Dictionary.* Oxford: Blackwell.

———. 2008. 'Meaning, Rules, and Conventions.' In *Wittgenstein's Enduring Arguments,* edited by D.K. Levy & E. Zamuner, 156–78. London & New York: Routledge.

Glüer, K. & Pagin, P. 1999. 'Rules of Meaning and Practical Reasoning.' *Synthese* 117: 207–27.

Glüer, K. & Wikforss. Å. 2009. 'Against Content Normativity.' *Mind* 118: 31–70.

  2010. '*Es braucht die Regel nicht*: Wittgenstein on Rules and Meaning.' In *The Later Wittgenstein on Language*, edited by D. Whiting, 148–66. New York: Palgrave MacMillan.

Goldfarb, W. 1983. 'I Want You to Bring Me a Slab: Remarks on the Opening Sections of the *Philosophical Investigations*.' *Synthese* 56 (3): 265–82.

  1985. 'Kripke on Wittgenstein and Rules.' Reprinted in *Rule-Following and Meaning*, edited by A. Miller & C. Wright, 92–108. Chesham: Acumen.

  2012. 'Rule-Following Revisited.' In *Wittgenstein and the Philosophy of Mind*, edited by J. Ellis & D. Guevara, 73–90. Oxford: Oxford University Press.

Goodman, R.B. 2002. *Wittgenstein and William James*. Cambridge: Cambridge University Press.

Hacker, P.M.S. 1972. *Insight and Illusion*. Oxford: Oxford University Press.

  1990. *Wittgenstein: Meaning and Mind. Volume 3 of An Analytical Commentary on the Philosophical Investigations*. Oxford: Blackwell.

Hanna, R. 2010. 'From Referentialism to Human Action: the Augustinian Theory of Language.' In *Wittgenstein's Philosophical Investigations: A Critical Guide*, edited by A. Ahmed, 11–29. Cambridge: Cambridge University Press.

Hattiangadi, A. 2006. 'Is Meaning Normative?' *Mind and Language* 21 (2): 220–40.

  2007. *Oughts and Thoughts: Rule Following and the Normativity of Meaning*. Oxford: Oxford University Press.

  2009. 'Some More Thoughts on Semantic Oughts: A Reply to Daniel Whiting.' *Analysis* 69 (1): 54–63.

Haukioja, J. 2004. 'Is Solitary Rule-Following Possible?' *Philosophia* 32: 1–25.

Horwich, P. 2005. *Reflections on Meaning*. Oxford: Oxford University Press.

  2012. *Wittgenstein's Metaphilosophy*. Oxford: Oxford University Press.

Hume, D. 1975a. *Enquiries Concerning Human Understanding and Concerning the Principles of Morals*. 3rd Edition. Edited by L.A. Selby-Bigge. Revised by P.H. Nidditch. Oxford: Clarendon Press.

  1975b. *A Treatise of Human Nature*. 2nd Edition. Edited by L.A. Selby-Bigge. Revised by P.H. Nidditch. Oxford: Clarendon Press.

James, W. 2007. *The Principles of Psychology*. Cambridge, MA: Harvard University Press.

Kahane, G., Kanterian, E., & Kuusela, O. eds. 2007. *Wittgenstein and His Interpreters*. Malden, MA, Oxford & Victoria: Blackwell.

Kenny, A. 1971. 'The Verificationist Principle and the Private Language Argument.' Reprinted in *The Philosophy of Wittgenstein: The Private Language Argument*, edited by J.V. Canfield, 208–33. New York & London: Garland Publishing.

  2006. *Wittgenstein*. 2nd Edition. Oxford: Blackwell.

Kölbel, M. & Weiss, B. eds. 2004. *Wittgenstein's Lasting Significance*. London and New York: Routledge.

Kripke, S. 1980. *Naming and Necessity*. Cambridge, MA: Harvard University Press.

  1982. *Wittgenstein on Rules and Private Language*. Cambridge, MA: Harvard University Press.

Kusch, M. 2006. *A Sceptical Guide to Meaning and Rules. Defending Kripke's Wittgenstein*. Chesham: Acumen.

Kuusela, O. 2008. *The Struggle Against Dogmatism: Wittgenstein and the Concept of Philosophy*. Cambridge, MA: Harvard University Press.

Kuusela, O. & McGinn, M. ed. 2011. *The Oxford Handbook of Wittgenstein*. Oxford: Oxford University Press.

Lear, J. 1984. 'The Disappearing "We".' *Aristotelian Society* 58: 219–42.

Lepore, E. & Smith, B. eds. 2006. *The Oxford Handbook of Philosophy of Language*. Oxford: Oxford University Press.

Levy, D.K. & Zamuner, E. eds. 2008. *Wittgenstein's Enduring Arguments*. London & New York: Routledge.

Locke, J. 1975. *An Essay Concerning Human Understanding*. Edited by P.H. Nidditch. Oxford: Clarendon Press.

Lycan, W.G. 1971. 'Noninductive Evidence: Recent Work on Wittgenstein's "Criteria".' *American Philosophical Quarterly* 8: 109–25.

2000. *Philosophy of Language: A Contemporary Introduction*. London & New York: Routledge.

Malcolm, N. 1954. 'Wittgenstein's *Philosophical Investigations*.' *The Philosophical Review* 63 (4): 530–59.

1986. *Nothing is Hidden: Wittgenstein's Criticism of his Early Thought*. Oxford: Blackwell.

McDowell, J. 1984. 'Wittgenstein on Following a Rule.' *Synthese* 58 (3): 325–63.

1998. *Mind, Value, and Reality*. Cambridge, MA: Harvard University Press.

2009a. 'How Not to Read *Philosophical Investigations*: Brandom's Wittgenstein.' In *The Engaged Intellect: Philosophical Essays*, J. McDowell, 96–111. Cambridge, MA: Harvard University Press.

2009b. 'Are Meaning, Understanding, etc., Definite States?' In *The Engaged Intellect: Philosophical Essays*, edited by J. McDowell, 79–95. Cambridge, MA: Harvard University Press.

2009c. *The Engaged Intellect: Philosophical Essays*. Cambridge, MA: Harvard University Press.

McGinn, C. 1984. *Wittgenstein on Meaning: An Interpretation and Evaluation*. Oxford: Blackwell.

McNally, T. 2013. 'Dummett's Radical Conventionalist Reading of Wittgenstein.' *Teorema: International Journal of Philosophy* 32 (1): 111–24.

2016a. 'Wittgenstein's Anti-Platonist Argument.' *Philosophical Investigations* 39 (3): 281–301.

2016b. 'More Than a Feeling: Wittgenstein and William James on Love and Other Emotions.' *British Journal of the History of Philosophy* 24 (4): 720–41.

Mill, J.S. 1961. *A System of Logic*. 8th Edition. London: Longmans.

Miller, A. & Wright, C. eds. 2002. *Rule-Following and Meaning*. Chesham: Acumen.

Miller, A. 2006. 'Meaning Scepticism.' In *The Blackwell Guide to the Philosophy of Language*, edited by M. Devitt & R. Hanley, 91–113. Oxford: Blackwell.

2007. *Philosophy of Language*. 2nd Edition. London & New York: Routledge.

2010. 'Kripke's Wittgenstein, Factualism, and Meaning.' In *The Later Wittgenstein on Language*, edited by D. Whiting, 167–90. Hampshire & New York: Palgrave MacMillan.

Moore, A.W. 1985. 'Transcendental Idealism in Wittgenstein, and Theories of Meaning.' *The Philosophical Quarterly* 35 (139): 134–155.

2007. 'Wittgenstein and Transcendental Idealism.' In *Wittgenstein and His Interpreters*, edited by G. Kahane, E. Kanterian, & O. Kuusela, 174–99. Malden, MA, Oxford & Victoria: Blackwell.

Morris, M. 2007. *An Introduction to the Philosophy of Language.* Cambridge: Cambridge University Press.

Mulhall, S. 2009. 'Hopelessly Strange: Bernard Williams' Portrait of Wittgenstein as a Transcendental Idealist.' *European Journal of Philosophy* 17 (3): 386–404.

Pears, D. 1988. *The False Prison.* Volume 2. Oxford: Clarendon Press.

Pitcher, G. ed. 1966. *Wittgenstein: Philosophical Investigations.* New York: Doubleday.

Pichler, A. & S. Säätelä, eds. 2006. *Wittgenstein: The Philosopher and his Works.* Frankfurt: Ontos Verlag.

Reeve, C.D.C. 1997. Plato, *Cratylus: Translated with Introduction and Notes.* In *Plato, Complete Works,* edited by J.M. Cooper. Indianapolis & Cambridge: Hackett.

Rhees, R. 1954. 'Can there be a Private Language?' *Proceedings of the Aristotelian Society,* Supp. Vol. 28: 63–94.

Rundle, B. 1990. *Wittgenstein and Contemporary Philosophy of Language.* Oxford: Blackwell.

Russell, B. 1905. 'On Denoting.' *Mind* 14: 479–93.

Shoemaker, S. 1963. *Self-Knowledge and Self-Identity.* Ithaca, NY: Cornell University Press.

Schroeder, S. 2006. *Wittgenstein: The Way Out of the Fly Bottle.* Cambridge: Polity Press.

Searle, J. 1958. 'Proper Names.' *Mind* 67: 166–73.

Soames, S. 1998. 'Facts, Truth-Conditions, and the Skeptical Solution to the Rule-Following Paradox.' *Philosophical Perspectives* 12: 313–48.

Stern, D. 2004. *Wittgenstein's Philosophical Investigations: An Introduction.* Cambridge: Cambridge University Press.

——— 2010. 'Another Strand in the Private Language Argument.' In *Wittgenstein's Philosophical Investigations: A Critical Guide,* edited by A. Ahmed, 178–96. Cambridge: Cambridge University Press.

——— 2011. 'Private Language.' In *The Oxford Handbook of Wittgenstein,* edited by O. Kuusela & M. McGinn, 333–50. Oxford: Oxford University Press.

Stroud, B. 1965. 'Wittgenstein and Logical Necessity.' *Philosophical Review* 74: 504–18.

Thomson, J.J. 1964. 'Private Languages.' *American Philosophical Quarterly* 1: 20–31.

Urmson, J.O & Warnock, G.J. eds. 1979. *Austin's Collected Papers,* 3rd Edition. Oxford: Oxford University Press.

Whiting, D. 2007. 'The Normativity of Meaning Defended.' *Analysis* 67 (2): 133–40.

——— 2010. *The Later Wittgenstein on Language.* Hampshire & New York: Palgrave MacMillan.

Williams, B. 1974. 'Wittgenstein and Idealism.' Reprinted in *Moral Luck: Philosophical Papers 1973–1980,* edited by B. Williams, 144–63. Cambridge: Cambridge University Press.

——— 1981. *Moral Luck: Philosophical Papers 1973–1980.* Cambridge: Cambridge University Press.

Williams, M. 1999. *Wittgenstein, Mind and Meaning: Toward a Social Conception of Mind.* London and New York: Routledge.

——— 2007. 'Blind Obedience: Rules, Community, and the Individual.' In *Wittgenstein's Philosophical Investigations: Critical Essays,* edited by M. Williams, 61–92. Plymouth: Rowman and Littlefield.

——— 2007. *Wittgenstein's Philosophical Investigations: Critical Essays.* Plymouth: Rowman and Littlefield.

Williamson, T. 1996. *Vagueness*. London & New York: Routledge.

Wilson, G. 1994. 'Kripke on Wittgenstein on Normativity.' Reprinted in *Rule-Following and Meaning*, edited by A. Miller & C. Wright, 234–59. Chesham: Acumen.

——— 1998. 'Semantic Realism and Kripke's Wittgenstein.' *Philosophy and Phenomenological Research* 58 (1): 99–122.

——— 2006. 'Rule-Following, Meaning and Normativity.' In *The Oxford Handbook of Philosophy of Language*, edited by E. Lepore & B. Smith, 151–74. Oxford: Oxford University Press.

——— 2011. 'On the Skepticism about Rule-Following in Kripke's Version of Wittgenstein.' In *The Cambridge Companion to Kripke*, edited by A. Berger, 253–89. Cambridge: Cambridge University Press.

Witherspoon, E. 2011. 'Wittgenstein on Criteria and the Problem of Other Minds.' In *The Oxford Handbook of Wittgenstein*, edited by O. Kuusela & M. McGinn, 472–98. Oxford: Oxford University Press.

Wittgenstein, L. 1956. *Remarks on the Foundations of Mathematics*. Edited by G.H. von Wright, R. Rhees, & G.E.M. Anscombe. Translated by G.E.M. Anscombe. Oxford: Blackwell.

——— 1958. *The Blue and Brown Books*. Oxford: Blackwell.

——— 1974a. *Philosophical Grammar*, edited by R. Rhees. Translated by A. Kenny. Oxford: Blackwell.

——— 1974b. *On Certainty*. Revised Edition. Edited by G.E.M. Anscombe & G.H. von Wright. Translated by D. Paul & G.E.M. Anscombe. Oxford: Blackwell.

——— 1975. *Philosophical Remarks*, edited by R. Rhees. Translated by R. Hargreaves & R. White. Oxford: Blackwell.

——— 1979a. *Lectures: Cambridge 1932–35. From the Notes of Alice Ambrose and Margaret MacDonald*, edited by A. Ambrose. Oxford: Blackwell.

——— 1979b. *Notebooks 1914–1916*. 2nd Edition, edited by G.H. von Wright & G.E.M. Anscombe. Translated by G.E.M. Anscombe. Chicago: University of Chicago Press.

——— 1980a. *Lectures: Cambridge 1930–1932. From the Notes of J. King and D. Lee*, edited by D. Lee. Chicago: University of Chicago Press.

——— 1980b. *Remarks on the Philosophy of Psychology*, Volume I, edited by G.E.M. Anscombe & G.H. von Wright. Translated by G.E.M. Anscombe. Oxford: Blackwell.

——— 1980c. *Remarks on the Philosophy of Psychology*, Volume II, edited by G.H. von Wright & Heikki Nyman. Translated by C.G. Luckhardt & M.A.E. Aue. Oxford: Blackwell.

——— 1981. *Zettel*. 2nd Edition, edited by G.E.M. Anscombe & G.H. von Wright. Translated by G.E.M. Anscombe. Oxford: Blackwell.

——— 2001. *Philosophical Investigations*. 3rd Edition. Translated by G.E.M. Anscombe. Oxford: Blackwell.

——— 2005a. *Big Typescript*, edited and translated by C.G. Luckhardt & M.A.E. Aue. Oxford: Blackwell.

——— 2005b. *Tractatus Logico-Philosophicus*. Translated by C.K. Ogden. London & New York: Routledge.

Wright, C. 1980. *Wittgenstein on the Foundations of Mathematics*. Cambridge, MA: Harvard University Press.

——— 2001. *Rails to Infinity*. Cambridge, MA: Harvard University Press.

——— 2007. 'Rule-Following without Reasons: Wittgenstein's Quietism and the Constitutive Question.' *Ratio* 20 (4): 481–502.

Index